Olympiad Champs
English Class 7

with **Chapter-wise Previous 10 Year** (2013 - 2022) Questions

In the interest of student community

DISHA Publication Inc.

45, 2nd Floor, Maharishi Dayanand Marg,
Corner Market, Malviya Nagar, new Delhi –110017
Tel: 49842349/ 49842350

Typeset By

DISHA DTP Team

Buying books from DISHA

Just Got A Lot More Rewarding!!!

We at DISHA Publication, value your feedback immensely and to show our apperciation of our reviewers, we have launched a review contest.

To participate in this reward scheme, just follow these quick and simple steps:

- Write a review of the product you purchase on Amazon/Flipkart.
- Take a screenshot/photo of your review.
- Mail it to *disha-rewards@aiets.co.in*, along with all your details.

Each month, selected reviewers will win exciting gifts from DISHA Publication. Note that the rewards for each month will be declared in the first week of next month on our website.

https://bit.ly/review-reward-disha.

Write To
Us At
feedback_disha@aiets.co.in

Preface

We are pleased to launch the 4th edition of **Olympiad Champs English Class 7** which is the first of its kind book on Olympiad in many ways.

The Unique Selling Proposition of this new edition is the inclusion of past year questions till 2022 of different Olympiad exams held in schools.

The book is aimed at achieving not only success but deep rooted learning in children. It is prepared on content based on National Curriculum Framework prescribed by NCERT. All the text books, syllabi and teaching practices within the education programme in India must follow NCF. Hence, Olympiad Champs become an ideal book not only for the Olympiad Exams but also for strengthening the concepts for Class 7.

There is an exhaustive range of thought provoking questions in MCQ format to test the student's knowledge thoroughly. The questions are designed so as to test the knowledge, comprehension, evaluation, analytical and application skills. Solutions and explanations are provided for all questions. The questions are divided into two levels-Level 1 and Level 2. The first level, Level 1, is the beginner's level which comprises of questions like fillers, analogy and odd one out. When the child covers Level 1, it means his basic knowledge about the subject is clear and now it is ready for Level 2. The second level is the advanced level. Level 2 comprises of techniques like matching, chronological sequencing, picture, passage and feature based, statement correct/ incorrect, integer based, puzzle, grid based, crossword, venn diagram, table/ chart based and much more.

The first concern which each parent faces is how to make their children read a book especially when it is based on academics. Keeping this in mind interesting facts, real life examples, historical preview, short cut to problem solving, charts, diagrams, illustrations and poems are added. In addition to this, we have introduced comic strip which increases the readability quotient and make the reading experience for the children more exciting.

With the vision to remove all the misconception a child may have pertaining to the subject, to relate his knowledge to the real world and to develop a deeper understanding of the subject this book will cater all the requirements of the students who are going to appear in Olympiads.

While preparing this book, some errors might have crept in. We request our readers to identify those errors and send it across on **feedback_disha@aiets.co.in.**

We wish you all the best for your Olympiads and happy reading.......

Team Disha

For feedback : feedback_disha@aiets.co.in.

CONTENTS

TYPES OF SENTENCES

PHRASES AND CLAUSES

The various parts of speech are grouped into phrases and clauses which make up the basic sentence.

PHRASES

Phrases are groups of related words that do not contain a subject-verb combination or express a complete thought. There are noun, prepositional, participial, verb and infinitive phrases.

EXAMPLE

- Noun: my brand new car, the sad old dog
- Prepositional: over the wall, around the world
- Participial: playing the fool, buying the book
- Verb: will be given, is coming
- Infinitive: to think, to draw

CLAUSES

Clauses are groups of related words that contain a subject-verb combination. Independent clauses express a complete thought and can stand by themselves as sentences. Subordinate clauses serve as part of a sentence but do not express a complete thought and cannot stand by themselves. They are subordinate to independent clauses.

INDEPENDENT CLAUSES

- The weather was warm and dry.
- Ram got free tickets to the play.
- They took the wrong road.

SUBORDINATE CLAUSES

- By the time June arrived.
- Because he works at the theatre.
- When they came to the turn.

COMPLETE SENTENCES

- *By the time June arrived*, the weather was warm and dry.
- Ram got free tickets to the play, *because he works at the theatre.*
- *When they came to the turn*, they took the wrong road.

NOTE

The following words are commonly used **subordinate conjunctions** and **relative pronouns**. If a group of words that has a subject and a verb, begins with one of these subordinate conjunctions or relative pronouns, then the clause is a dependent clause.

Subordinate Conjunctions	Relative Pronouns
After	That
Although	Which
As	Whichever
As if	Who
Because	Whoever
Before	Whom
Even though	Whomever
How	Whose
If	
Since	
So that	
Than	
Though	
Unless	
Until	
What	
When	
Whenever	
Where	
Whereas	
Wherever	
Whether	
While	

However, many of the words in the list are also **adverbs** or **prepositions**. As such, they will not precede a subject and a verb; hence, the group of words will not be a dependent clause.

EXAMPLE

- While running for the train. (Participial phrase)
- Because of her competence. (Prepositional phrase)

TYPES OF SENTENCES

There are five types of sentences that are used in writing - declarative, exclamatory, imperative, optative and interrogative. Each type is used in a specific situation and each has its own punctuation mark.

1.   DECLARATIVE

Declarative sentences make a statement or state universal truths. They end with a full stop.

EXAMPLE

- The cake is delicious.
- Delhi is the capital of India.

2.   EXCLAMATORY

Exclamatory sentences contain a strong emotion and end with an exclamation mark.

EXAMPLE

- I am excited to watch this movie!
- It's a great day!

3.   IMPERATIVE

Imperative sentences make a command or request. They typically end with a period, but sometimes end with an exclamation mark.

EXAMPLE

- Take out the trash.
- Please be quiet.
- Give me your wallet!

4.   INTERROGATIVE

Interrogative sentences ask a question and end with a question mark.

EXAMPLE

- Where did you go yesterday?
- Did you finish your homework?

5.   OPTATIVE

Optative sentences express a desire or a wish. They end with an exclamation mark but may also use a full stop sometimes.

EXAMPLE

- May God bless you!
- Have a great day.

SENTENCE CONSTRUCTION

We need to construct our sentences in the right way and a combination of differently constructed sentences make the writing more interesting.

1.   SIMPLE SENTENCE

The simple sentence is an independent clause without subordinate clause. It begins with a capital letter and closes with an end mark. Simple sentences can vary considerably in length.

EXAMPLE

- I bought four apples at the farmers' market.
- I bought four apples, a basket of tomatoes, a bag of green beans, and three squashes at the farmers' market.
- The farmers' market is a classic example of producers selling directly to consumers and avoiding the attempts of agents to control the supply or to manipulate the price.

2. COMPOUND SENTENCE

The compound sentence contains two or more independent clauses but no subordinate clauses. The two independent clauses are joined by a comma (,) followed by a conjunction (for, and, nor, but…). They may also be joined by a semicolon (;), a semicolon followed by a linking adverb (therefore, however, because, since…), or a colon (:).

EXAMPLE

- I don't know where she went, and no one has seen her since this afternoon. (conjunction)
- Rahul Gandhi represents the youth of the country; his campaigns generally were successful. (semicolon)
- Chavi wanted to stay another week in Lucknow; however, her parents refused to send her more money. (linking adverb)
- You must have heard the news: we all are getting bonuses this year! (colon)

COMPOUND SENTENCES WITH COORDINATORS

> Independent Clause + , + Coordinators + Independent Clause

The two independent clauses are joined by a comma and one of the seven coordinating conjunctions: *for, and, nor, but, or, yet,* and *so.*

You can remember the coordinating conjunctions by remembering the word FANBOYS.

F → for

A → and

N → nor

B → but

O → or

Y → yet

S → So

- The following sentences illustrate their meanings.

1. The Japanese have the longest life expectancy than any other people, for their diet is extremely healthy.

   (**for** expresses reason.)

2. The Indians consume a lot of rice and they eat more grains than vegetables. (expresses equal related ideas).

COMPOUND SENTENCES WITH LINKING ADVERBS (CONJUNCTIVE ADVERBS)

> Independent Clause; + Conjunctive Adverb, + Independent Clause

The two independent clauses are joined by a **semicolon** (;), a **conjunctive adverb** and a **comma**. Just like the *FANBOYS* coordinators, conjunctive adverbs express the relationship of the second clause to the first clause. The chart below shows the coordinators and conjunctive adverbs which express similar relationship.

Coordinating Conjunctions	Conjunctive Adverbs	Meaning
And	Furthermore, besides, moreover, also	Additional idea
But, yet	However, nonetheless, nevertheless, still	Opposite idea
Or	Otherwise	Choice
So	Consequently, thus, therefore, hence, accordingly	Result

EXAMPLE

- Few coaching centers offer preparation for the professions, business and industry; moreover, they prepare students to get an admission into a college. (equal related ideas)
- Students must take the final exam; otherwise, they will have to repeat the year. ("or else")

COMPOUND SENTENCES WITH SEMICOLON

> Independent Clause + ; + Independent Clause

The two independent clauses are joined by a **semicolon** (;). Use a semicolon only when the two independent clauses are closely related and the relationship is implied.

EXAMPLE

My older brother is a lawyer; my younger sister studies fashion designing.

3. COMPLEX SENTENCES

A complex sentence contains one independent clause and one or more dependent clauses. In a complex sentence, one idea is generally more important than the other one. The more important idea is placed in the independent clause, and the less important idea is placed in the dependent clause.

Independent Clause + Dependent Clause
Dependent Clause + , + Independent Clause

In the following sentences, the independent clause is underlined and the dependent clause is in italics.

EXAMPLE

- *If you are not good at figures,* it is pointless to apply for a job in a bank.
- *When he saw the door open,* the stranger entered the house.
- Holiday resorts *which are very crowded* are not very pleasant.
- *That the Earth's temperature is raising* concerns scientists.

NOTE: There are three kinds of dependent clauses used in complex sentences: *adverb, adjective* and *noun.*

1. **A dependent adverb clause** begins with an adverbial subordinator such as *when, while, because, even though, so that, etc.*

2. **A dependent adjective clause** begins with a relative pronoun such as *who, whom, which, whose,* or a relative adverb *where, when* and *why.*

3. **A dependent noun clause** begins with *that, a wh-question word, whether* and *if.*

LEVEL 1

1. He said, "I like this song."
   - (a) request
   - (b) statement
   - (c) command
   - (d) question

2. "Where is your sister?" she asked me.
   - (a) request
   - (b) statement
   - (c) command
   - (d) question

3. "I don't speak Italian," she said.
   - (a) request
   - (b) statement
   - (c) command
   - (d) question

4. "Say hello to Jim," they said.   **(2014)**
   - (a) request
   - (b) statement
   - (c) command
   - (d) question

5. "The film began at seven o'clock," he said.
   - (a) request
   - (b) statement
   - (c) command
   - (d) question

6. "Don't play on the grass, boys," she said.
   - (a) request
   - (b) statement
   - (c) command
   - (d) question

7. "Where have you spent your money?" she asked him.   **(2013)**
   - (a) request
   - (b) statement
   - (c) command
   - (d) question

8. "I never make mistakes," he said.
   - (a) request
   - (b) statement
   - (c) command
   - (d) question

9. "Does she know Robert?" he wanted to know.
   - (a) request
   - (b) statement
   - (c) command
   - (d) question

10. "Don't try this at home," the stuntman told the audience.   **(2014)**
    - (a) request
    - (b) statement
    - (c) command
    - (d) question

11. Why aren't you going to the party?
    - (a) Imperative
    - (b) Optative
    - (c) Declarative
    - (d) Interrogative

12. We are very excited about going on a field trip!
    - (a) Optative
    - (b) Declarative
    - (c) Interrogative
    - (d) Exclamatory

13. Make sure you pay your bills on time.
    - (a) Declarative
    - (b) Interrogative
    - (c) Optative
    - (d) Exclamatory

14. Quit being so cautious!   **(2015)**
    - (a) Imperative
    - (b) Exclamatory
    - (c) Declarative
    - (d) Interrogative

15. Did Sahil achieve his goals?   **(2012)**
    - (a) Exclamatory
    - (b) Interrogative
    - (c) Optative
    - (d) None

16. May you attain the maximum height in your life!
    - (a) Exclamatory
    - (b) Interrogative
    - (c) Optative
    - (d) None

17. How many beans are there in the jar?
    - (a) Declarative
    - (b) Exclamatory
    - (c) Optative
    - (d) Interrogative

18. Go get my screwdriver out of the workshop for me.   **(2016)**
    - (a) Imperative
    - (b) Declarative
    - (c) Exclamatory
    - (d) Optative

19. That's my favourite song.   **(2016)**

    (a) Declarative   (b) Optative

    (c) Exclamatory   (d) Interrogative

20. It's Renu's birthday today.   **(2012)**

    (a) Imperative   (b) Interrogative

    (c) Exclamatory   (d) Declarative

DIRECTIONS (Qs. 21-24) : *Read the sentences and correct the ending punctuation. Also state what type of sentence it is.*

---

21. He's so dishonest _________   **(2015)**

    (a) Optative   (b) Exclamatory

    (c) Declarative   (d) Imperative

22. Put the roti's on the table next to the curry _________   **(2017)**

    (a) Imperative   (b) Declarative

    (c) Exclamatory   (d) Optative

23. Why are you playing in the hot sun _________

    (a) Declarative   (b) Interrogative

    (c) Exclamatory   (d) Optative

24. She loves to swim and bask in the sun _________

    (a) Imperative   (b) Declarative

    (c) Exclamatory   (d) Interrogative

DIRECTIONS (Qs. 25-29) : *Read the sentences and state the type of sentence based on structure*

---

25. The power was off until they fixed it.   **(2014)**

    (a) Simple   (b) Compound

    (c) Complex   (d) None

26. I felt dizzy after I spun around.   **(2012)**

    (a) Simple   (b) Complex

    (c) Compound   (d) None

27. I read the right book, but it was the wrong day.

    (a) Compound   (b) Simple

    (c) Complex   (d) None

28. The stone was heavy.   **(2013)**

    (a) Compound   (b) Complex

    (c) Simple   (d) None

29. We can go, or you can go.   **(2017)**

    (a) Compound

    (b) Simple

    (c) Complex

    (d) None

30. If you ______ a mobile phone on the street, what would you do with it?   **(2018)**

    (a) find   (b) finds

    (c) finding   (d) found

31. If we ______ him tomorrow, we'll return his books.   **(2018)**

    (a) meet

    (b) 'll meet

    (c) meets

    (d) were meeting

32. My dad would have ______ more if he had had the time.   **(2018)**

    (a) had writing

    (b) been written

    (c) written

    (d) wrote

33. If we all manage to play our best, we______ with a chance of wining.   **(2019)**

    (a) can in   (b) was in

    (c) have in   (d) are in

LEVEL 2

1. Which of the following is not a complex sentence?

   (a) I felt dizzy after I spun around.

   (b) We will take a bus.

   (c) We will take a bus when we visit them.

   (d) We will take a bus as it is raining today.

2. Which of the following is a compound sentence?

   (a) They had a tough job, yet they stopped trying.

   (b) They had a tough job.

   (c) They had a tough job after they stopped trying.

   (d) None of the above.

3. Which of the following is a complex sentence?

   (a) I got there on time.   **(2016)**

   (b) I got there, so everyone else got there.

   (c) I got there before everyone else got there.

   (d) None of the above.

4. Which of the following sentence is a compound sentence?   **(Critical Thinking, 2014)**

   (a) The house was destroyed in the fire, but none of them was hurt.

   (b) She said that she was so disappointed that she would not try again.

   (c) The men who rule the world with their pens are like knights in a shining armour.

   (d) The good that men do never dies.

5. Which of the following is a simple sentence?

   (a) All that glitters is not gold.   **(Tricky)**

   (b) Neither the colour nor the fabric appeals to me.

   (c) Rose will be competing in the next tournament.

   (d) If we do not change our ways of treating nature then we shall soon suffer the undesirable consequences.

6. Since decomposition of some materials takes many years, recycling them helps the environment.   **(2014)**

   (a) declarative-compound

   (b) declarative-complex

   (c) imperative-compound

   (d) imperative-complex

7. If we can't get tickets to the show, we can always watch it on T.V.

   (a) declarative-complex

   (b) imperative-complex

   (c) interrogative-compound

   (d) declarative-compound

8. The platypus is a mammal, isn't it?

   (a) interrogative-complex

   (b) interrogative-compound

   (c) interrogative-simple

   (d) exclamatory-simple

9. When I go swimming, I always take a shower.

   (a) imperative-complex

   (b) imperative-compound

   (c) declarative-complex

   (d) declarative-compound

10. People who become blind after birth can see images in their dreams.   **(2013)**

    (a) imperative-simple

    (b) declarative-simple

    (c) optative-compound

    (d) declarative-complex

11. What is the most common emotion experienced in dreams? **(Tricky, 2017)**
    - (a) interrogative-simple
    - (b) interrogative-compound
    - (c) interrogative-complex
    - (d) optative-compound

12. Please leave your footwear outside. **(2015)**
    - (a) imperative-compound
    - (b) imperative complex
    - (c) declarative-simple
    - (d) imperative-simple

13. Will you take these books and drop them at the reception? **(2015)**
    - (a) interrogative-simple
    - (b) imperative-complex
    - (c) interrogative-compound
    - (d) interrogative-complex

14. This is the most-beautiful lawn I have ever seen!
    - (a) imperative-simple
    - (b) declarative-simple
    - (c) exclamatory-compound
    - (d) exclamatory-simple

15. I can't get down! **(2017)**
    - (a) declarative-simple
    - (b) imperative-simple
    - (c) imperative-compound
    - (d) exclamatory-simple

16. If you eat a lot of chocolate, you______. **(2018)**
    - (a) will gain weight
    - (b) graining weight
    - (c) would gain weight
    - (d) had gain weight

17. The test was so easy that most people ______ finished after 45 minutes, I think. **(2018)**
    - (a) would have
    - (b) will have
    - (c) have
    - (d) was

HINTS & EXPLANATIONS

LEVEL - 1

1. (b) statement
2. (d) question
3. (b) statement
4. (c) command
5. (b) statement
6. (c) command
7. (d) question
8. (b) Statement
9. (d) question
10. (a) command
11. (d) Interrogative
12. (d) Exclamatory
13. (a) Declarative
14. (a) Imperative
15. (b) Interrogative
16. (c) Optative
17. (d) Interrogative
18. (a) Imperative
19. (a) Declarative sentence
20. (d) Declarative
21. (c) Declarative, full stop (.)
22. (b) Imperative, full stop (.)
23. (b) Question mark (?) Interrogative
24. (b) Declarative, full stop (.)
25. (c) Conjunction (until) $\rightarrow$ Complex
26. (b) Conjunction (after) $\rightarrow$ Complex
27. (a) Conjunction (but) $\rightarrow$ Compound
28. (c) Simple sentence
29. (a) Conjunction (or) $\rightarrow$ Compound
30. (d) found
31. (a) meet
32. (c) written
33. (d) are in

LEVEL - 2

1. (b)
2. (a)
3. (c)
4. (a)
5. (c)
6. (b)
7. (a)
8. (c)
9. (c)
10. (d)
11. (a)
12. (d)
13. (c)
14. (d)
15. (d)
16. (a) will gain weight
17. (a) would have

NOUNS/ PRONOUNS/ VERBS/ADVERBS

NOUNS

A noun is a word that identifies:
* a person (*woman, boy, doctor, neighbour*)
* a thing (*dog, building, tree, country*)
* an idea, quality, or state (*truth, danger, birth, happiness*).

There are several different types of nouns, which are as follows:

COMMON NOUN

A common noun is a noun that refers to people or things in general, e.g., *boy, country, bridge, city, birth, day, happiness*.

PROPER NOUN

A proper noun is a name that identifies a particular person, place, or thing, e.g., *Rohit, Africa, Tower Bridge, London, Monday*. In written English, proper nouns begin with capital letters.

CONCRETE NOUN

A concrete noun is a noun which refers to people and to things that exist physically and can be seen, touched, smelled, heard, or tasted. Examples include, *dog, building, tree, rain, beach, tune, Tower Bridge*.

ABSTRACT NOUN

An abstract noun is a noun which refers to ideas, qualities, and conditions – things that cannot be seen or touched and things which have no physical reality, e.g., *truth, danger, happiness, time, friendship, humour*.

COLLECTIVE NOUNS

Collective nouns refer to groups of people or things, e.g., *audience, family, government, team, jury*. Collective nouns can usually be treated as singular or plural, with either a singular or plural verb.

Both the following sentences are grammatically correct.
* The whole family **was** at the table.
* The whole family **were** at the table.

A noun may belong to more than one category. For example, *happiness* is both a common noun and an abstract noun, while *Tower Bridge* is both a concrete noun and a proper noun.

COUNTABLE AND UNCOUNTABLE NOUNS

Nouns can be either countable or uncountable. Countable nouns (or count nouns) are those that refer to something that can be counted. Uncountable nouns (or mass nouns) do not typically refer to things that can be counted and so they do not have a plural form.

PRONOUNS

Pronouns are used in place of a noun that has already been mentioned or that is already known, often to avoid repeating the noun.

EXAMPLE

- Rita was tired so **she** went to bed.
- Kiran sent the children with **him**.
- Rajat's face was close to **mine**.
- **That** is a good idea.
- **Anything** might happen.

PERSONAL PRONOUNS

Personal pronouns are used in place of nouns referring to specific people or things, for example *I, me, mine, you, yours, his, her, hers, we, they*, or *them*. They can be divided into various categories according to their role in a sentence, as follows:

* subjective pronouns	* objective pronouns
* possessive pronouns	* reflexive pronouns

SUBJECTIVE PRONOUNS

The personal pronouns *I, you, we, he, she, it, we*, and *they* are known as subjective pronouns because they act as the subjects of verbs.

EXAMPLE

- **She** saw Manjula.
- **We** drove Rakesh home.
- **I** waved at her.

OBJECTIVE PRONOUNS

The personal pronouns *me, you, us, him, her, it,* and *them* are called objective pronouns because they act as the objects of verbs and prepositions.

EXAMPLE

- Raghav saw **her**.
- Rita drove **us** home.
- She waved at **me.**

Here's a table setting out the different forms:

	SINGULAR		PLURAL	
	subjective	objective	subjective	objective
first person	I	me	we	us
second person	you	you	you	you
third person	he/she/it	him/her/it	they	them

Notice that the personal pronouns *you* and *it* stay the same, whether they are being used in the subjective or objective roles.

POSSESSIVE PRONOUNS

The personal pronouns *mine, yours, hers, his, ours*, and *theirs* are known as possessive pronouns: they refer to something owned by the speaker or by someone or something previously mentioned.

EXAMPLE

- That book is **mine.**
- John's eyes met **hers.**
- **Ours** is a family farm.

REFLEXIVE PRONOUNS

Reflexive personal pronouns include *myself, himself, herself, itself, ourselves, yourselves*, and *themselves*. These are used to refer back to the subject of the clause in which they are used:

EXAMPLE

- **I** fell and hurt **myself.**
- **Daisy** prepared **herself** for the journey.
- **The children** had to look after **themselves.**

VERBS

A verb describes what a person or thing does or what happens.

For example, verbs describe:

an action – *run, hit, travel*

an event – *rain, occur*

a situation – *be, seem, have*

a change – *become, grow, develop*

The basic form of a verb is known as the **infinitive.** It's often preceded by the word 'to'.

EXAMPLE

- *Molly decided **to follow** him.*
- *He began **to run** back.*

Regular and Irregular Verbs

In the context of verbs, we use the term *inflection* to talk about the process of changing a verb form to show tense, mood, number (i.e., singular or plural), and person (i.e., first person, second person, or third person). This section deals with inflecting verbs to show tenses and participles, and is divided into two main sections:

* Regular verbs
* Irregular verbs

REGULAR VERBS

Many English verbs are *regular*, which means that they form their different tenses according to an established pattern. Such verbs work like this:

Verb	3rd person singular present tense	3rd person singular past tense	past participle	present participle
laugh	he/she laughs	he/she laughed	laughed	laughing
love	he/she loves	he/she loved	loved	loving
boo	he/she boos	he/she booed	booed	booing

Present tense formation

In the present simple tense, the basic form of a regular verb only changes in the 3rd person singular, as follows:

Most verbs just add -*s* to the basic form (e.g. *take/takes, seem/seems, look/looks*).

Verbs that end with a vowel other than *e* add -*es* (e.g., go/goes, veto/vetoes, do/does).

Verbs that end with -*s*, -*z*, -*ch*, -*sh*, and -*x* add -*es* (e.g. *kiss/kisses, fizz/fizzes, punch/punches, wash/washes, mix/mixes*).

If the verb ends in a consonant plus -*y*, change the *y* to an *i* before adding -*es* (e.g. *hurry/hurries, clarify/clarifies*). But if the verb ends in a vowel plus -*y*, just add -*s* (e.g. *play/plays, enjoy/enjoys*).

Past Tense Formation

Forming the past simple tense of regular verbs is mostly straightforward, and you use the same form for the first, second, and third persons, singular and plural:

If the basic form of the verb ends in a consonant or a vowel other than *e*, add the letters -*ed* to the end (e.g. *seem/seemed, laugh/laughed, look/looked*).

For verbs that end in -*e*, add -*d* (e.g. *love/loved, recede/receded, hope/hoped*).

If the verb ends in a consonant plus *-y*, change the *y* to an *i* before adding *-ed* (e.g. *hurry/hurried, clarify/ clarified*). But if the verb ends in a vowel plus *-y*, just add *-ed* (e.g. *play/played, enjoy/enjoyed*).

Forming participles

To form the past participle of regular verbs, follow the same rules as for the past simple tense above.

To make the present participle of regular verbs:

If the basic form of the verb ends in a consonant or a vowel other than *e*, add the ending *-ing* (e.g., *laugh/ laughing, boo/booing*).

If the verb ends in *e*, drop the *e* before adding -ing (e.g., *love/loving, hope/hoping*).

If the basic form ends in *y* just add *-ing* (e.g., *hurry/hurrying, clarify/clarifying*).

IRREGULAR VERBS

There are many *irregular* verbs that don't follow the normal rules. Here are the forms of some of the most common irregular verbs:

Verb	3rd person singular past tense	past participle	present participle	3rd person singular present tense
be	was	been	being	is
begin	began	begun	beginning	begins
bite	bit	bitten	biting	bites
break	broke	broken	breaking	breaks
buy	bought	bought	buying	buys
choose	chose	chosen	choosing	chooses
come	came	come	coming	comes
dig	dug	dug	digging	digs
do	did	done	doing	does
drink	drank	drunk	drinking	drinks
eat	ate	eaten	eating	eats
fall	fell	fallen	falling	falls
feel	felt	felt	feeling	feels
find	found	found	finding	finds
get	got	got	getting	gets
go	went	gone	going	goes
grow	grew	grown	growing	grows
have	had	had	having	has
hide	hid	hidden	hiding	hides
keep	kept	kept	keeping	keeps
know	knew	known	knowing	knows
lay	laid	laid	laying	lays
lead	led	led	leading	leads
leave	left	left	leaving	leaves
lie	lay	lain	lying	lies
lose	lost	lost	losing	loses
make	made	made	making	makes

meet	met	met	meeting	meets
put	put	put	putting	puts
read /ri:d/	read /red/	read /red/	reading	reads
ride	rode	ridden	riding	rides
ring	rang	rung	ringing	rings
rise	rose	risen	rising	rises
run	ran	run	running	runs
say	said	said	saying	says
see	saw	seen	seeing	sees
sell	sold	sold	selling	sells
set	set	set	setting	sets
sing	sang	sung	singing	sings
sit	sat	sat	sitting	sits
stand	stood	stood	standing	stands
stick	stuck	stuck	sticking	sticks
take	took	taken	taking	takes
teach	taught	taught	teaching	teaches
think	thought	thought	thinking	thinks
wake	woke	woken	waking	wakes

Note that sometimes the spelling doesn't change but the pronunciation does (e.g. read).

Auxiliary Verbs

Auxiliary verbs are so called because they help to form the various tenses, moods, and voices of other verbs. The principal ones are *be*, *do*, and *have*.

'Be' is used with other verbs to form continuous tenses and the passive voice.
- *She **is** reading a magazine.*
- *We **were** talking to them for ages.*
- *England **were** beaten by Germany in the final.*

'Have' is used to make perfect tenses:
- *The judge **had** asked her to speak up.*
- *In two years, we will **have** established community gardens.*

Do is used:

For emphasis- *He **did** look tired.*

To make questions - **Do** *you want a coffee?*

To form negative statements or questions
- *I **don't** like meat.*
- ***Didn't** he know how to play football?*

Modal Verbs

There is a further set of auxiliary verbs known as *modal verbs* or *modal auxiliary verbs*. These combine with other verbs to express necessity, possibility, intention, or ability. The modal auxiliary verbs are *must, shall, will, should, would, ought (to), can, could, may,* and *might*.

EXAMPLE
* *You **must** act promptly.*
* ***Can** you speak Spanish?*
* *I would go if I **could** afford it.*
* *He said he **might** reconsider his decision.*
* *I **ought** to visit my family.*
* *We **should** get to London before midday.*
* ***May** I come in?*

Subject Verb Agreement
Having understood verbs, it is also essential to understand subject - verb agreement. This implies that the subjects and verbs must agree in number.

> **For example :**
> * The **cat mews** when it **is** hungry.
> * The **cats mew** when they **are** hungry.

The sentence may have either a singular or plural noun or pronoun as subject. Make sure you accurately indentify the subject before deciding on the proper verb form to use.

Points to remember
* Subjects don't always come before the verb.

EXAMPLE
> * Where is the coat?
> * Where are the girls?

* If there is more than one subject operated with 'or; 'nor' neither/nor, either/or the verb is singular

EXAMPLE
Neither Ram nor Rahim is coming to the party.
* If the subjects are plural and connected with or, nor, neither/nor, either/or, the verb is plural.

EXAMPLE
Either girls or boys are going for the picnic.
* Collective nouns usually take a singular verb.

ADVERBS
An adverb is a word that's used to give information about a verb, adjective, or other adverb.
When used with a verb, adverbs can give information about:
* How something happens or is done:
  * *She stretched lazily.*
  * *He walked slowly.*
  * *The town is easily accessible by road.*
* Where something happens:
  * *I live here.*
  * *She's travelling abroad.*
  * *The children tiptoed upstairs.*
* When something happens:
  * *They visited us yesterday.*
  * *I have to leave soon.*
  * *He still lives in London.*

Adverbs can make the meaning of a verb, adjective, or other adverb stronger or weaker:
* With a verb:
  * *I almost fell asleep.*
  * *He really means it.*
* With an adjective:
  * *These schemes are very clever.*
  * *This is a slightly better result.*
* With another adverb:
  * *They nearly always get home late.*
  * *The answer to both questions is really rather simple.*
* Adverbs are often found between the subject and its verb:
  * *She carefully avoided my eye.*
* They can also come between an auxiliary verb (such as *be* or *have*) and a main verb:
  * *The concert was suddenly cancelled.*
  * *He had **quickly** eaten his dinner.*

LEVEL 1

DIRECTONS (Qs. 1-5) : *Select the answer choice that identifies the noun in the sentence.*

1. Many of these people have been ignored.
   - (a) Many
   - (b) These
   - (c) People
   - (d) Ignored
2. Most of the calls to this company are placed on lengthy holds. **(2014)**
   - (a) Most
   - (b) Placed
   - (c) Lengthy
   - (d) Holds
3. Rosemary, come and meet our new dog! **(2015)**
   - (a) Come
   - (b) Meet
   - (c) Our
   - (d) Dog
4. Keeping warm in the winter is both more difficult and more important for elderly persons.**(2013)**
   - (a) Keeping
   - (b) Difficult
   - (c) Persons
   - (d) Elderly
5. Tom and Dave were in the same platoon during the Gulf War. **(2015)**
   - (a) War
   - (b) And
   - (c) Were
   - (d) During

DIRECTIONS (Qs. 6-10) : *Tick the right option to identify what kinds of Nouns the words in bold are.*

6. I have to attend an important **conference** tomorrow. **(2012)**
   - (a) Abstract
   - (b) Common
   - (c) Proper
   - (d) Collective
7. The friends promised to stay together in **sickness and death**. **(2016)**
   - (a) Both Common
   - (b) Both Collective
   - (c) Both Abstract
   - (d) Both Proper
8. Dresses are made of **cotton, wool and silk**.
   - (a) All Collective
   - (b) All Common
   - (c) All Abstract
   - (d) All Material
9. The school **committee** has selected him as secretary by unanimous vote. **(2015)**
   - (a) Proper Noun
   - (b) Common
   - (c) Abstract
   - (d) Collective
10. **Work** is worship.
   - (a) Common
   - (b) Abstract
   - (c) Collective
   - (d) Material

DIRECTIONS (Qs. 11-15) : *Fill in the blanks with the most suitable pronoun from the options given below.*

11. The man _______ gave me the gift was quite young.
   - (a) which
   - (b) whose
   - (c) who
   - (d) whom
12. The father _______ son was crying since long, tried to calm him. **(2017)**
   - (a) which
   - (b) whose
   - (c) who
   - (d) whom
13. Would _______ buy some nice gifts for your friend?
   - (a) she
   - (b) her
   - (c) he
   - (d) you
14. All of _______ went to fetch her friend from the airport. **(2014)**
   - (a) we
   - (b) them
   - (c) our
   - (d) none of these
15. My parents live in Bengal. _______ often come to see me. **(2013)**
   - (a) He
   - (b) Them
   - (c) They
   - (d) None of these

DIRECTIONS (Qs. 16-30) : *Fill the blanks with correct alternatives.*

16. We _______ not go to the movie next Sunday.
   - (a) will
   - (b) does
   - (c) have
   - (d) has
17. Each of you _______ to collect a few rupees.
   - (a) do
   - (b) does
   - (c) have
   - (d) has
18. The earth _______ round the sun.
   - (a) go   **(Critical Thinking)**
   - (b) goes
   - (c) both A and B
   - (d) none of these above
19. Ritesh _______ French very fluently.
   - (a) speak
   - (b) speaking
   - (c) speaks
   - (d) none of these

20. You _______ not clean the dining table. The servant will do it.   **(2013)**
    (a) could   (b) shall
    (c) need   (d) might

21. My friend _______ not read without glasses.
    (a) can   (b) need
    (c) must   (d) should

22. We _______ not oppose you if you say so.
    (a) could   (b) will
    (c) ought to   (d) used to

23. We _______ buy things on installments.
    (a) shall   (b) dare
    (c) ought to   (d) would

24. Gandhiji _______ advise all freedom fighters.   **(2015)**
    (a) ought to   (b) would
    (c) used to   (d) could

25. _______ you lend me your camera, please?
    (a) shall   (b) may
    (c) will   (d) dare

26. Those who live in glass houses _______ not throw stones at others.   **(2014)**
    (a) ought to   (b) used to
    (c) should   (d) might

27. I found his home very _______.
    (a) easily   (b) difficultly
    (c) frequently   (d) oftenly

28. Rohan behaves very _______ with his elders.   **(2012)**
    (a) goodly   (b) badly
    (c) easily   (d) eagerly

29. My father will be _______ of town this weekend.
    (a) inside   (b) outside
    (c) out   (d) beyond

30. Rohan plays football _______.
    (a) aggressively   (b) sympathetically
    (c) hardly   (d) cruely

DIRECTIONS (Qs. 31-46) : *Read the sentences and match the subject with a suitable verb by choosing the correct option.*

31. The President, together with his wife, _______ the press cordially.   **(2014)**
    (a) greets   (b) greet
    (c) greeting   (d) greetings

32. The students _______ the questions carefully.
    (a) debates   (b) debate
    (c) debating   (d) none

33. Each of these books _______ a classic.   **(2015)**
    (a) were   (b) was
    (c) is   (d) are

34. Nobody _______ her house.
    (a) knowing   (b) knows
    (c) know   (d) known

35. One of my neighbours _______ going on a trip to Thailand.   **(Tricky)**
    (a) are   (b) is
    (c) be   (d) none

36. Renuka _______ the answer.
    (a) know   (b) knows
    (c) knowing   (d) known

37. Either my books or your bag _______ always on the floor.   **(2016)**
    (a) is   (b) are
    (c) be   (d) none

38. Mathematics _______ my favourite subject.
    (a) are   (b) is
    (b) be   (d) none

39. He skidded on his bicycle and _______ up in hospital.   **(2018)**
    (a) caught   (b) ended
    (c) set   (d) fixed

40. Sea birds often avoid _______ over the city because of the pollution.   **(2019)**
    (a) flying   (b) flighted
    (c) flown   (d) fly

41. I really only need _______ of these pens to complete my homework.   **(2019)**
    (a) a lot   (b) one
    (c) many   (d) most

42. Bill _______ back to the class about his holiday and the adventures he went on   **(2019)**
    (a) reported   (b) explained
    (c) reviewed   (d) spoke

43. _______ dress should I wear for the party tonight?   **(2020)**
    (a) How   (b) Who
    (c) Which   (d) When

44. I hurt a _______ in my knee, but it isn't serious.   **(2020)**
    (a) ligament   (b) mainland
    (c) convoy   (d) blitz

45. Rajesh speaks Japanese _______ fluently.   **(2020)**
    (a) such (b)   too
    (c) very (d)   just

46. Have _______ ever been to the Netherlands? **(2020)**
    - (a) he
    - (b) she
    - (c) them
    - (d) you

DIRECTIONS (Qs. 47-49) : *Choose the correct option to fill in the blank.* **(2021)**

47. Rama has ______ that she will help me in my work.
    - (a) assure
    - (b) assured
    - (c) assures
    - (d) assuring

48. Jay is so smart, his teachers have decided to accelerate ______ studies.
    - (a) him
    - (b) his
    - (c) its
    - (d) himself

49. The school management acts _________ with its staff and the students.
    - (a) protection
    - (b) protect
    - (c) protectively
    - (d) perfect

50. The rat_______ in the rat-trap. **(2022)**
    - (a) catch
    - (b) traps
    - (c) got caught
    - (d) was catching

51. The _______ committee was yet to review the proceeds from the industry. **(2022)**
    - (a) possible
    - (b) potential
    - (c) standing
    - (d) politician

52. This is the cycle ________ I bought yesterday. **(2022)**
    - (a) whom
    - (b) that
    - (c) whose
    - (d) what

53. Which one of the following is/are irregular verb(s)? **(2022)**
    - (a) Know
    - (b) Take
    - (c) Go
    - (d) All of these

54. Fill in the blanks with correct pronouns. **(2022)**

    Mr. Gupta knows _____ better than _____.
    - (a) me, he
    - (b) I, him
    - (c) me, him
    - (d) None of these

LEVEL 2

DIRECTIONS (Qs. 1-10) : *Select the word from the options that identifies the noun in the sentences given below.*

1. It will take all of your energy and you will be able to walk again.
   (a) Take   (b) All
   (c) Your   (d) Energy

2. The works of many great poets have been placed on reserve. **(2014)**
   (a) Many   (b) Great
   (c) Placed   (d) Reserve

3. The Brooklyn Bridge was opened in 1883.
   (a) Bridge   (b) Was
   (c) Opened   (d) In

4. Sparta and Athens were enemies during the Peloponnesian War. **(Critical Thinking, 2015)**
   (a) And   (b) Were
   (c) During   (d) War

5. Sharks and lampreys are not true fish because their skeletons are made of cartilage rather than bone. **(2015)**
   (a) True   (b) Because
   (c) Their   (d) Bone

6. John, have you met your new boss?
   (a) Have   (b) Met
   (c) Your   (d) Boss

7. Her parents tried living in the north India, but they could not adapt to the cold. **(2013)**
   (a) North   (b) But
   (c) Not   (d) Adapt

8. Mastering basic mathematics is an important goal for younger students. **(2016)**
   (a) Mastering   (b) Important
   (c) Younger   (d) Students

9. To seize a foreign embassy and its inhabitants is flagrant disregard for diplomatic neutrality.
   (a) Seize   (b) Its
   (c) Flagrant   (d) Neutrality

10. The Trojans' rash decision to accept the wooden horse led to their destruction. **(2012)**
    (a) Their   (b) Led
    (c) Accept   (d) Destruction

DIRECTIONS (Qs. 11-56) : *Fill the blanks with correct alternatives.*

11. Is that the bus _______ we`re waiting for?
    (a) whom   (b) where
    (c) whose   (d) that

12. He's the man with _______ we spoke a few days ago. **(2015)**
    (a) whom   (b) who
    (c) which   (d) that

13. Are they looking for the book _______ was here? **(Tricky, 2016)**
    (a) which   (b) whose
    (c) who   (d) whom

14. Is he the same person _______ we met last week ?
    (a) which   (b) who
    (c) that   (d) whom

15. An aeroplane is a machine _______ flies.
    (a) which   (b) whom
    (c) who   (d) when

16. The people _______ work in the house are very friendly. **(2016)**
    (a) who   (b) whom
    (c) when   (d) which

17. A salesman is a man ______ works in a shop.
    (a) who   (b) whom
    (c) when   (d) which

18. They live in the house ____ windows are broken.
    (a) who   (b) whom
    (c) whose   (d) which

19. My wife's mother, _______ I haven't seen for several years, speaks too much. **(2017)**
    (a) who   (b) whom
    (c) when   (d) which

20. I don't like the town _______ you work.
    (a) who   (b) whom
    (c) when   (d) where

21. The girl _______ lives next door is very boring.
    (a) who   (b) whom
    (c) when   (d) which

22. This is the lady _________ husband died last year.

(Tricky, 2014)

   (a) who   (b) whose
   (c) when   (d) which

23. They _____ getting ready when she arrived.
   (a) did   (b) have
   (c) were   (d) do

24. I _____ use to make so many mistakes.
   (a) didn't   (b) don't
   (c) hadn't   (d) wouldn't

25. They _____ been waiting for more than three hours. **(2012)**
   (a) were   (b) has
   (c) have   (d) did

26. What time _____ the plane leave? **(2015)**
   (a) is   (b) do
   (c) does   (d) have

27. She _____ have finished the work by the time you get back.
   (a) does   (b) is
   (c) had   (d) will

28. We _____ sitting on the beach this time next week. **(2017)**
   (a) are   (b) will be
   (c) will have   (d) are going to

29. I _____ met him for lunch had I known he was coming.
   (a) would   (b) had
   (c) would have (d) will

30. If I _____ you, I'd think twice about that! **(2016)**
   (a) am   (b) are
   (c) will be   (d) were

31. _________ I met my childhood friend Meeta.
   (a) Yesterday   (b) Today
   (c) Tomorrow   (d) This Sunday

32. You need to run _____ to win this race.
   (a) slow   (b) steadily
   (c) fast   (d) lazily

33. I won't say it _______. **(2014)**
   (a) progressively (b) repeatedly
   (c) necessarily   (d) correctly

34. Speak _______, I cannot hear you.
   (a) loudly   (b) slowly
   (c) hardly   (d) quickly

35. You should _______ smoke as it is dangerous for your health. **(2016)**
   (a) always   (b) usually
   (c) never   (d) hardly

36. We searched _______ but were unable to find her lost jewellery.
   (a) nowhere   (b) anywhere
   (c) everywhere (d) all where

37. I hope to see you _______!
   (a) soon   (b) never
   (c) randomly   (d) occasionally

38. Deepak never dresses _______ for work. **(2015)**
   (a) formally   (b) coolly
   (c) dirtily   (d) casually

39. The manager looked at me with an _______ expression when I reached late! **(Tricky)**
   (a) sad   (b) regret
   (c) angry   (d) polite

40. Ranjit speaks _______ good French, he can be of great help to you.
   (a) he   (b) great
   (c) quite   (d) English

41. The elephants were _______ the village when they came through the forest. **(2018)**
   (a) avoid   (b) avoidable
   (c) avoiding   (d) avoided

42. I _______ since I was about 5 years old. **(2018)**
   (a) have been played
   (b) have been playing
   (c) played
   (d) was playing

43. Now always it _______ cost a fortune to own a laptop. Ten years ago they used to cost a lot. **(2018)**
   (a) mustn't   (b) hasn't
   (c) needn't   (d) couldn't

44. The quiz will not test your _______, but it will test your knowledge of the game. **(2019)**
   (a) Coordinated   (b) coordinately
   (c) coordination (d) coordinate

45. _______ at the end is the best way of telling a funny story. **(2019)**
   (a) Begins
   (b) Beginning
   (c) Began
   (d) Having begun

46. I think you _______ go to a doctor as you've been unwell more than a week now. **(2020)**
   (a) may be   (b) should
   (c) might   (d) oughtn't

47. When it _________ raining, the flow of river water will be _________ .   **(2020)**
    (a) cease, more weak
    (b) stops, weaker
    (c) commence, weaker
    (d) leads, weakly
48. We couldn't _____ to keep our scooter, so we sold it.   **(2020)**
    (a) afford   (b) afforded
    (c) affordable   (d) affording
49. _______ you think footballers are paid way too much?   **(2020)**
    (a) Does   (b) Were
    (c) Do   (d) Have
50. The teacher is satisfied with our daughter 's progress in _____ term.   **(2020)**
    (a) this   (b) these
    (c) those   (d) there
51. If you heat ice, it _______ .   **(2020)**
    (a) could melt   (b) be melting
    (c) melt (d)   melts
52. A few of the girls______join the foreign language course.   **(2021)**
    (a) wants
    (b) want to
    (c) to wanting
    (d) have want to
53. Tania invited my friend and _______ to _______birthday party.   **(2021)**
    (a) I, my   (b) me, her
    (c) me, hers   (d) I, their
54. The food is cold. You can _______ it _______in the microwave.   **(2021)**
    (a) keep, out   (b) warm, up
    (c) move, on   (d) take, off
55. _______ were playing cricket when _____ saw a snake near the bushes.   **(2021)**
    (a) Them, he   (b) They, they
    (c) Their, we   (d) He, he
56. He said he _______ look after my parrots while I was away.   **(2021)**

(a) can   (b) may
(c) might   (d) would

DIRECTIONS (Qs. 57-65) : *choose the correct option to fill in the blank.*   **(2021)**

57. This report is urgent, so please _________ the process as much as you can
    (a) habilitate   (b) expedite
    (c) brandish   (d) 1mpasse
58. The brochure, _______ is available on the website will give you all the information that you are looking for.
    (a) which   (b) what
    (c) whose   (d) when
59. Santosh is _______ athletic for his age.
    (a) coincidence   (b) unusually
    (c) contagious   (d) passively
60. The two mountain goats fought _________ .
    (a) fiercely   (b) quietly
    (c) dutifully   (d) orderly
61. The rats hid under the _________ in the garden.
    (a) house   (b) light
    (c) vegetation   (d) sanitation
62. Judith : He should have _______ from making unnecessary comments.
    (a) refrained   (b) reduced
    (c) designed   (d) deliberate
63. Grace : She excused _______ before she left the dinner table.
    (a) himself   (b) itself
    (c) herself   (d) ourselves
64. The point of a story is to invoke __________ in the reader.
    (a) catheter   (b) catharsis
    (c) composition   (d) condition
65. Fill in the blank as per the subject-verb agreement.
    The pair of shoes _______ good.
    (a) looks   (b) look
    (c) have looked   (d) are looking

HINTS & EXPLANATIONS

LEVEL - 1

1. (c) "People" is the only noun in this sentence. It is the plural of "person." A noun identifies a person, place, or thing, "Many," although the subject of the sentence, is an adverb indicating amount. "These" is an adjective modifying the noun "people." "Ignored" is a transitive verb; in the plural past participle used to form the passive voice.

2. (d) In this sentence context, "holds" is a plural noun. ("Calls" and "company" are also nouns but are not choices here.) B (placed) is a verb. C (lengthy) is an adjective modifying the noun.

3. (d) "Dog" is a noun. "Come" (A) is a verb (imperative). "Meet" (B) is also a verb "Our" (C) is a possessive pronoun modifying the noun "dog."

4. (c) "Persons" is a plural noun. "Keeping" (A) is the gerund form of a verb in this sentence (i.e. it functions as the subject like a noun, but it is not a noun). "Difficult" (B) is an adjective modifying the noun phrase "Keeping warm in the winter." "Elderly" (D) is an adjective modifying the noun "persons."

5. (a) War is the only choice offered that is a noun. (Nouns in the sentence are proper nouns Tom, Dave; platoon; and War) "And" is a conjunction. "Were" is a verb (past tense). "During" is a preposition indicating a relationship of time between the verb "were" and the noun "War".

6. (d) Collective Noun is a count noun that denotes a group of individuals (e.g. assembly, family, crew).

7. (c) Abstract Noun denotes an idea, quality, or state rather than a concrete object, e.g., truth, danger, happiness.

8. (d) Material Noun is the name of a material or a substance or an ingredient of an alloy.

9. (d) Collective Noun is a count noun that denotes a group of individuals (e.g., assembly, family, crew).

10. (a) Common Noun is a noun denoting a class of objects or a concept as opposed to a particular individual. Often contrasted with proper noun.

11. (c) 'Who' the interrogative Pronoun refers to what or which person or people

12. (b) 'Whose' is the interrogative Possessive determiner and pronoun refers to belonging to or associated with which person.

13. (d) You, the pronoun is used to refer to the person or people that the speaker is addressing.

14. (b) 'them' as a pronoun is used to as the object of a verb or preposition to refer to two or more people or things previously mentioned or easily identified.

15. (c) 'They' the pronoun is used to refer to two or more people or things previously mentioned or easily identified.

16. (a) 'Will' verb is used to perform action in future.

17. (d) Subject is singular

18. (b) Third person singular present of go is used for earth.

19. (c) Third person singular

20. (c) Not want to be subjected to something

21. (a) Modal verb means be able to

22. (b) Modal verb expressing the future tense.

23. (d) Modal verb past of will here expressing a desire.

24. (c) Adjective meaning made familiar with; accustomed to

25. (c) Modal verb expressing a request

26. (c) Modal verb referring to a possible event or situation

27. (a) Adverb here means without difficulty or effort

28. (b) Adverb here means in an unacceptable or unpleasant way

29. (c) Adverb means moving or appearing to move away from a particular place

30. (a) Adverb here means in a determined and forceful way

31. (a)   32. (b)   33. (c)   34. (b)
35. (b)   36. (b)   37. (a)   38. (b)

39. (b) ended
40. (a) flying
41. (b) one
42. (c) reviewed
43. (c) Which
44. (a) ligament
45. (c) very
46. (d) you
47. (b) assured
48. (b) his
49. (c) protectively (adverb of manner)
50. (c) got caught
51. (c) standing
52. (b) that
53. (d)
54. (c)

LEVEL - 2

1. (d) Energy is a noun, as is will here. Take (a) is a verb. All (b) is an adverb modifying take. Your (c) is an adjective modifying energy and will.

2. (d) Reserve is the only noun of the choices. Many (a) and great (b) are adjectives modifying the noun poets. Placed (c) is a verb.

3. (a) Bridge is a proper noun here. Was (b) is the auxiliary verb for the past perfect tense of the verb opened (c). In (d) is a preposition.

4. (d) War is a proper noun here. And (a) is a conjunction. Were (b) is a verb. During (c) is a preposition.

5. (d) Bone is a noun. True (a) is an adjective modifying the noun fish. Because (b) is a conjunction. Their (c) is a plural possessive third-person pronoun modifying the noun skeletons.

6. (d) Boss is a noun. Have (a) is the auxiliary verb for the present perfect tense of the verb met (b). Your (c) is a possessive second-person pronoun modifying the noun boss.

7. (a) North is a noun here. But (b) is a conjunction. Not (c) is an adverb modifying the verb adapt (d).

8. (d) Students is a plural noun. NOTE: Mastering (a) is a gerund, i.e. a verb form functioning as a noun. But since (d) is already a noun, it is the better choice. Important (b) is an adjective modifying the noun goal. Younger (c) is an adjective modifying the noun students.

9. (d) Neutrality is a noun. Seize (a) is a verb. Its (b) is a possessive pronoun modifying the noun inhabitants. Flagrant (c) is an adjective modifying the noun disregard.

10. (d) Destruction is a noun. Their (a) is a plural possessive pronoun modifying destruction. Led (b) and accept (c) are verbs.

11. (d) Relative pronoun used to identify a specific person or thing observed or heard by the speaker.

12. (a) Relative pronoun used instead of 'who' as the object of a verb or preposition.

13. (a) Relative pronoun asking for information specifying one or more people or things from a definite set.

14. (d) Relative pronoun used instead of 'who' as the object of a verb or preposition.

15. (a) Relative pronoun used referring to something previously mentioned when introducing a clause giving further information.

16. (a) Relative pronoun used to introduce a clause giving further information about a person or people previously mentioned.

17. (a) Relative pronoun used to introduce a clause giving further information about a person or people previously mentioned.

18. (c) Relative pronoun of whom or which used to indicate that the following noun belongs to or is associated with the person or thing mentioned in the previous clause.

19. (b) Relative pronoun used instead of 'who' as the object of a verb or preposition.

20. (d) Relative pronoun means in or to what place or position.

21. (a) Relative pronoun used to introduce a clause giving further information about a person or people previously mentioned.

22. (b) Relative pronoun means of whom or which (used to indicate that the following noun belongs to or is associated with the person or thing mentioned in the previous clause.

23. (c) 24. (a) 25. (c) 26. (c) 27. (d)
28. (b) 29. (c) 30. (d) 31. (a) 32. (c)

33. (b) 34. (a) 35. (c) 36. (c) 37. (a)

38. (a) 39. (c) 40. (c)

41. (c)

42. (b)

43. (c) needn't

44. (c) coordination

45. (d) having begun

46. (b) should

47. (b) stops, weaker

48. (a) afford

49. (c) 'Do' auxialiary verb is used when the sentence is in 'present tense' and the subject is 'you'.

50. (a) this

51. (d) melts

52. (b) want to

53. (b) me, her

54. (b) warm, up

55. (b) They, they

56. (d) would

57. (b) "expedite" which means "to make something happen more quickly".

58. (a) which

59. (b) unusually

60. (a) "fiercely" which means "in a frightening, violent, or powerful way".

61. (c) vegetation

62. (a) refrained

63. (c) herself

64. (b) "catharsis" which means "the process of releasing strong emotions through a particular activity or experience".

65. (a)

CHAPTER 3

ADJECTIVES/ DETERMINERS/ PREPOSITIONS/ CONJUNCTIONS

ADJECTIVES

An adjective is a word that describes a noun, giving extra information about it.

EXAMPLE

- *a* **sweet** taste
- *a* **red** *apple*
- *a* **technical** *problem*
- *an* **Italian** *woman*

POSITIONS OF ADJECTIVES

Most adjectives can be used in two positions: **attributive** adjectives occur before the noun they describe, while **predicative** adjectives are used after certain verbs:

a **black** *cat*   [attributive]

The cat was **black**.   [predicative]

Comparative and superlative adjectives

Most adjectives have three forms: the **positive** (e.g. *sad*); the **comparative** (e.g. *sadder*); and the **superlative** (e.g. *saddest*). The formation of comparative and superlative adjectives (and adverbs) is known as **comparison**.

Gradable and non-gradable adjectives

Most adjectives are **gradable**. This means that you can modify (strengthen, weaken, or otherwise change) their meanings by placing one or more adverbs in front of them (e.g. *a* **very** *expensive car*).

Non-gradable adjectives are those with meanings which cannot be modified by adverbs (e.g., western, electric).

Qualitative and classifying adjectives

Adjectives can also be divided into two other types:

Qualitative adjectives describe the qualities of someone or something (e.g. *tall, long, hot*)

Classifying adjectives are used to put people or things into categories or classes (e.g. *weekly, northern, external*)

DETERMINERS

Determiners are used to either refer to something or to quantify. Referring means showing us who or what the noun is pointing to or talking about. We use articles, possessives and demonstratives to refer.

EXAMPLE

Where's **the** *new house?*

It's on **the** main road.

*Have you seen **my** brown shoes anywhere?*
*Yes. It's under **the** sofa.*

Quantifying

'Quantifying' is to show how much of something there is, or how many.

EXAMPLE

Many people died in the blast near the subway.

You have got **two** new messages.

Different types of determiners include:

Articles: *a/an, the*

Demonstratives: *this, that, these, those*

Possessives: *my, your, his, her, its, our, their*

Quantifiers: *(a) few, fewer, (a) little, many, much, more, most, some, any*, etc.

Numbers: *one, two, three*, etc.

Demonstratives

Demonstratives are used to state the distance from the speaker. The distance can be either psychological or physical.

Demonstratives can be used as *pronouns* or *adjectives*. They are sometimes referred to as demonstrative adjectives or demonstrative pronouns. When they are used as adjectives they modify the *noun*. A determiner is always used before a noun.

This – is used with singular nouns when referring to an object that is close to the speaker

This car is parked very close to my driveway.

Is **this** Soumya's dog?

This is not Soumya's book.

That – is used with singular nouns when referring to an object or person that is far to the speaker

That dog across the street is really sweet.

Is **that** Soumya's car across the street?

That is not Soumya's house.

These - is used with plural nouns when referring to an object that is close to the speaker

These cars are parked very close to my driveway.

Are **these** Soumya's dogs?

These are not Soumya's books.

Those - is used with plural nouns when referring to an object or person that is far to the speaker

I really like **those** cars.

Are **those** Soumya's friends?

Those are not Soumya's brothers.

Possessive determiners

Possessive determiners, or possessive adjectives, tell us who owns something.

We use a possessive determiner before a noun to show who owns the noun we are talking about.

EXAMPLE

Jane gave me **your** address.

Would you please return **my** book?

It's his sister's wedding.

Our new home is very airy.

Subject	Possessive Determiner
I	my
we	our
you	your
they	their
he	his
she	her
it	its

Quantifiers

Quantifiers answer the following two questions:

1. How much? – this is used with only uncountable nouns. The words used with uncountable nouns are: a little, a bit of, much, a great deal of, and a large amount of.

EXAMPLE

*   What you need is to put **a little** more salt to make it taste like soup.
*   There is **a bit of** broken glass under the chair.
*   I haven't brought **much** money with me.
*   **A great deal of** her work is massaging the back of patients.
*   The drugs were sold for **a large amount of** hard cash.

2. How many? – this is used with countable nouns. The words used with countable nouns are: a, an, one, each, every, both, a couple of, a few, several, many, a number of, a large number of, and a great number of.

EXAMPLE

*   **A** rubber duck is floating in the bath.
*   **An** evil monster like him has no friends.
*   **One** page is missing from the book.
*   **Each** item is carefully checked.
*   **Every** child was given a lollipop.
*   **Both** donkeys are braying at the same time.
*   After **a couple of** drinks, he was unable to control his speech.
*   She cracked **a few** eggs into the mixture.
*   Someone stole **several** pigs from his farm.
*   I think he is putting too **many** eggs in one basket.
*   **A number of** you think I look overweight.

Quantifiers can be used with countable or uncountable nouns with such words as: no, any, some, plenty of, a lot of, lots of, most, and all.

EXAMPLE

*   There is a lot of work I have to do this week. (Uncountable noun)
*   There were a lot of people watching the cockfight. (Countable noun)

PREPOSITIONS

A preposition is a word such as *after, in, to, on*, and *with*. Prepositions are usually used in front of nouns or pronouns and they show the relationship between the noun or pronoun and other words in a sentence. They describe, for example:

*   *The position of something*:
    *   Her bag was **under** the chair.
    *   The dog crawled **between** us and lay down at our feet.
*   *The time when something happens:*
    *   They arrived **on** Sunday.
    *   The class starts **at** 9 a.m.
    *   Shortly **after** their marriage they moved to Mumbai.

*   *The way in which something is done*:
  - We went **by** train.
  - They stared at each other **without** speaking.
*   *Some prepositions are made up of more than one word* .
  - They moved here **because of** the baby.
  - We sat **next to** each other.
  - The hotel is perched **on top** of a cliff.

CONJUNCTIONS

A conjunction (also called a connective) is a word such as *and, because, but, for, if, or* and *when*. Conjunctions are used to connect phrases, clauses, and sentences.

There are two main kinds of conjunction.

Coordinating Conjunctions

Coordinating conjunctions join items that are of equal importance in a sentence.
- You can have ice cream **or** strawberries.
- He plays football **and** cricket.
- The weather was cold **but** clear.

Subordinating Conjunctions

Subordinating conjunctions connect subordinate clauses to the main clause of a sentence.
- I waited at home **until** she arrived.
- He went to bed **because** he was tired.

Starting a sentence with a conjunction

You might have been taught that it's not good English to start a sentence with a conjunction such as *and* or *but*. It's not grammatically incorrect to do so, however, and many respected writers use conjunctions at the start of a sentence to create a dramatic or forceful effect.

EXAMPLE

What are the government's chances of winning in court? **And** what are the consequences?

Beginning a sentence with a conjunction can also be a useful way of conveying surprise.
- **And** are you really going?
- **But** didn't she tell you?

It's best not to overdo it, but there is no reason for completely avoiding the use of conjunctions at the start of sentences.

LEVEL 1

1. The Arabic language is **difficult** to learn.
   - (a) quality
   - (b) quantity
   - (c) Numeral
   - (d) demonstrative
2. **Many** people work but **few** deserve to work.
   - (a) distributive
   - (b) numeral **(2012)**
   - (c) emphasising
   - (d) quantity
3. **These** fruits are juicy and sweet. **(2016)**
   - (a) Numeral
   - (b) quality
   - (c) demonstrative
   - (d) distributive
4. **Such** people like Tendulkar are exceptional.
   (2014)
   - (a) emphasising
   - (b) demonstrative
   - (c) numeral
   - (d) quantity
5. **Every** object in the Universe has its value.
   - (a) distributive
   - (b) interrogative
   - (c) numeral
   - (d) quantity

6. The Math paper was very ________. **(2014)**
   - (a) simplified
   - (b) correct
   - (c) tough
   - (d) tougher
7. Don't take or give ________ help to anyone.
   - (a) finance
   - (b) financial
   - (c) financed
   - (d) money
8. Mountains and Rivers are Nature's ________ gifts to human-beings. **(Tricky)**
   - (a) most precious
   - (b) more precious
   - (c) very precious
   - (d) prettier
9. Most of the South Indians are ________ in their domestic expenditure. **(2014)**
   - (a) economic
   - (b) economics
   - (c) economical
   - (d) most economic
10. My father is very ________ about my joining in the Banking.
    - (a) enthusiasm
    - (b) enthusiastic
    - (c) enthusing
    - (d) enthuse

11. Rekha is ________ prettiest girl in our class.
    - (a) a
    - (b) the **(2012)**
    - (c) no article
    - (d) an
12. Which shirt do you like? ________ blue one?
    - (a) the
    - (b) one
    - (c) no article
    - (d) a
13. Mr. Joshi is ________ best teacher in our school.
    - (a) an
    - (b) a
    - (c) no article
    - (d) the
14. There is ________ party at Raman's house tonight.
    - (a) a
    - (b) an **(2015)**
    - (c) no article
    - (d) the
15. She has ________ very nice cat.
    - (a) no article
    - (b) the
    - (c) an
    - (d) a
16. Keep ________ eye on him and make sure he doesn't steal anything. **(2017)**
    - (a) no article
    - (b) the
    - (c) a
    - (d) an
17. What time are we going to ________ party?
    - (a) the
    - (b) no article
    - (c) a
    - (d) an
18. I have ________ test tomorrow morning. **(2014)**
    - (a) the
    - (b) a
    - (c) an
    - (d) no article
19. Hurry up! ________ movie starts in 15 minutes!
    - (a) no article
    - (b) the
    - (c) a
    - (d) an
20. Sarah is ________ excellent teacher! **(2015)**
    - (a) a
    - (b) an
    - (c) no article required
    - (d) the

The chameleon is a relative ___21___ the lizard. It is a reptile. It can be found ___22___ Africa and Madagascar. You can also find it in some parts of Asia and southern Europe. Some varieties of chameleons can grow ___23___ a length of 60 centimeters. However, the most common variety does not grow more than 30 centimeters long.

The most interesting thing ___24___ the chameleon is that it is able to change colour. It is able to change quickly ___25___ white to yellow, black, green or brown. It is able to do this because of the differences ___26___ light and temperature of its surroundings.

The chameleon lives in trees. Its tail and feet can hold on ___27___ the branches while it is reaching ___28___ to catch its prey.

The chameleon can remain very still ___29___ a branch ___30___ hours. As a result, when it is hunting, its prey will not even know it is there.

The chameleon has a long, sticky tongue. It can shoot ___31___ its tongue ___32___ a distance of 10 centimeters. the chameleon also has interesting eyes. Each eye can turn 180 degrees. Furthermore, each eye can turn independently. Thus, the right eye can look right while the left one is looking left.

21. (a) to (b) on (c) of (d) out

22. (a) in (b) for (c) but (d) against

23. (a) between (b) to (c) on (d) in

24. (a) around (b) in (c) about (d) of

25. (a) for (b) on (c) in (d) from

26. (a) out (b) between (c) in (d) on

27. (a) to (b) of (c) on (d) in

28. (a) around (b) across (c) out (d) in

29. (a) in (b) on (c) of (d) out

30. (a) of (b) to (c) for (d) in

31. (a) across (b) above (c) out (d) on

32. (a) towards (b) on (c) in (d) to

DIRECTIONS (Qs. 33-40): *Fill in the blanks with appropriate conjunctions from the given options.*

---

33. He is not _______ clever as his brother.
    (a) and (b) so **(2012)**
    (c) yet (d) but

34. He must be punished _______ he is guilty.
    (a) because (b) after
    (c) although (d) as

35. A fool _______ his money are soon parted.
    (a) than (b) that **(2015)**
    (c) while (d) and

36. He was not punished _______ he was guilty.
    (a) since (b) than
    (c) though (d) that

37. He worked hard _______ he might pass the examination. **(2014)**
    (a) not only (b) that
    (c) but (d) than

38. Give every man thy ear, _______ few thy voice.
    (a) but (b) before **(2016)**
    (c) because (d) for

39. I waited for him _______ the clock struck seven.
    (a) till (b) until
    (c) that (d) before

40. You will not get the prize _______ you deserve it.
    (a) for (b) but
    (c) and (d) unless

DIRECTIONS (Qs. 41-45): Fill in the blanks with the most suitable determiner.

---

41. __________ rivers in India are not polluted.
    (a) Few (b) Fewest **(2013)**
    (c) Fewer (d) None of these

42. In India, __________ time and resources are spent on education. **(2014)**
    (a) many (b) most
    (c) more (d) much

43. I would like to buy __________ sugar, please.
    (a) any (b) much
    (c) some (d) many

44. Do you have __________ new pen for tomorrow's competition? **(2012)**
    (a) any (b) much
    (c) some (d) most

45. The principal spoke separately to __________ student. **(2015)**
    (a) every (b) each
    (c) any (d) some

46. To complete the task you need _________ the tools not just a few.   **(2018)**
    (a) most   (b) some
    (c) any   (d) all

47. The cat is always left ________ when we are away.   **(2018)**
    (a) about   (b) roundabout
    (c) right on   (d) indoors

48. The match will be excellent ________ we all play well.   **(2018)**
    (a) and   (b) so
    (c) if   (d) but

49. I generally go by ______ bus to school but sometimes 1 cycle.   **(2018)**
    (a) the   (b) a
    (c) an   (d) no article

50. There were ______ than fifty people in the whole auditorium.   **(2018)**
    (a) little   (b) few
    (c) fewer   (d) no lesser

51. ______I'm not mistaken, that's certainly my uncle in the taxi. Wonder where he is going.   **(2018)**
    (a) If   (b) Till
    (c) Except   (d) Until

52. The farm we visited last week was really far out ______ the countryside.   **(2019)**
    (a) on   (b) in
    (c) over   (d) besides

53. Most things in life are ________, so there is little need to worry too much.   **(2019)**
    (a) solving   (b) solution
    (c) solvability   (d) solvable

54. The correct way to write ______ sentence is to start with ________ pronoun and make sure the verb matches.   **(2019)**
    (a) no article, the   (b) a, a
    (c) the, no article   (d) the, the

55. We are all in need of ______ rest and a hot coffee after such a long walk.   **(2019)**
    (a) a lot   (b) some
    (c) many   (d) too much

56. Watch ________ ! There is a pothole.   **(2020)**
    (a) off   (b) out
    (c) over   (d) for

57. ________ you answer back to me like that.   **(2020)**
    (a) Need   (b) Ought
    (c) Dare   (d) Would

58. Overall, it has been noticed that ______ saddest people live ______ shortest.   **(2020)**
    (a) a, the   (b) the, the
    (c) the, a   (d) the, no article

59. My mother is ______ my uncle.   **(2020)**
    (a) generous than
    (b) more generous that
    (c) most generous then
    (d) more generous than

60. I asked __________ , if anyone had seen my wallet in the cafeteria.   **(2020)**
    (a) above   (b) around
    (c) over   (d) on

61. You are __________ to switch off your mobile-phones.   **(2020)**
    (a) questioned   (b) suggest
    (c) wished   (d) requested

62. Oprah Winfrey who is an intelligent and bright woman __________ a heart of gold.   **(2020)**
    (a) had   (b) has
    (c) have   (d) having

63. Much of our time ______ now wasted in attending to the visitors.   **(2021)**
    (a) is   (b) are
    (c) were   (d) has

64. The director and the principal of the school ______ present in the assembly.   **(2021)**
    (a) was   (b) has
    (c) were   (d) will

65. Sushil ______ eating sweets because the doctor has advised him to.   **(2021)**
    (a) avoids   (b) has avoid
    (c) avoiding   (d) were avoiding

66. The police arrived in the nick of time ______ rescue the kidnapped child.   **(2021)**
    (a) for   (b) to
    (c) from   (d) and

67. I will finish my work ________ an hour. Then, I will go to park to play badminton.   **(2021)**
    (a) on   (b) at
    (c) in   (d) from

68. Penguins cannot fly ______ they can swim very well.   **(2021)**
    (a) but   (b) and
    (c) of   (d) so

69. Excuse me. Could you show me ______ way to ______ bus stop?   **(2021)**
    (a) a, a   (b) the, the
    (c) an, an   (d) the, no article

70. Father gave me _______ ten rupee note. **(2021)**
    (a) an   (b) a
    (c) the   (d) no article
71. I will go to the fair ________ we can all go together.   **(2021)**
    (a) only if   (b) unless
    (c) in order   (d) even if
72. ________ you check this document before I ____ print it, please?   **(2021)**
    (a) May   (b) Should
    (c) Can   (d) Have
73. Manju: I was up past my bedtime __________ I tried to keep my voice low.   **(2021)**
    (a) yet   (b) through
    (c) so   (d) or

DIRECTIONS (Qs. 74-82) : *Choose the correct option to fill in the blank.*   **(2022)**

74. Peninsula is a piece of land surrounded _______ water but is joined to a larger piece of land on one side.
    (a) by   (b) of
    (c) from   (d) for
75. The petals of balsam are soft and ___________
    (a) delicate   (b) droll
    (c) determinate   (d) dismal
76. The old man was as good as ________ word.
    (a) him   (b) them
    (c) himself   (d) his
77. Swift told his teammates that this _______ was last chance at the game.
    (a) there   (b) their
    (c) its   (d) him
78. She was_______in her criticism of the health policy.

79. ________ girl who called me up is from Kerala.
    (a) A   (b) An
    (c) The   (d) No article
80. Alan has __________ good command on Mathematics.
    (a) a   (b) an
    (c) the   (d) no article
81. Fill in the blank with the most appropriate filler.
    He ________ insulted his parents.
    (a) should not has
    (b) should have not
    (c) should not have
    (d) should not had
82. Fill in the blanks with the correct articles.
    ______ DM of our district came to our village yesterday and told us about _______ importance of discipline in life.
    (a) An, the   (b) An, a
    (c) The, a   (d) The, the

DIRECTIONS (Qs. 83-84) : *Fill in the blanks with appropriate prepositions.*   **(2022)**

83. I have no acquaintance ________ the members of her family.
    (a) to   (b) with
    (c) for   (d) on
84. He takes pride ________ his work.
    (a) in   (b) by
    (c) at   (d) for
85. Fill in the blank with the correct conjunction.
    ________I was hungry, I didn't eat anything.
    (a) And   (b) If
    (c) Although   (d) Or

(a) forthright   (b) grateful
(c) bright   (d) inclined

LEVEL 2

DIRECTIONS (Qs. 1-10) : *Choose the correct option to complete the sentences with the correct form of adjectives.*

1. When we visited Kerala the people were very
   _______.   **(2014)**
   - (a) friendly
   - (b) friends
   - (c) befriending
   - (d) friending

2. The play was quite _______.
   - (a) amuse
   - (b) amusing
   - (c) amused
   - (d) amusable

3. The smooth air after the pinching heat of Delhi
   was very _______.   **(2014)**
   - (a) refresh
   - (b) refreshed
   - (c) refreshing
   - (d) refreshable

4. The kids were _______ to see the water park
   and the various rides.
   - (a) excited
   - (b) excite
   - (c) excitable
   - (d) exciting

5. Little babies are so _______   **(2013)**
   - (a) adoring
   - (b) adored
   - (c) adory
   - (d) adorable

6. Whenever I am complemented I always feel
   _________.   **(2015)**
   - (a) embarrassing
   - (b) embarrass
   - (c) embarrassed
   - (d) embarrassingly

7. My father has a huge collection of _______ bed
   time stories.
   - (a) interested
   - (b) interesting
   - (c) interest
   - (d) interestingly

8. Mother is women of _______ words.
   - (a) few
   - (b) fewer
   - (c) little
   - (d) small

9. The _______ words made Ragini blush up to
   her ears.   **(2012)**
   - (a) whisper
   - (b) whisperingly
   - (c) whispery
   - (d) whispering

10. My _______ parents are still very active.**(2016)**
    - (a) aged
    - (b) age
    - (c) agedly
    - (d) ageing

DIRECTIONS (Qs. 11-20) : *Choose the correct articles given from the options.*

11. Never tell _______ lie.
    - (a) a
    - (b) an
    - (c) the
    - (d) none of the above

12. I have lost _______ pen that you gave me.
    - (a) a
    - (b) the
    - (c) an
    - (d) none of the above

13. I am in _______ hurry.
    - (a) the
    - (b) no article
    - (c) a
    - (d) an

14. She is _______ honest girl.   **(2017)**
    - (a) an
    - (b) the
    - (c) a
    - (d) no article

15. He has _______ headache.
    - (a) no article required
    - (b) the
    - (c) an
    - (d) a

16. It is time to take _______ tea.   **(2015)**
    - (a) a
    - (b) the
    - (c) no article
    - (d) an

17. The man is _______ mortal.
    - (a) no article
    - (b) a
    - (c) the
    - (d) an

18. Please give me _______ one-rupee note. **(2014)**
    - (a) a
    - (b) an
    - (c) the
    - (d) no article

19. She is _______ M. A. in Geography.   **(2015)**
    - (a) zero article
    - (b) the
    - (c) an
    - (d) a

20. He is going to _______ University.
    - (a) the
    - (b) none of the options
    - (c) no article
    - (d) a

DIRECTIONS (Qs. 21-30) : *Fill the blanks with appropriate prepositions from the given alternatives.*

21. We regret that we cannot comply _______ your
    request.   **(2016)**
    - (a) with
    - (b) at
    - (c) to
    - (d) for

22. The best candidate should be appointed _______ the post.
    (a) to   (b) at
    (c) with   (d) in

23. He is addicted _______ gambling.
    (a) on   (b) at
    (c) to   (d) for

24. I was amazed _______ her stupendous ignorance. **(2013)**
    (a) with   (b) on
    (c) at   (d) to

25. We must be grateful for the blessings that God has bestowed _______ us. **(2015)**
    (a) on   (b) with
    (c) for   (d) to

26. We called _______ a friend's house on the way.
    (a) at   (b) on
    (c) for   (d) to

27. On the way we came _______ an old beggar.
    (a) along   (b) across   **(2014)**
    (c) on   (d) to

28. We agreed _______ a certain course of action.
    (a) with   (b) upon
    (c) in   (d) on

29. People in many villages don't have access _______ electricity. **(2012)**
    (a) with   (b) to
    (c) at   (d) for

30. He was accused _______ theft.
    (a) of   (b) for
    (c) with   (d) by

DIRECTIONS (Qs. 31-40) : *Fill in the blanks with correct conjunctions from the options given below.*

31. She is noble _______ kind too. **(2015)**
    (a) and   (b) but
    (c) or   (d) otherwise

32. We eat _______ we remain healthy.
    (a) therefore   (b) so that
    (c) as well as   (d) since

33. Raj is poor _______ he is honest **(2014)**
    (a) since   (b) or
    (c) but   (d) otherwise

34. The sun rose _______ the fog disappeared.
    (a) as soon as   (b) thus
    (c) as well as   (d) therefore

35. _______ she saw the tiger, she shouted. **(2014)**
    (a) as soon as   (b) since
    (c) so that   (d) as well as

36. Work hard _______ you will fail.
    (a) since   (b) therefore
    (c) otherwise   (d) but

37. Robin worked very hard _______ he didn't stand first. **(2016)**
    (a) still   (b) but
    (c) therefore   (d) as well as

38. She must cry _______ she will die.
    (a) but   (b) otherwise
    (c) or   (d) therefore

39. He _______ his brother is coming. **(2017)**
    (a) as soon as   (b) but
    (c) so   (d) as well as

40. The box was heavy _______ he could not lift it.
    (a) therefore   (b) so
    (c) otherwise   (d) but

DIRECTIONS (Qs. 41-45) : *Choose the correct option and fill in the blanks.*

41. Did you take _______ photos? Yes, but not _______. **(Tricky, 2015)**
    (a) many, much   (b) a lot of, a lot
    (c) any, many   (d) much, many

42. Did you get _______ work done? Yes, but not _______.
    (a) some, much
    (b) any much
    (c) some, a lot of
    (d) any a lot of

43. _______ of the kids had ever been abroad before.
    (a) None   (b) Many
    (c) Some   (d) Much

44. I'm afraid I made _______ mistakes; I hope I've corrected _______ of them. **(2012)**
    (a) many, much   (b) many, some
    (c) a lot of, all   (d) a lot of, none

45. I've tried _______ possible method but I've had _______ success. **(2016)**
    (a) many, much   (b) every, no
    (b) some, no   (d) every, any

46. The house is _______ the rear _________ the new school.   **(2018)**
    (a) to, of
    (b) on, with (c) at, alone
    (d) next to, in

47. A baby needs at least ten-hour of _______ sleep.   **(2018)**
    (a) undisputed
    (b) undisturbed
    (c) undivided
    (d) undisclosed

48. Why the painter decided to add such a lot of color to this painting ______ me.   **(2019)**
    (a) behind
    (b) within
    (c) ahead
    (d) beyond

49. I moved to a new house last week. My new house is _________ there beside the park ________ a little cul-de-sac.   **(2019)**
    (a) over, in
    (b) near, with (c) alone, for
    (d) up, at

50. The newspaper reported their belief _________material possessions.   **(2020)**
    (a) off
    (b) inside
    (c) in
    (d) after

51. Rati stormed ________of the hall______ angel.   **(2020)**
    (a) out, in
    (b) for, at
    (c) in, by
    (d) by, of

52. Tourist Guide: Come guys, let's get going or we _______ late.   **(2020)**
    (a) could
    (b) will be
    (c) can have
    (d) should been

53. The _________ mountaineers who scaled the peak in winter should be specially congratulated   **(2020)**
    (a) cowardly
    (b) intrepid
    (c) garrulous
    (d) pompous

54. Little Kezia ________ the manuscript her dad had been working on for six months.   **(2021)**
    (a) cut in
    (b) pulled apart
    (c) fall apart
    (s) drop back

55. It didn't at any ______ to us that we point had left the iron on.   **(2021)**
    (a) dawn
    (b) think
    (c) mind
    (d) occur

56. Leo : ________ all practical purposes, they are one and the same thing.   **(2021)**
    (a) Form
    (b) For
    (c) But
    (d) And

57. Davis : There is a new bridge that connects the old_____new stations.   **(2021)**
    (c) or
    (c) so
    (c) and
    (c) too

58. Her presentation was so long and dull had a hard time staying awake.   **(2021)**
    (a) or
    (b) that
    (c) whether
    (d) when

59. The lawyer seemed all_______during the proceedings at the court.   **(2022)**
    (a) put through
    (b) put up
    (c) put to
    (d) put together

60. Modern day anxieties have _________ the increasing level of stress among people.
    (a) led to
    (b) lead on   **(2022)**
    (c) let in
    (d) let down

DIRECTIONS (Qs. 61-63) : *Choose the correct option to complete each conversation.*   **(2022)**

61. Shruti :_______you like another cup of tea?
    Niveda : No, thank you.
    (a) Should
    (b) Would
    (c) Can
    (d) Must

62. Samuel : _________ knowledgeable is not the same thing as being wise.
    (a) Been
    (b) An
    (c) Being
    (d) Do

63. Joe : I got drenched _____ the rain yesterday.
    (a) on
    (b) at
    (c) in
    (d) along\

DIRECTIONS (Qs. 64-66) : *Find the usage of the words underlined in the following sentences:*   **(2022)**

64. I eat these pastries.
    (a) Adjective
    (b) Pronoun
    (c) Infinitive
    (d) Adverb

65. The actor agreed to dance with me.
    (a) Gerund
    (b) Infinitive
    (c) Adverb
    (d) Adjective

66. Walking on the lawns is forbidden.
    (a) Infinitive
    (b) Adjective
    (c) Adverb
    (d) Gerund

HINTS & EXPLANATIONS

LEVEL - 1

1. (a) Qualitative adjective relates to the quality or standard of something rather than the quantity

2. (b) Adjective which expresses the number of persons or things are called the Adjective of Number or Numeral Adjective.

3. (c) Demonstrative adjectives are especially helpful when you want to make it clear which noun (which thing) you would like to talk about.

4. (b) Such the demonstrative adjective demonstrates of the kind, character, degree, extent, etc., of that or those indicated or implied.

5. (a) This distributive adjective implies being one of a group or series taken collectively; each.

6. (c) Difficult to solve

7. (b) Relating to finance

8. (a) Of great value because of being rare, expensive, or important.

9. (c) Giving good value or return in relation to the money, time, or effort extended.

10. (b) Having or showing intense and eager enjoyment, interest, or approval.

11. (b) Nouns with superlative adjectives normally have the article *the*.

12. (a) Here the is used for a particular or definite shirt.

13. (d) Definite article is used before superlative degree.

14. (a) Indefinite article-a- is used before a consonant sound.

15. (d) Indefinite article-a- is used before a consonant sound and again the object is singular.

16. (d) The form an--is used before words starting with a vowel sound, regardless of whether the word begins with a vowel letter.

17. (a) Asking a definite time.

18. (b) 'a' is used before consonant sound and singular number.

19. (b) Referring a definite movie.

20. (b) An is used before vowel sound.

21. (c) The chameleon is a relative of the lizard.

22. (a) It can be found in Africa and Madagascar.

23. (b) Some varieties of chameleons can grow to a length of 60 centimeters.

24. (c) The most interesting thing about the chameleon is that it is able to change colour.

25. (d) It is able to change quickly from white to yellow, black, green or brown.

26. (c) It is able to do this because of the differences in light and temperature of its surroundings.

27. (a) The chameleon lives in trees. Its tail and feet can hold on **to** the branches while it is reaching ___28___ to catch its prey.

28. (c) The chameleon lives in trees. Its tail and feet can hold on to the branches while it is reaching out to catch its prey.

29. (b) The chameleon can remain very still on a branch ___30___ hours.

30. (c) The chameleon can remain very still on a branch for hours.

31. (c) It can shoot out its tongue ___32___ a distance of 10 centimeters.

32. (d) It can shoot out its tongue to a distance of 10 centimeters.

33. (b) He is not **so** clever as his brother.

34. (a) He must be punished **because** he is guilty.

35. (d) A fool **and** his money are soon parted.

36. (c) He was not punished **though** he was guilty.

37. (b) He worked hard **that** he might pass the examination.

38. (a) Give everyman thy ear, **but** few thy voice.

39. (b) I waited for him **until** the clock struck seven.

40. (d) You will not get the prize **unless** you deserve it.

41. (a)

42. (d)
43. (c)
44. (a)
45. (b)
46. (d)
47. (d)
48. (c)
49. (d)   no article
50. (c)   fewer
51. (a)   If
52. (b)   in
53. (d)   solvable
54. (b)   a, a
55. (b)   some
56. (b)   "Watch out" means "to be careful because of possible danger or trouble".
57. (c)   Dare
58. (b)   the, the
59. (d)   more generous than
60. (b)   around
61. (d)   requested
62. (b)   has
63. (a)   is
64. (c)   were
65. (a)   avoids
66. (b)   to
67. (c)   in
68. (a)   but
69. (b)   the, the
70. (b)   a
71. (a)   "only if" is used because the sentence expresses a strong condition.
72. (c)   Can
73. (c)   so
74. (a)   by
75. (a)   delicate
76. (d)   his

77. (b)   their
78. (a)   "forthright" which means "to be straightforward and direct".
79. (c)   "The" is used here to specify a particular girl.
80. (a)   a
81. (c)
82. (d)
83. (b)
84. (a)
85. (c)

LEVEL - 2

1. (a)   Friendly the adjective means kind and pleasant.
2. (b)   Amusing the adjective here means causing laughter and providing entertainment.
3. (c)   Refreshing the adjective here means serving to refresh or reinvigorate someone.
4. (a)   Excited in adjective form means serving to refresh or reinvigorate someone.
5. (d)   Adorable the adjective here implies inspiring great affection or delight.
6. (c)   Embarrassed the adjective here means feeling or showing embarrassment.
7. (b)   Interesting the adjective here means arousing curiosity or interest; holding or catching the attention.
8. (a)   The adjective here means a small number of.
9. (c)   Whispery in adjective for means like a whisper.
10. (a)   The adjective form means having lived for a specified length of time; of a specified age.
11. (a)   Never tell a lie.
12. (b)   I have lost the pen that you gave me.
13. (c)   I am in a hurry.
14. (a)   She is an honest girl.
15. (d)   He has a headache.
16. (c)   It is time to take tea.
17. (a)   Man is mortal.
18. (a)   Please give me a one rupee note.
19. (c)   She is an M. A. in Geography.
20. (d)   He is going to a University.

21.	(a)	Comply with	49.	(a)	over, in
22.	(a)	Appointed to	50.	(c)	in
23.	(c)	Addicted to	51.	(a)	out, in
24.	(c)	Amazed at	52.	(b)	will be
25.	(a)	Bestowed on	53.	(b)	intrepid
26.	(a)	Called at (= visit)	54.	(b)	"pulled apart" which means "to be separated into pieces by pulling".
27.	(b)	Came across			
28.	(b)	Agreed upon	55.	(d)	occur
29.	(b)	Access to	56.	(b)	For
30.	(a)	Accused of	57.	(c)	and
31.	(a)	and---cumulative conjunction	58.	(b)	that
32.	(b)	so that----purpose, subordinating	59.	(d)	"put together" which means "to prepare something by collecting ideas or information".
33.	(c)	but----adversative conjunction, contrast			
34.	(d)	therefore/so---result, illative conjunction			
35.	(a)	as soon as -subordinating conjunction, time	60.	(a)	"led to" which means "to cause something to happen".
36.	(c)	otherwise---subordinating conjunction, contrast			
37.	(a)	still---contrast	61.	(b)	Would
38.	(c)	or---alternative, coordinating conjunction	62.	(c)	Being
39.	(d)	as well as	63.	(c)	in
40.	(b)	so---result,	64.	(a)	
41.	(c)	42. (b) 43. (a) 44. (c) 45. (b)	65.	(b)	
46.	(a)		66.	(a)	
47.	(b)	undisturbed			
48.	(d)	beyond			

TENSES

The concept of time can be split into:
1. **The Present -** What you are currently doing.
   I eat, I am eating
2. **The Past -** What you did some time back.
   I ate, I was eating
3. **The Future -** What you will do later.
   I will eat, I will be eating

In the English language, tenses play an important role in sentence formation.

The tense of a verb shows the time of an event or action.

Types of Tenses and Their Subcategories

As we have already discussed in the introduction, there are primarily three types of tenses. These three tenses are again subcategorized based on continuance and completeness of action:

- Ø Simple/Indefinite Tense
- Ø Continuous tense
- Ø Perfect tense
- Ø Perfect continuous tense

Simple Tense: It is utilized for ongoing or routine activities in the Present Tense, activity which is over in the Past Tense and activity to occur in the Future Tense.

Continuous Tense: The activity is fragmented or consistent or going on.

Perfect Tense: The activity is finished, completed or wonderful regarding a specific purpose of time.

Perfect Continuous Tense: The activity is going on persistently throughout an extensive stretch of time and is yet to be done.

Rules For Tenses

Rules of Tenses make it easier to comprehend how to use the various tenses in a sentence without making grammatical errors and by clearly stating when an event or action has taken place. There are a few rules to remember to use these tenses correctly and meaningfully.

Tenses	Tenses Rule
Past Simple Tense	Subject + V_2 + Object
Past Perfect Tense	Subject + had + V_3 + Object
Past Continuous Tense	Subject + was + V_1 + ing + Object (Singular)
	Subject + were + V_1 + ing + Object (Plural)
Past Perfect Continuous Tense	Subject + had been + V_1 + ing + Object
Present Simple Tense	Subject + V_1 + s/es + Object (Singular)
	Subject + V_1 + Object (Plural)
Present Perfect Tense	Subject + has + V_3 + Object (Singular)
	Subject + have + V_3 + Object (Plural)

Present Continuous Tense	Subject + is/am/are + V_1 + ing + object
Present Perfect Continuous Tense	Subject + has been + V_1 + ing + Object (Singular)Subject + have been + V_1 + ing + Object (Plural)
Future Simple Tense	Subject + will/shall + V_1 + Object
Future Perfect Tense	Subject + will have/shall have + V_3 + Object
Future Continuous Tense	Subject + will be/shall be + ing + V_1 + Object
Future Perfect Continuous Tense	Subject + will have been + V_1 + ing + Object

V_1 = First form of the verb
V_2 = Second form of the verb
V_3 = Third form of the verb
Let's discuss in details about their rules for each tense with examples.

PRESENT TENSE

Present Tense can be defined as an expression for an activity that is currently in action or is habitually performed. It is used for a state that generally exists or is currently ongoing.

SIMPLE PRESENT TENSE

Singular:
Rule – Subject + V_1 + s/es + Object
Example – The child plays a guitar.
Here the subject 'child' is singular and so we use 's' with the verb 'play'

Plural:
Rule – Subject + V_1 + object
Example – The children play guitar.
Here the subject 'children' is plural and we use the plural form of the verb 'play' (without "s")

PRESENT CONTINUOUS TENSE

Rule – Subject + is/am/are + V_1 + ing + object
While employing the tense rules for present continuous, all the verb form for singular or plural subject stays in its first form V_1
Example: Mary is dancing.
            They are dancing.
Here the subject "Mary" or "they" is followed by 'is' or 'are' respectively. The first form of verb (V_1) here is "dance" and we added "ing" to it to make it continuous.

PRESENT PERFECT TENSE

Singular:
Rule – Subject + has + V_3 + Object
Example – Mary has washed the clothes.
Here, "Mary" is the subject + has "washed" followed by the third form of verb "wash"

Plural:
Rule – Subject + have + V_3 + Object
Example – They have washed the clothes.
Here, "They" is the subject + have followed by the third form of verb "wash"

PRESENT PERFECT CONTINUOUS TENSE

Singular:

Rule – Subject + has been + V_1 + ing + Object
Example – Mary has been studying since morning.
Here, the subject "Mary" + has been is followed the the first form of verb "study" + ing

Plural:

Rule – Subject + have been + V_1 + ing + Object
Example – The students have been studying since morning.
Here the subject "students" + have been is followed by the first form of verb "study" + ing

PAST TENSE

Any event or action that took place in the past can be referred to as the past tense.

SIMPLE PAST TENSE

Rule – Subject + V_2 + Object
For past tense, the verb is always plural irrespective of the subject (without "s").
Example – He swam across the river.
　　　　　They swam across the river.
Here, the subject "He" and "They" is followed by "swam", the second form of verb (V_2) of "swim"

PAST CONTINUOUS TENSE

Singular

Rule – Subject + was + V_1 + ing + Object
Example – Mary was cleaning the house.
Here, the subject "Mary" + 'was' is followed by the first form of verb (V_1) "clean" + "ing"

Plural
Rule – Subject + were + V_1 + ing + Object
Example – They were cleaning the house.
Here, the subject is "They" + were is followed by the first form of verb (V_1) "clean" + "ing"

PAST PERFECT TENSE

Rule – Subject + had + V_3 + Object
Example – Mary had pulled the rope.
Here the subject "Mary" + had is followed by the third form of verb (V_3) "pull"

PAST PERFECT CONTINUOUS TENSE

Rule – Subject + had been + V_1 + ing + Object
Example – Mary had been taking care of her mother from last two weeks.
Here the subject "Mary" + had been is followed the first form of verb (V_1) of "take" + ing

FUTURE TENSE

The actions that are to take place in the future fall in the category of the future tense.

SIMPLE FUTURE TENSE

Rule – Subject + will/shall + V_1 + Object
For future tense, the verb is always plural irrespective of the subject (without "s").
Example – I shall go to the market tomorrow.
In this example, the subject "I" + shall is followed by the first form of verb (V_1) "go"

FUTURE CONTINUOUS TENSE

Rule –　Subject + will be/shall be + V_1 + ing + Object
Example –　Mary will be coming to my house tomorrow.
　　　　　They will be coming to my house tomorrow.
Here the subject "Mary" / "They" + will be is followed by the first form of verb (V_1) "come"+ing

FUTURE PERFECT TENSE

Rule – Subject + will have/shall have + V_3 + Object

Example –   Mary shall have covered all the notebooks in brown paper by tomorrow.

Here, the subject is "Mary" + shall have is followed by the third form of Verb (V_3) "covered"

FUTURE PERFECT CONTINUOUS TENSE

Rule – Subject + will have been + V_1 + ing + Object

Example –   He shall have been living here since 2001.

Here, the subject "he" + will have been is followed by the first form of verb "work"+ing

LEVEL 1

DIRECTIONS (Qs. 1-10) : *Fill in the blanks by writing appropriate tense form of the verbs given in brackets. Choose the tense from the options given below.*

1.   Fashion is important to Shyam, so he always _______ the latest and most popular style. (to select)   **(2014)**
    (a) present continuous
    (b) present tense
    (c) present perfect
    (d) present indefinite

2.   While Radha _______ new clothes, her fashion consultant is busy on the sidelines, recommending stripes and long 'kurtas' to minimize the bulge factor. (to buy)
    (a) present continuous
    (b) simple present
    (c) present perfect
    (d) Present Perfect Continuous

3.   Shyam hopes that the next fashion _______ fad a more mature, oval figure like his own. (to flatter)
    (a) Future Continuous   **(2012)**
    (b) Future Perfect
    (c) Future Perfect Continuous
    (d) simple future

4.   She once _______ a purple suede pantsuit, which lashed with her orange "I Love Motorcycle" tattoo. (to purchase)   **(2015)**
    (a) Past Continuous
    (b) simple past
    (c) Past Perfect
    (d) Past Perfect Continuous

5.   Two minutes after she received the award, Maya _______ it on a self next to her "Best dressed, Considering" medal. (to place)   **(2013)**
    (a) simple past
    (b) Past Continuous
    (c) Past Perfect
    (d) Past Perfect Continuous

6.   Rita _______ it to me in detail Yesterday. (to explain)
    (a) Past Continuous
    (b) Past Perfect

    (c) Simple past
    (d) Past Perfect Continuous

7.   Reema _______ an acceptance speech, but the "Leader of the Year" title went to Henna instead. (to prepare)
    (a) Past Continuous
    (b) Past Perfect Continuous
    (c) Simple past
    (d) Past perfect

8.   Mike _______ on thin ice for two hours when he heard the first crack. (to skate)   **(2016)**
    (a) Simple past
    (b) Past Perfect Continuous
    (c) Past Continuous
    (d) Past perfect

9.   Reema _______ Shyam for years about his smoking habits, but he just won't listen. (to warn)
    (a) Simple past   **(2014)**
    (b) Past Continuous
    (c) Present Perfect Continuous
    (d) Present perfect

10.   Garima _______ to speak to Micky ever since he declared that a little thin ice shouldn't scare anyone. (to refuse)   **(2017)**
    (a) Present perfect
    (b) Present Continuous
    (c) Present Perfect
    (d) Present Continuous

DIRECTIONS (Qs. 11-25) : *Fill in the blanks with the correct tense form of the verbs in the brackets.*

11.   It _______ (rain) since last night, and it _______ (look) as if it may rain for the rest of the day.
    (a) has been raining, looks
    (b) had been raining, looked
    (c) raining, looked
    (d) had rained, looks

12.   My school _______ (hold) a food-and-fun fair next month to raise money for the school building-fund.   **(2016)**
    (a) holds   (b) will hold
    (c) is holding   (d) was hold

13. Look! Those bees _______ (buzz) round the flowers. The bees _______ not only _______ (collect) honey, but they _______ (pollinate) the flowers as well.
    - (a) buzzed, are, collecting, are pollinating
    - (b) are buzzing, are, collected, are pollinating
    - (c) are buzzing, were, collecting, are pollinating
    - (d) are buzzing, are, collecting, are pollinating

14. Mary told him what _______ (happen) to his dog, so he _______ (run) home to see how it _______ (be). **(2014)**
    - (a) have happened, ran, was
    - (b) had happened, ran, was
    - (c) had happened, ran, is
    - (d) had happened, run, is

15. _______ the taxi _______ (come) yet ? It _______ (be) already ten minutes late. I hope it _______ (be) here soon.
    - (a) Has, come, is, will be
    - (b) Have, came, is, would be
    - (c) Had, came, was, would be
    - (d) Has, come, is, will being

16. We _______ (go) shopping last weekend. There _______ (be) a great crowd at the shopping center. Most of the people _______ (do) their New Year's shopping. **(2015)**
    - (a) gone, was, were doing
    - (b) went, were, were doing
    - (c) went, is, was doing
    - (d) went, was, were doing

17. It _______ (be) a fine morning today. The birds _______ (sing) in the trees, and there _______ (be) not a cloud in the sky.
    - (a) is, are sung, is
    - (b) is, are singing, is
    - (c) is, are sung, was
    - (d) was, are singing, is

18. That child _______ always _______ (ask) questions. Sometimes he _______ (ask) such complicated questions that I _______ (become) puzzled, too. **(2016)**
    - (a) asked, asked, became
    - (b) is, asking, asks, become
    - (c) will, ask, has been asking, become
    - (d) asked, asking, became

19. I thought that the grass _______ (need) cutting, but the lawnmower _______ (be) out of order. Therefore, I _______ (cut) the grass with a pair of shears.
    - (a) needs, would, cut
    - (b) needing, will, cut
    - (c) needed, was, cut
    - (d) needed, were, cut

20. Your friends _______ (wait) for you for over an hour. Where _______ you _______ (be) all this time ? You _______ (be) out for almost four hours. **(2013)**
    - (a) have been waiting, have, been, were
    - (b) had been waiting, have, been, being, was
    - (c) had been waiting, had been, being, is
    - (d) have been waiting, had been, being, is

21. She _______ (mop) the floor when her cousin came in. She _______ (scold) him angrily because he _______ (make) the floor dirty with his muddy shoes.
    - (a) was mopping, scolded, will make
    - (b) was mopping, scolded, made
    - (c) is mopping, scolded, made
    - (d) is mopping, scolds, made

22. The police _______ (investigate) the robbery that _______ (take) place last week. So far, they _______ (discover) nothing and _______ (arrest) no one. **(2013)**
    - (a) are investigated, took, have discovered, have arrested
    - (b) were investigating, took, have discovered, have arrested
    - (c) are investigating, took, have discovered, have arrested
    - (d) were investigating, take, have discovered, have arrested

23. She _______ (look) very worried for the past few days; but when I _______ (ask) what the matter was, she _______ (say) that it _______ (be) nothing. **(2017)**
    - (a) had been looking, asked, said, was
    - (b) have been looking, asked, said, was
    - (c) had been looking, asks, said, was
    - (d) had been looking, asked, said, were

24. She says that she _______ (send) the letter a month ago; but, so far, she _______ (not receive) any reply. She _______ (think) that her letter _______ (be) lost in the post. **(Tricky)**
    - (a) had sent, has not received, thinks, were
    - (b) has sent, had not received, thinks, was
    - (c) had sent, has not received, thinks, was
    - (d) has sent, has not received, thinks, were

25. He walked along the road, wondering what ________ (happen) and where all the people ________ (go). The streets ________ (be) deserted, and the stalls ________ (be leave) as they ________ (be), with fruit and vegetables arranged in neat rows. **(2013)**
    (a) had happened, had gone, were, were left, were
    (b) have happened, had gone, were, were left, were
    (c) had happened, had gone, was, were left, was
    (d) had happened, gone, were, was left, were

DIRECTIONS (Qs. 26-30) : *Fill the correct present perfect or simple past of the verb form, from the options given below.*

26. This pen ________ to me for ten years.
    (a) belongs
    (b) has belonged
    (c) belonged
    (d) has been belonging
27. The slow boy ________ very little today.
    (a) do   (b) done
    (c) has done   (d) had done
28. I ________ the tragedy today. I don't know the man. **(2016)**
    (a) see   (b) saw
    (c) has seen   (d) had seen
29. England ________ the T20 match yesterday.
    (a) win   (b) wins
    (c) won   (d) had won
30. India ________ 405 for six wickets on the third day of the match. **(2015)**
    (a) score   (b) scored
    (c) has scored   (d) had scored

DIRECTIONS (Qs. 31-35) : *Change the sentence as directed in the bracket and choose the correct option.*

31. The Principal of our school keeps the school compound clean. (Present continuous)
    (a) The Principal of our school has been keeping the compound clean.
    (b) The Principal of our school is keeping the school compound clean.
    (c) The Principal of our school did keep the school compound clean.
    (d) None

32. Is Kusum singing a song? (Present-simple negative) **(2014)**
    (a) Kusum does not sing a song.
    (b) Kusum doesn't sing.
    (c) Kusum is singing a song, isn't it?
    (d) None of the above.
33. Ali has finished his work in time. (Simple past)
    (a) Ali finishes his work in time.
    (b) Ali finished his work.
    (c) Ali has been finishing his work.
    (d) Correct as is.
34. The house is far away from dust, noise and smoke (Past simple) **(2014)**
    (a) The house was far away from the dust, noise and smoke.
    (b) The house was far away.
    (c) The house wasn't far away from the dust, noise and smoke.
    (d) None of the above.
35. We are taught honesty. (Past perfect) **(2017)**
    (a) We had been teaching honesty.
    (b) We had been taught honesty.
    (c) We were taught honesty.
    (d) Correct as is.
36. History tell us that we always ________ to do the right thing. **(2018)**
    (a) was tried   (b) trying
    (c) have been tried   (d) try
37. I ________ one of those since I was a kid. **(2019)**
    (a) saw   (b) have been seen
    (c) haven't seen   (d) was seeing
38. The bandits were ________ the village when they came through the forest. **(2020)**
    (a) avoid   (b) avoidable
    (c) avoiding   (d) avoided
39. My sister ____ studying for two hours now. **(2020)**
    (a) is being   (b) has been
    (c) have been   (d) was been
40. Someone ________ my mobile when I was in the supermarket. **(2021)**
    (a) stolen
    (b) steals
    (c) stole
    (d) stealing

41. The director _______ the biweekly meeting for tomorrow. **(2021)**
    (a) scheduling
    (b) have scheduled
    (c) will be scheduling
    (d) schedule

DIRECTIONS (Qs. 42-45) : *Choose the correct option to complete each conversation.* **(2021)**

---

42. Tarun: Please convey to him that today's meeting _______ because the director is not well. The same will be held next week. **(2021)**
    (a) has been cancelled　　(b) are cancelled
    (c) were cancelled　　(d) cancelling

43. Shebin : Steven _______ a brand new toaster robot. **(2021)**
    (a) invented
    (b) were inventing
    (c) will be invent
    (d) has invent

44. It _______ a lot to be a pioneer in any field. **(2022)**
    (a) take up
    (b) take
    (c) takes
    (d) taking

45. Due to heavy rainfall, there _______ in the area.
    (a) were waterlog　　**(2022)**
    (b) was waterlogging
    (c) have waterlogged
    (d) has waterlogging

LEVEL 2

DIRECTIONS (Qs. 1-12) : *Put the given verb into the correct form, positive or negative and complete the sentences.*

1. It was warm, so I _______ off my coat. (take)
   (a) didn't take
   (b) take
   (c) took
   (d) will take
2. The film wasn't very good. I _______ it very much. (enjoy) **(Tricky)**
   (a) enjoyed
   (b) enjoying
   (c) will enjoy
   (d) didn't enjoy
3. I knew Sarah was very busy, so I _______ her. (disturb) **(2016)**
   (a) didn't disturb
   (b) disturbing
   (c) disturbed
   (d) will disturb
4. I was very tired, so I _______ to bed early. (go)
   (a) went
   (b) didn't go
   (c) will go
   (d) go
5. The bed was very uncomfortable. I _______ very well. (sleep)
   (a) slept
   (b) will sleep
   (c) didn't sleep
   (d) sleep
6. Sue wasn't hungry, so she _______ anything. (eat)
   (a) eat   (b) didn't eat
   (c) ate   (d) would eat
7. We went to Kate's house but she _______ at home. (be) **(2014)**
   (a) was   (b) wasn't
   (c) is   (d) has been

8. It was a funny situation but nobody _______. (Laugh)
   (a) laughed
   (b) didn't laugh
   (c) laughing
   (d) will laugh
9. The window was open and a bird _______ into the room. (fly) **(2013)**
   (a) fly   (b) didn't fly
   (c) flew   (d) can fly
10. The hotel wasn't very expensive. It _______ very much. (cost) **(2017)**
    (a) costs
    (b) will cost
    (c) didn't cost
    (d) is costing
11. I was in a hurry, so I _______ time to phone you. (have)
    (a) didn't have
    (b) have
    (c) hadn't
    (d) will have
12. It was hard work carrying the bags. They _______ very heavy. (be)
    (a) was   (b) were
    (c) are   (d) weren't

DIRECTIONS (Qs. 13-22): *Read the following passage carefully. Fill in each blank with the correct form of the verb in the bracket* **(Critical Thinking, 2013)**

Coffee is a beverage ___13___ (drink) by many past generations of people. What most people do not realize is that coffee is ___14___ (make) from beans ___15___ (pick) from trees.

Coffee trees ___16___ (grow) either from seeds or cuttings. These trees will begin to ___17___ (bear) crops when they are about four years old.

Workers on coffee plantations have to pick the beans by hand. After the beans ___18___ (gather), they are

___19___ (roast) at high temperatures. This process ___20___ (give) them their fragrance.

The best coffee is made from freshly ___21___ (grinding) beans. There are many different ways of ___22___ (prepare) coffee. Coffee can be served either with or without milk.

13. (a) drunk
    (b) drink
    (c) drinking
    (d) drinks
14. (a) make
    (b) made
    (c) have made
    (d) have been made
15. (a) picking
    (b) will pick
    (c) have been picked
    (d) picked
16. (a) are grown
    (b) was grown
    (c) is growing
    (d) was growing
17. (a) beared
    (b) will bear
    (c) bear
    (d) has been bearing
18. (a) gathered
    (b) will gather
    (c) have been gathered
    (d) gathering
19. (a) will roast
    (b) roasted
    (c) roasting
    (d) would have roasted
20. (a) gave   (b) given
    (c) gives   (d) is given
21. (a) ground   (b) grounded
    (c) grounding   (d) will ground
22. (a) prepared
    (b) preparing
    (c) will not prepare
    (d) is prepared

DIRECTIONS (Qs. 23-32) : *Read the following passage carefully. Fill in each blank with the correct form of the verb from the given options.*   **(Tricky)**

Falconry is the art of ___23___ (catch) animals by using specially ___24___ (train) hawks and falcons. It is a very old sport ___25___ (date) back to 2000 B.C. However, it is not very popular now.

After the bird is ___26___ (tame) and ___27___ (train), it is ___28___ (take) out to hunt. It ___29___ (perch) on the owner's gloved left hand and wears a hood which keeps it quiet. If the owner wants the bird to ___30___ (attack) an animal, he will cast the bird off by ___31___ (throw) his left arm forward.

The bird then ___32___ (fly) towards its prey, pounces on it and kills it.

23. (a) catching   (b) caught
    (c) catch   (d) to catch
24. (a) training   (b) trained
    (c) have trained   (d) have been training
25. (a) dated   (b) to date
    (c) dating   (d) have been dating
26. (a) taming   (b) tamed
    (c) tame   (d) have tamed
27. (a) training   (b) have been trained
    (c) had been trained (d) trained
28. (a) taken
    (b) take
    (c) has been taking
    (d) took
29. (a) perching   (b) perches
    (c) perched   (d) have perched
30. (a) attack
    (b) attacked
    (c) attacking
    (d) had attacked
31. (a) threw
    (b) thrown
    (c) throwing
    (d) have been throwing
32. (a) fly
    (b) flies
    (c) flew
    (d) have been flying

DIRECTIONS (Qs. 33–40) : *Indicate whether the following sentences are simple present (SP), present continuous (PC), present perfect (PP) or present perfect continuous (PPC), by choosing the correct option.*

33. The full moon always shines with a glow.
    (2014)
    - (a) SP
    - (b) PC
    - (c) PP
    - (d) PPC

34. Ranjit is not going to the coaching classes.
    - (a) PC
    - (b) PPC
    - (c) SP
    - (d) PP

35. Historians say, dogs have been pets to man for ages. **(Tricky)**
    - (a) PC
    - (b) PPC
    - (c) SP
    - (d) PP

36. I have been wanting my own bike for years.
    (2015)
    - (a) SP
    - (b) PP
    - (c) PPC
    - (d) PC

37. I have been taking music classes for a month now. **(2016)**
    - (a) PPC
    - (b) PP
    - (c) PC
    - (d) SP

38. We have known the Mishras for many years.
    - (a) PC
    - (b) PP   **(2012)**
    - (c) SP
    - (d) PPC

39. I have seen the movie four times.
    - (a) PP
    - (b) PC
    - (c) PPC
    - (d) SP

40. It has been raining since yesterday.   **(2014)**
    - (a) PP
    - (b) PPC
    - (c) SP
    - (d) PC

41. My mum ______ always ______ to instill good values in us so far. **(2019)**
    - (a) will, be tried
    - (b) was, try
    - (c) has, tried
    - (d) may, try

DIRECTIONS (Q. 42) : *Choose the correct option to fill in the blank.*

42. Isn't it quite fortunate that the stolen jewellery and money ______ before the ______ ? **(2020)**
    - (a) reappears, arriving police
    - (b) reappeared, police arrived
    - (c) reappearing, police will be arrive
    - (d) reappear, arrived police

HINTS & EXPLANATIONS

LEVEL - 1

1. (b) selects, simple present
2. (a) is buying, present continous
3. (d) will flatter, simple future
4. (b) purchased, simple past
5. (a) placed, hint after see received
6. (c) explained, hint--yesterday
7. (d) had prepared, two events happened in the past
8. (b) had been skating
9. (c) has been warning
10. (a) has refused
11. (a) It *has been raining* since last night, and it *looks* as if it may rain for the rest of the day.
12. (c) My school *is holding* a food-and-fun fair next month to raise money for the school building-fund
13. (d) Look! Those bees *are buzzing* round the flowers. The bees *are not* only *collecting* honey, *but* they *are* pollinating the flowers as well.
14. (b) Mary told him what had *happened* to his dog, so he *ran* home to see how it was.
15. (a) *Has* the taxi *come* yet ? It *is* already ten minutes late. I hope *it will be* here soon.
16. (d) We *went* shopping last weekend. There *was* a great crowd at the shopping center. Most of the people *were doing* their New Year's shopping.
17. (b) It *is a fine* morning today. The birds *are singing* in the trees, and there *is* not a cloud in the sky.
18. (b) That child *is* always *asking* questions. Sometimes he *asks* such complicated questions that I *become* puzzled, too.
19. (c) I thought that the grass *needed* cutting, but the lawnmower *was out* of order. Therefore, I *cut* the grass with a pair of shears.
20. (a) Your friends *have been* waiting for you for over an hour. Where *have* you *been* all this time? You *were out* for almost four hours.
21. (b) She *was mopping* the floor when her cousin came in. She *scolded* him angrily because he *made* the floor dirty with his muddy shoes.
22. (c) The police *are investigating* the robbery that *took* place last week. So far, they have *discovered* nothing and *have arrested* no one.
23. (a) She *had been looking* very worried for the past few days; but when I *asked* what the matter was, she *said* that it *was* nothing.
24. (c) She says that she *had sent* the letter a month ago; but, so far, she *has not received* any reply. She *thinks* that her letter was lost in the post.
25. (a) He walked along the road, wondering what *had happened* and where all the people *had gone*. The streets *were* deserted, and the stalls *were* left as they *were*, with fruit and vegetables arranged in neat rows.
26. (b) has belonged, present perfect
27. (c) has done, present perfect
28. (b) saw, simple past
29. (c) won, simple past
30. (c) has scored, present perfect
31. (b)   32. (a)   33. (b)
34. (a)
35. (b)
36. (d) try
37. (c) haven't seen
38. (c) avoiding
39. (b) hasbeen
40. (c) stole (past form of steal)
41. (c) will be scheduling

42. (a) has been cancelled

43. (a) invented

44. (c) takes

45. (b) was waterlogging

LEVEL - 2

1. (c) took, positive
2. (d) didn't enjoy, negative
3. (a) didn't disturb, negative
4. (a) went, positive
5. (c) didn't sleep, negative
6. (b) didn't eat, negative
7. (b) wasn't, negative
8. (a) laughed, positive
9. (c) flew, positive
10. (c) didn't cost, negative
11. (a) didn't have, negative
12. (b) were, positive
13. (a) drunk
14. (b) made
15. (d) picked
16. (a) are grown
17. (c) bear
18. (c) have been gathered
19. (b) roasted
20. (c) gives
21. (a) ground
22. (b) preparing
23. (a) catching

24. (b) trained
25. (c) dating
26. (b) tamed
27. (d) trained
28. (a) taken
29. (b) perches
30. (a) attack
31. (c) throwing
32. (b) flies
33. (a) Simple Present, a universal truth (shines is the verb)
34. (a) Present Continuous ---is not going---action continuing
35. (d) have been denotes a complete action, Present Perfect Tense
36. (c) have been waiting-Present Perfect continuous Tense. Action which started earlier is still going on.
37. (a) have been taking---Present Perfect Continuous-Action is going on though it started earlier.
38. (b) have known, Present Perfect, denotes an action completed in the present.
39. (a) have seen present perfect
40. (b) has been raining is present perfect continuous, Action started earlier is still going on.
41. (c) has, tried
42. (b) reappeared, police arrived

CHAPTER 5

VOICES AND NARRATIONS

VOICES

Depending on the way in which you word a sentence, a verb can be either **active** or **passive**.

When the verb is active, the subject of the verb is doing the action, as in these examples.

> *France* **beat** *Brazil in the final.*
>
> [subject]   [active verb]
>
> *More than 300 million people* **speak** *Spanish.*
>
> [subject]   [active verb]
>
> *Ravi* **will take** *the matter forward.*
>
> [subject]   [active verb]

When the verb is passive, the subject undergoes the action rather than doing it:

> *Brazil* **was beaten** *by France in the final.*
>
> [subject]   [passive verb]
>
> *Spanish* **is spoken** *by more than 300 million people worldwide.*
>
> [subject]   [passive verb]
>
> *The matter* **will be taken** *forward by Ravi.*
>
> [subject]   [passive verb]

Here, the sentences' points of view have changed: *Brazil, Spanish,* and *the matter* have become the subjects of the passive verbs was *beaten, is spoken,* and *will be* taken. In the first example, you can see that the subject of the active verb (*France*) does not appear in the corresponding passive version of the sentence. In the other two passive examples, the former subjects of the active verbs (*more than 300 million people; Ravi*) are now introduced with the word 'by'.

The person or thing in a passive sentence that does or causes something is called the **agent**: *more than 300 million people* and *Ravi* are the agents of the second and third passive examples.

These two different ways of using verbs are known as **voices**. In everyday writing, the active voice is much more common than the passive. The passive tends to be used in formal documents such as official reports or scientific papers, often where an action or situation is regarded as more significant than who or what did or caused it.

- *The results* **were published** *in the Journal of the American Medical Association.*
- *A fair grading system* **was found** *to be important to all students.*

RULES TO CHANGE VOICES

1. Only 3rd form of the verb/past participle is used as a main verb in passive voice.
2. The structure for changing modals Can, Could, may, might, shall, will, etc is–

Active voice	**Passive voice**
S + can + infinitive (v₁) + object	O + can + be + past + participle (v₃) + by subject

Example	
I can solve <u>this sum</u>	<u>This sum</u> <u>can be</u> solved by me
(s) (modal) (vi) (O)	O (m + be) V₃

3.   Subjective case in active voice changes to objective case in passive voice.

Active voice	**Passive voice**
He	him
She	her
We	us
I	me
You	You
if	if
they	them

4.   Passive structure for imperative sentence is : let + object + be/not be + v₃
      example : Do it. (active voice)
            Let it be done. (passive voice)

5.   Change in the infinitive verbs
      (– 0 + V₁) active voice
      (+ 0 + be + V₃) passive voice
      eg. I have to do this work. (active)
      This work has to be done. (passive)

PASSIVE VERB FORMS

The passive is formed with tenses of the auxiliary verb 'to be' and the past participle of the main verb. Here is a table showing the passive forms for most English verbs.

Tense	Passive	Example
present simple	am/are/is + past participle	*He* **is taken** *to school by his mother.*
present continuous	am/are/is being + past participle	*They* **are being bullied**.
present perfect	have/has been + past participle	*Have you* **been interviewed** *for many jobs?*
past simple	was/were + past participle	*We* **were told** *not to touch anything.*
past continuous	was/were being + past participle	*Our computers* **were being attacked** *by hackers.*
past perfect	had been + past participle	*His mother* **had been brought up** *in India.*
future	will be + past participle	*Arrangements* **will be made** *to move them to other locations.*
future perfect	will have been + past participle	*All the merchandise* **will have been shipped** *by tomorrow.*

NARRATIONS

There are two ways to convey a message of a person, or the words spoken by a person to other person.

1.   Direct speech
2.   Indirect speech

Suppose your friend whose name is John tells you in school, "I will give you a pen". You come to home and you want to tell your brother what your friend told you. There are two ways to tell him.

Direct Speech: John said, "I will give you a pen".

Indirect Speech: John said that he would give me a pen.

In direct speech the original words of person are narrated (no change is made) and are enclosed in quotation mark. While in indirect speech some changes are made in original words of the person because these words have been uttered in past so the tense will change accordingly and pronoun may also be changed accordingly. In indirect speech the statement of the person is not enclosed in quotation marks, the word "that" may be used before the statement to show that it is indirect speech. Indirect speech is also called reported speech because reported speech refers to the second part of indirect speech in which something has been told by a person.

Reporting Verb: The verb of first part of sentence (i.e. he said, she said, he says, they said, she says,) before the statement of a person in sentence is called reporting verb.

EXAMPLE

In all of the following example the reporting verb is "said".

- He **said**, "I work in a factory"   (Direct speech)
- He **said** that he worked in a factory.   (Indirect speech)
- They **said**, "We are going to cinema"   (Direct speech)
- They **said** that they were going to cinema.   (Indirect speech)

Reported Speech. The second part of indirect speech in which something has been told by a person (which is enclosed in quotation marks in direct speech) is called reported speech. For example, a sentence of indirect speech is, *He said that he worked in a factory*. In this sentence the second part "*he worked in a factory*" is called reported speech and that is why the indirect speech as a whole can also be called reported speech.

Fundamental rules for indirect speech.

1.   Reported speech is not enclosed in quotation marks.
2.   **Use of word "that":** The word "that" is used as a conjunction between the reporting verb and reported speech.
3.   **Change in pronoun:** The pronoun (subject) of the reported speech is changed according to the pronoun of reporting verb or object (person) of reporting verb (first part of sentence). Sometimes the pronoun may not change.

In the following example the pronoun of reported speech is "I" which will be changed in indirect speech into the pronoun (Subject) of reporting verb that is "he".

EXAMPLE

- **Direct speech:** He said, "I am happy".
- **Indirect Speech:** He said that **he** was happy.
- **Direct speech:** I said to him, "You are intelligent".
- **Indirect Speech:** I told him that he was intelligent. ("You" changed to "he" the person of object of reporting verb)

4.   **Change in time:** Time is changed according to certain rules like now to then, today to that day, tomorrow to next day and yesterday to previous day.

EXAMPLE
- **Direct speech:** He said, "I am happy today".
- **Indirect Speech:** He said that he was happy **that day**.

5. **Change in the tense of reported speech:** If the first part of sentence (reporting verb part) belongs to past tense the tense of reported speech will change. If the first part of sentence (reporting verb part) belongs to present or future tense, the tense of reported speech will not change.

EXAMPLE
- **Direct speech:** He said, "I am happy".
- **Indirect Speech:** He said that he was happy. (Tense of reported speech changed)
- **Direct speech:** He says, "I am happy".
- **Indirect Speech:** He says that he is happy. (Tense of reported speech didn't change)

TENSE CHANGE IN INDIRECT SPEECH
* Present simple tense *into* Past simple
* Present Continuous tense *into* Past continuous
* Present Perfect tense *into* Past perfect
* Present Perfect Continuous *into* Past perfect continuous
* Past simple *into* Past Perfect
* Past Continuous *into* Past Perfect Continuous
* Past Perfect *into* Past Perfect
* In Future tense change only 'shall/will' into 'would'.

EXAMPLE

DIRECT SPEECH	INDIRECT SPEECH
PRESENT TENSE	
Present Simple *changes into* **Past Simple**	
He said, "I write a letter"	He said that he wrote a letter.
She said, "She goes to school daily"	She said that she went to school daily.
They said, "We love our country"	They said that they loved their country
He said, "He does not like computer"	He said that he did not like computer.
Present Continuous *changes into* **Past Continuous**	
He said, "He is listening to the music"	He said that he was listening to the music.
She said, "I am washing my clothes"	She said that she was washing her clothes.
They said, "We are enjoying the weather"	They said that they were enjoying the weather.
She said, "I am not laughing"	She said that she was not laughing.
Present Perfect *changes into* **Past Perfect**	
She said, "He has finished his work"	She said that he had finished his work.
He said, "I have started a job"	He said that he had started a job.
I said, "She has eaten the meal"	I said that she had eaten the meal.
They said, "We have not gone to New York.	They said that they had not gone to New York.
Present Perfect Continuous *changes into* **Past Perfect Continuous**	
He said, "I have been studying since 3 O'clock"	He said that he had been studying since 3 O'clock.
She said, "It has been raining for three days."	She said that it had been raining for three days.
I said, "She has been working in this office since 2007"	I said that she had been working in this office since 2007.

PAST TENSE	
Past Simple *changes into* **Past Perfect**	
He said to me, "You answered correctly"	He told me that I had answered correctly.
John said, "They went to cinema"	John said that they had gone to cinema.
He said, "I made a table"	He said that he had made a table.
She said, "I didn't buy a car"	She said that she had not bought a car.
Past Continuous *changes into* **Past Perfect Continuous**	
They said, "We were enjoying the weather"	They said that they had been enjoying the weather.
He said to me, " I was waiting for you"	He told me that he had been waiting for me.
I said, "It was raining"	I said that it had been raining.
She said, "I was not laughing"	She said that she had not been laughing.
Past Perfect *changes into* **Past Perfect (tense does not change)**	
She said, "She had visited a doctor"	She said that she had visited a doctor.
He said, "I had started a business"	He said that he had started a business.
I said, "She had eaten the meal"	I said that she had eaten the meal.
They said, "We had not gone to New York.	They said they had not gone to New York.
FUTURE TENSE	
Future Simple Tense *Will changes into Would*	
He said, "I will study the book"	He said that he would study the book.
She said, "I will buy a computer"	She said that she would buy a computer.
They said to me, "We will send you gifts"	They told me that they would send me gifts.
I said, "I will not take the exam"	I said that I would not take the exam.
Future Continuous Tense *Will be changes into Would be*	
I said to him, " I will be waiting for him"	I told him that I would be waiting for him.
She said," I will be shifting to a new home"	She said that she would be shifting to a new home.
He said, "I will be working hard"	He said that he would be working hard.
He said, "He will not be flying kite"	She said that he would not be flying kites.
Future Perfect Tense *Will have changes into Would have*	
He said, "I will have finished the work"	He said that he would have finished the work.
She said, "They will have passed the examination"	She said that they would have passed the examination.
He said, "I will have gone"	He said that he would have gone.

Note : The tense of reported speech may not change, if reported speech is a universal truth, even though its reporting verb belongs to past tense.

EXAMPLE

- **Direct speech:** He said, "Mathematics is a science"
- **Indirect Speech:** He said that mathematics is a science.
- **Direct speech:** He said, "the Sun rises in the east"
- **Indirect Speech:** He said that sun rises in east. (Tense didn't change because reported speech is a universal truth though its reporting verb belongs to past tense)

Indirect speech for Interrogative (question) sentence

For changing interrogative (question) sentence into indirect speech we have to observe the nature of question and then change it into indirect speech according to rules for indirect speech. A question can be of two types. One type which can be answered in only YES or NO and other type which needs a little bit explanation for its answer and cannot be answered in only YES or NO.

EXAMPLE

*   Do you like music? (It can be answered in YES or NO)
*   How are you? (It cannot be answered in YES or NO but it needs a little bit explanation i.e, I am fine.)

Questions which can be answered in YES/NO.

To change questions (which can be answered in yes or no) into indirect speech, word "if" or "whether" is used before the question in indirect speech. Rules for change in tense of question sentences are same as for change in normal tenses in indirect speech but sentence will not start with the auxiliary verb of the tense. The word "that" is not used between reporting verb and reported speech as conjunction in indirect speech for question sentence. Question mark is not used in indirect speech.

EXAMPLE

*   **Direct speech:** He said to me, "Do you like music?"
*   **Indirect Speech:** He asked me if I liked music. (Not, did I like music)
*   **Indirect Speech:** He asked me whether I liked music.
*   **Direct speech:** She said, "Will he participate in the quiz competition?"
*   **Indirect Speech:** She asked me if he would participate in quiz competition.
*   **Direct speech:** I said to him, "Are you feeling well?"
*   **Indirect Speech:** I asked him if he was feeling well.
*   **Direct speech:** They said to me, "Did you go to school?"
*   **Indirect Speech:** They asked me if I had gone to school.
*   **Direct speech:** He said to me, "Have you taken the breakfast?"
*   **Indirect Speech:** He asked me if I had taken the breakfast

Question which cannot be answered in YES/NO.

To change such questions into indirect speech, the words "if" or "whether" is not used. The tense of the question is changed according to the rules for change in normal tenses in indirect speech but sentence will not start with the auxiliary verb of the tense. The word "that" is not used between reporting verb and reported speech as conjunction, in indirect speech for question sentence. Question mark is not used in indirect speech.

EXAMPLE

*   **Direct speech:** He said to me, "How are you?"
*   **Indirect speech:** He asked me how I was. (Not, how was I)
*   **Direct speech:** Teacher said to him, "What is your name?"
*   **Indirect speech:** Teacher asked him what his name was.
*   **Direct speech:** She said to him, "Why did you come late?"
*   **Indirect speech:** She asked him why he had come late.
*   **Direct speech:** He said, "When will they come?"
*   **Indirect speech:** He asked when they would come.
*   **Direct speech:** She asked his son, "Why are you crying?"
*   **Indirect speech:** She asked her son why he was crying.

Indirect speech for sentence having MODALS, "can, may, must"
Present modals are changed to past modals.

Direct Speech	Indirect Speech
Indirect speech for sentence having MODALS, "can, may, must, should, ought to"	
CAN changes into COULD	
He said, "I can drive a car"	He said that he could drive a car.
She said, "He can play a violin."	She said that he could play a violin.
They said, "We can climb on a hill"	They said that they could climb on a hill.
MAY changes into MIGHT	
He said, "I may buy a computer"	He said that he might buy a computer.
She said, "He may visit a doctor."	She said that he might visit a doctor.
They said, "They may go to zoo"	They said that they might go to zoo.
MUST changes into HAD TO	
He said, "I must work hard"	He said that he had to work hard.
She said, "They must carry on their work"	She said that they had to carry on their work.
I said to him, "You must learn the test-taking strategies"	I told him that he had to learn the test-taking strategies.

Indirect speech for sentence having MODALS, should, ought to, might, would, and could"
The modal will not change in indirect speech.

Direct Speech	Indirect Speech
THESE MODALS DO NOT CHANGE "would, could, might, should, ought to"	
Would	
They said, "we would apply for a visa"	They said that they would apply for a visa.
He said, "I would start a business.	He said that he would start a business.
She said, "I would appear in exam"	She said that she would appear in the exam.
Could	
She said, "she could play a piano"	She said that she could play a piano.
They said, "we couldn't learn the lesson"	They said they couldn't learn the lesson.
He said, "I could run faster"	He said that he could run faster.
Might	
He said, "Guests might come"	He said that guests might come.
She said, "It might rain"	She said that it might rain.
John said, "I might meet him"	John said that he might meet him.
Should	
He said, "I should avail the opportunity"	He said that he should avail the opportunity.
She said, "I should help him"	She said that she should help him.
They said, "We should take the exam"	They said that they should take the exam.
Ought to	
He said to me, "You ought to wait for him"	He told me that I ought to wait for him.
She said, "I ought to learn method of study"	She said that she ought to learn method of study.
They said, "We ought to attend our classes"	They said that they ought to attend their classes.

Indirect speech for imperative and exclamatory sentences
Indirect speech of imperative sentence
A sentence which expresses command, request, advice or suggestion is called *imperative sentence.*

EXAMPLE

*   Open the door.
*   Please help me.
*   Learn your lesson.

To change such sentences into indirect speech, the word "ordered" or "requested" or "advised" or "suggested" or "forbade" or "not to do" is added to reporting verb depending upon nature of imperative sentence in reported speech.

EXAMPLE

*   **Direct speech:** He said to me, "Please help me."
*   **Indirect Speech:** He *requested* me to help him.
*   **Direct speech:** She said to him, "You should work hard for exam."
*   **Indirect Speech:** She *suggested* him to work hard for exam.
*   **Direct speech:** They said to him, "Do not tell a lie"
*   **Indirect Speech:** They said to him *not to* tell a lie.
*   **Direct speech:** He said, "Open the door."
*   **Indirect Speech:** He *ordered* to open the door.
*   **Direct speech:** The teacher said to students, "Do not waste time."
*   **Indirect Speech:** The teacher *advised* the students not to waste time.
*   **Direct speech:** He said, "Please give me a glass of water."
*   **Indirect Speech:** He *requested* to give him a glass of water.
*   **Direct speech:** Doctor said to me, "Do not smoke"
*   **Indirect Speech:** Doctor *advised* me not to smoke.
*   **Direct speech:** The teacher said to him, "Get out."
*   **Indirect Speech:** The teacher *ordered* him to get out.

Indirect speech of exclamatory sentences

Sentence which expresses state of joy or sorrow or wonder is called exclamatory sentence.

EXAMPLE

*   Hurrah! We won the match.
*   Alas! I failed the test.
*   Wow! What a nice shirt it is.

To change such sentences, the words "exclaimed with joy" or "exclaimed with sorrow" or "exclaimed with wonder" is added in the reporting verb depending upon the nature of exclamatory sentence in indirect speech.

EXAMPLE

*   **Direct speech:** He said, "Hurrah! I won a prize."
*   **Indirect Speech:** He *exclaimed with joy* that he had won a prize.
*   **Direct speech:** She said, "Alas! I failed in exam."
*   **Indirect Speech:** She *exclaimed with sorrow* that she had failed in the exam.
*   **Direct speech:** John said, "Wow! What a nice shirt it is."
*   **Indirect Speech:** John *exclaimed with wonder* that it was a nice shirt.
*   **Direct speech:** She said, "Hurrah! I am selected for the job."
*   **Indirect Speech:** She *exclaimed with joy* that she was selected for the job.
*   **Direct speech:** He said, "Oh no! I missed the train."
*   **Indirect Speech:** He *exclaimed with sorrow* that he had missed the train.
*   **Direct speech:** They said, "Wow! What a pleasant weather it is."
*   **Indirect Speech:** They *exclaimed with wonder* that it was a pleasant weather.

Changes in pronoun in Indirect Speech

The pronoun (subject) of the reported speech is changed according to the pronoun of reporting verb or object (person) of reporting verb (first part of sentence). Sometimes the pronoun may not change.

1. First person pronoun in reported speech i.e. I, we, me, us, mine, or our, is changed according to the pronoun of reporting verb if pronoun in reporting verb is third person pronoun i.e. he, she, it, they, him, his, her, them or their.

EXAMPLE

- **Direct speech:** He said, "I live in New York."
- **Indirect speech:** He said that he lived in New York.
- **Direct speech:** They said, "We love our country."
- **Indirect speech:** They said that they loved their country

2. First person pronoun in reported speech i.e. I, we, me, us, mine, or our, is not changed if the pronoun (Subject) of reporting is also first person pronoun i.e. I or we.

EXAMPLE

- **Direct speech:** I said, "I write a letter."
- **Indirect speech:** I said that I wrote a letter.
- **Direct speech:** We said, "We had completed our work."
- **Indirect speech:** We said that we had completed our work.

3. Second person pronoun in reported speech i.e. you, yours is changed according to the person of object of reporting verb.

EXAMPLE

Direct speech: She said to him, "You are intelligent."
Indirect speech: She said to him that he was intelligent.
Direct speech: He said to me, "You are late for the party."
Indirect speech: He said to me that I was late for the party.

4. Third person pronoun in reported speech i.e. he, she, it, they, him, his, her, them or their, is not changed in indirect speech.

EXAMPLE

- **Direct speech:** They said, "He will come."
- **Indirect speech:** They said that he would come.
- **Direct speech:** You said, "They are waiting for the bus."
- **Indirect speech:** You said that they were waiting for the bus.

Changes in time and adverbs in indirect speech

Time and adverbs are changed in indirect speech.

EXAMPLE

- **Direct speech:** He said, "I will buy a book tomorrow."
- **Indirect speech:** He said that he would buy a book the **next day**.
- **Direct speech:** She said, "I am happy now."
- **Indirect speech:** She said that she was happy **then**.
- **Direct speech:** He said, "I like this book."
- **Indirect speech:** He said that he liked **that** book.

Common Rules

* **Today** changes to **that day**/the same day
* **Tomorrow** changes to **the next day/the following day**
* **Yesterday** changes to **the day before/the previous day**
* **Next week/month/year** changes to **the following week/month/year**
* **Last week/month/year** changes to **the previous week/month/year**
* **Now/just** changes to **then**
* **Ago** changes to **before**
* **Here** changes to **there**
* **This** changes to **that**

LEVEL 1

DIRECTIONS (Qs. 1-12) : *Fill in the blanks with suitable active and passive verb forms.*

1. This house ________ in 1970 by my grandfather.
    (a) built   (b) was built **(Tricky)**
    (c) was build   (d) has built
2. The robbers ________ by the police.   **(2013)**
    (a) have arrested   (b) have been arrested
    (c) was arrested   (d) had arrested
3. We ________ for the examination.
    (a) have preparing
    (b) are preparing
    (c) had preparing
    (d) have been prepared
4. It ________ since yesterday.   **(2014)**
    (a) is raining
    (b) has been raining
    (c) have been raining
    (d) was raining
5. I ________ for five hours.
    (a) have been working
    (b) has been working
    (c) was working
    (d) am working
6. The students ________ to submit their reports by the end of this week.   **(2015)**
    (a) have asked   (b) are asked
    (c) has asked   (d) are asking
7. She ________ for a while.
    (a) are ailing
    (b) is ailing
    (c) has been ailing
    (d) have been ailing
8. The teacher ________ the student for lying.
    (a) has been punished   **(2016)**
    (b) punished
    (c) is punished
    (d) was punished

9. I ________ to become a successful writer.
    (a) have always wanted
    (b) am always wanted
    (c) was always wanted
    (d) am always wanting
10. The inmates of the juvenile home ________ well by their caretakers.
    (a) were not being treated
    (b) were not treating
    (c) have not being treated
    (d) was not being treated
11. As the patient could not walk he ________ home in a wheel chair.
    (a) has carried   (b) has been carried
    (c) was carried   (d) was carrying
12. The injured ________ to the hospital in an ambulance.   **(2015)**
    (a) were taking   (b) was taking
    (c) were taken   (d) have taken

DIRECTIONS (Qs. 13-20) : *Choose the correct passive form of the following sentences.*

13. The teacher punished all the students.   **(2014)**
    (a) The students were all punished by the teacher.
    (b) All the students were punished by the teacher.
    (c) Punishment was given to all the students by the teacher.
    (d) Students were all punished by the teacher.
14. Has Ravi written this letter?
    (a) Is this letter being written by Ravi?
    (b) This letter is being written by Ravi.
    (c) This letter has been written by Ravi.
    (d) Has this letter been written by Ravi?
15. The students have eaten all the fruits.   **(2015)**
    (a) The fruits are been eaten by the students.
    (b) The fruits are being eaten by the students.
    (c) All the fruits have been eaten by the students.
    (d) The fruits had been eaten by the students.

16. The soldiers are defending the country bravely.
    (Tricky)
    (a) The country is being defended bravely by the soldiers.
    (b) The country has been defended bravely by the soldiers.
    (c) The country had been defended bravely by the soldiers.
    (d) The country was being defended by the soldiers bravely.

17. The farmer is ploughing this field.
    (a) This field had been ploughed by the farmer.
    (b) This field has been ploughed by the farmer.
    (c) This field is being ploughed by the farmer.
    (d) This field was being ploughed by the farmer.

18. They are plucking some flowers.   **(2016)**
    (a) Some flowers had been plucked by them.
    (b) Some flowers have been plucked by them.
    (c) Some flowers were being plucked by them.
    (d) Some flowers are being plucked by them.

19. The postman was delivering the parcels.
    (a) The parcels have been delivered by the postman.
    (b) The parcels were being delivered by the postman.
    (c) The parcels had been delivered by the postman.
    (d) The parcels are being delivered by the postman.

20. The girls were cooking dinner.   **(2015)**
    (a) The dinner is being cooked by the girls.
    (b) The dinner has been cooked by the girls.
    (c) The dinner had been cooked by the girls.
    (d) The dinner was being cooked by the girls.

DIRECTIONS (Qs. 21-32) : *Report the following dialogue.*

---

21. The headmistress says, "The young people of today are tomorrow's leaders." (An hour later, you report her statement.)   **(2012)**
    (a) The headmistress says that the young people of that day are the next day's leaders.
    (b) The headmistress says that the young people of today are tomorrow's leaders.
    (c) The headmistress said that the young people of yesterday are today's leaders.
    (d) The headmistress said that the young people of that day are the next day's leaders.

22. She said, "I have been sewing from morning until now." (The next day, you report her statement)
    (a) She said that she had been sewing from morning until now.
    (b) She said that she had been sewing from morning until then.
    (c) She said that she has been sewing from morning until now.
    (d) She said that she has been sewing from morning until then.

23. Rakesh said, "I am very happy today because my father has given me a car." (A month later, you report his statement.)   **(2013)**
    (a) Rakesh said that he was very happy that day because his father had given him a car.
    (b) Rakesh said that he was very happy that day because his father has given him a car.
    (c) Rakesh said that he is very happy today because his father has given him a car.
    (d) Rakesh said that he was very happy today because his father has given him a car.

24. "If you don't keep quiet I shall shoot you", he said to her in a calm voice.
    (a) Calmly he warned her that be quiet or else he will have to shoot her.
    (b) He said calmly that I shall shoot you if you don't be quiet.
    (c) He warned her to shoot if she didn't keep quiet calmly.
    (d) He warned her calmly that he would shoot her if she didn't keep quiet.

25. He exclaimed with joy that India had won the Sahara Cup.   **(2015)**
    (a) He said, "Wow! India won the Sahara Cup"
    (b) He said, "India has won the Sahara Cup"
    (c) He said, "Wow! India will win the Sahara Cup"
    (d) He said, "Wow! India will win the Sahara Cup"

26. Find the correct sentence in INDIRECT speech which matches to this sentence in DIRECT speech Mary asks, "Are you ok, Harry?" **(2014)**
    (a) Mary asks Harry if he was ok.
    (b) Mary told Harry he was ok.
    (c) Mary told Harry he is ok.
    (d) Mary asked if harry was ok?

27. Change the narration of the following sentences. I told him that he was not working hard.
    (a) I told to him, "You are not working hard."
    (b) I said, "You are not working hard."
    (c) I said to him, "You are not working hard."
    (d) I said to himorking hard."

28. Our house _______ when we were on holiday.
    (a) were broken in   **(2018)**
    (b) was broken into
    (c) will broken into
    (d) can be broken

29. 'Everything possible _______ to get things back to normal,' said the prime minister.   **(2018)**

    (a) is doing
    (b) was doing
    (c) done
    (d) is being done

30. If I'm not mistaken, that's certainly my uncle in the taxi. Wonder _______ .   **(2020)**
    (a) where he is went
    (b) where going is he
    (c) he is gone where
    (d) where he is going

31. Plastic containers _____________ more and more to package soft drinks, milk, oil, etc.
                                                   (2022)
    (a) 1s using   (b) was used
    (c) were using   (d) are being used

32. Change the narration.   **(2022)**
    Rita said, "I'm not feeling well."
    (a) Rita said that she was not feeling well.
    (b) Rita said she will not be feeling well.
    (c) Rita said that she is not feeling well.
    (d) Rita said that I'm not feeling well.

LEVEL 2

DIRECTIONS (Qs. 1-20) : *In the questions below, the sentences have been given in Active/Passive voice. From the given alternatives, choose the one which best expresses the given sentence in Passive/Active voice.*

---

1. I remember my sister taking me to the museum.
    (a) I remember I was taken to the museum by my sister. **(Tricky)**
    (b) I remember being taken to the museum by my sister.
    (c) I remember myself being taken to the museum by my sister.
    (d) I remember taken to the museum by my sister.

2. Who is creating this mess? **(2014)**
    (a) Who has been created this mess?
    (b) By whom has this mess been created?
    (c) By whom this mess is being created?
    (d) By whom is this mess being created?

3. Darjeeling grows tea.
    (a) Tea is being grown in Darjeeling.
    (b) Let the tea be grown in Darjeeling.
    (c) Tea is grown in Darjeeling.
    (d) Tea grows in Darjeeling.

4. Sahil sharma makes tea.
    (a) Tea is made by Sahil sharma.
    (b) Tea is made by the Sahil sharma.
    (c) Tea was made by Sahil sharma.
    (d) Tea has made by Sahil sharma.

5. Priyanka has written these notes.
    (a) These notes are written by Priyanka.
    (b) These notes has been written by Priyanka.
    (c) These notes have been written by Priyanka.
    (d) These notes had been written by Priyanka.

6. Someone has stolen his book. **(2015)**
    (a) His book is been stolen.
    (b) His book has been stolen.
    (c) His book is stolen.
    (d) His book has stolen.

7. Do you imitate others? **(2013)**
    (a) Are others being imitated by you?
    (b) Are others imitated by you?
    (c) Have others being imitated by you?
    (d) Were others being imitated by you?

8. Sahil spoke the lie.
    (a) The lie was spoke by Sahil.
    (b) The lie spoken by Sahil.
    (c) Lie was spoken by Sahil.
    (d) The lie was spoken by Sahil.

9. Rahul will pass the message.

    (2012)
    (a) The message will passed by Rahul.
    (b) The message would be passed by Rahul.
    (c) The message will pass by Rahul.
    (d) The message will be passed by Rahul.

10. The police will have caught the culprit. **(2014)**
    (a) The culprit will have caught by the police.
    (b) The culprit have been caught by the police.
    (c) The culprit will have been caught by the police.
    (d) The culprit would have been caught by the police.

11. I must help him. **(2016)**
    (a) He must helped by me.
    (b) I must held him.
    (c) He must get help from me.
    (d) He must be helped by me.

12. She spoke to the official on duty.
    (a) The official on duty was spoken to by her
    (b) The official was spoken to by her on duty.
    (c) She was spoken to by the official on duty.
    (d) She was the official to be spoken to on duty.

13. They may win the battle. **(2017)**
    (a) The battle may be win.
    (b) The battle may be won.
    (c) The battle may be won by them.
    (d) The battle may won.

14. We ought to have saved our environment.

(Tricky, 2013)

(a) Our environment ought to had been saved.

(b) Our environment ought to has been save.

(c) Our environment ought to have been saved.

(d) Our environment ought to have saved.

15. There is no book to read.

(a) To be read there is no book.

(b) To read there is no book.

(c) There is no book to read.

(d) There is no book to be read.

16. Does the police officer catch the thief?

(a) Is the thief caught by the police officer?

(b) Has the thief been caught by the police officer?

(c) The thief has been caught by the police officer

(d) Was the thief caught by the thief?

17. They pay a lot of money. **(Tricky, 2015)**

(a) A lot of money is paid

(b) A lot of money is paid by them.

(c) Money has been paid

(d) A lot of money is being paid.

18. Does your father pick you up?

(a) Who picks you up?

(b) You are picked up by your father.

(c) Are you picked up by your father?

(d) None of the above.

19. A cake was made by Geeta yesterday.

(a) Geeta made a cake yesterday

(b) Geeta has been making a cake.

(c) Cake has been made by Geeta.

(d) Geeta made a cake.

20. Her pen was stolen by somebody yesterday.

(a) The pen was stolen by someone.

(b) Somebody stole her pen yesterday.

(c) Somebody is stealing has pen.

(d) Somebody has been stealing her pen yesterday.

DIRECTIONS (Qs. 21-40) : *In the questions below, the sentences have been given in Direct/Indirect speech. From the given alternatives, choose the one which best expresses the given sentence in Indirect/ Direct speech.*

---

21. They said, "We can not live without oxygen".

(a) They said that we can not live without oxygen.

(b) They said that they can not live without oxygen.

(c) They said that they would not live without oxygen.

(d) They says that they can not live without oxygen.

22. He said to his father, "Please increase my pocket-money." **(Critical Thinking, 2014)**

(a) He told his father, "Please increase the pocket-money"

(b) He pleaded his father to please increase my pocket money.

(c) He requested his father to increase his pocket-money.

(d) He asked his father to increase his pocket-money.

23. Sahil said to Deepu, "I was going to buy milk".

(a) Sahil told Deepu that he were going to buy milk.

(b) Sahil told Deepu that he would going to buy milk.

(c) Sahil told Deepu that he had been going to buy milk.

(d) Sahil told Deepu that he was going to buy milk.

24. His father ordered him to go to his room and study. **(2016)**

(a) His father said, "Go to your room and study."

(b) His father said to him, "Go and study in your room."

(c) His father shouted, "Go right now to your study room"

(d) His father said firmly, "Go and study in your room."

25. The Indian express says, "We shall issue an astrology section in our Thursday's paper".

(2013)

(a) The Indian express says that it will issue an astrology section in their Thursday's paper.

(b) The Indian express says that they will issue an astrology section in their Thursday's paper.

(c)   The Indian express said that it will issue an astrology section in its Thursday's paper.

(d)   The Indian express says that it will issue an astrology section in its Thursday's paper.

26.   The boy said, "Who dare call you a thief?" **(2015)**

(a)   The boy enquired who dared call him a thief.

(b)   The boy asked who called him a thief.

(c)   The boy told that who dared call him a thief.

(d)   The boy wondered who dared call a thief.

27.   He said to you, "You may go out".   **(2017)**

(a)   He told you that you might be go out.

(b)   He said you that you might be go out.

(c)   He told you that you may go out.

(d)   He told you that you might go out.

28.   He said, "Honesty is the best policy."

(a)   He said that Honesty is the best policy.

(b)   He said that Honesty was the best policy.

(c)   He said that Honesty would be the best policy.

(d)   He said that Honesty will be the best policy.

29.   She said, "Madam, I have done homework."

(a)   She said respectfully that she had been done homework.

(b)   She said respectfully that she has done homework.

(c)   She said respectfully that she had done homework.

(d)   She said respectfully to her teacher that she had done homework.

30.   She exclaimed with sorrow that was a very miserable plight.   **(2014)**

(a)   She said with sorrow, "What a pity it is."

(b)   She said, "What a mystery it is."

(c)   She said, "What a miserable sight it is."

(d)   She said, "What a miserable plight it is."

31.   "Please don't go away," she said.

(a)   She said to please her and not go away.

(b)   She told me to go away.

(c)   She begged me not to go away.

(d)   She begged that I not go away.

32.   I said to my brother, "What are you playing today ?"   **(2013)**

(a)   I asked my brother what he will be playing that day.

(b)   I asked my brother what he was playing that day.

(c)   I asked my brother if he was playing that day.

(d)   I asked my brother what he would be playing that day.

33.   Baljider said to me, "I had been working on it for 5 days."   **(2015)**

(a)   Baljinder told me that he had been working on it for 5 days.

(b)   Baljinder told me that he has been working on it for 5 days.

(c)   Baljinder told me that he had worked on it for 5 days.

(d)   Baljinder told me that he was working on it for 5 days.

34.   Robert will say to me, "I am your classmate".

(a)   Robert will tell me that he is my classmate.

(b)   Robert will tell me that he was my classmate.

(c)   Robert will tell me that he will be my classmate.

(d)   Robert said me that he is my classmate.

35.   Mahesh **said**, "I am very busy now".

(a)   He said, that he was very busy.

(b)   He said that he was very busy.

(c)   Mahesh said that he was very busy.

(d)   Mahesh said that he was very busy then.

36.   Nita ordered her servant to bring her cup of tea.

(a)   Nita told her servant, "Bring a cup of tea."

(b)   Nita said, "Bring me a cup of tea."

(c)   Nita said to her servant, "Bring me a cup of tea."

(d)   Nita told her servant, "Bring her that cup of tea."

37.   The MLA said to people, "Ladies and gentlemen, your vote is my real power." **(2016)**

(a)   The MLA said that people your vote will my real power.

(b)   The MLA addressed the people as ladies and gentlemen and said that your vote will be my real power.

(c)   The MLA addressed the people as ladies and gentlemen and said that their vote is my real power.

(d)   The MLA addressed the people as ladies and gentlemen and said that their vote was his real power.

38. The Judge said to inspector, "Call the thieves."
    (a) The Judge urged inspector to call the thieves.
    (b) The Judge ordered inspector to get the thieves.
    (c) The Judge requested inspector to call the thieves.
    (d) The Judge ordered inspector to call the thieves.

39. I asked, "What happened?" **(2017)**
    (a) I enquired what happened.
    (b) I asked what happened.
    (c) I enquired that what happened.
    (d) I asked what had happened.

40. Garima said, "My father is a doctor."
    (a) Garima said that her father was a doctor.
    (b) Garima said that her father is a doctor.
    (c) Garima says that her father is a doctor.
    (d) None of the above

41. The TV _______ switched on in over a month because we just don't watch it anymore. **(2019)**
    (a) oughtn't be   (b) can't be
    (c) mustn't be   (d) hasn't been

42. The couple ___________ us that their marriage has been a success___________ the sacrifices made by them. **(2020)**
    (a) asked, in the end
    (b) told, in spite of
    (c) said, because
    (d) screamed, briefly

43. That book is so ambiguous that it_____ in any way. **(2022)**
    (a) could interpret
    (b) can be interpreted
    (c) should be interpreting
    (d) shall been interpreted

44. Change the voice. **(2022)**
    Who gave you the money?
    (a) Who gave the money to you?
    (b) Who was given the money by you?
    (c) By whom were you given the money?
    (d) By whom was you given the money?

HINTS & EXPLANATIONS

LEVEL - 1

1. (b) was built
2. (b) have been arrested
3. (b) are preparing
4. (b) Has been raining
5. (a) have been working
6. (b) are asked
7. (c) has been ailing
8. (b) punished
9. (a) have always wanted
10. (a) were not being treated
11. (c) was carried
12. (c) were taken
13. (b) All the students were punished by the teacher.
14. (d) Has this letter been written by Ravi?
15. (c) All the fruits have been eaten by the students.
16. (a) The country is being defended bravely by the soldiers.
17. (c) This field is being ploughed by the farmer.
18. (d) Some flowers are being plucked by them.
19. (b) The parcels were being delivered by the postman.
20. (d) The dinner was being cooked by the girls.
21. (b) The headmistress says that the young people of today are tomorrow's leaders.
22. (b) She said that she had been sewing from morning until then.
23. (a) Rakesh said that he was very happy that day because his father had given him a car.
24. (d) He warned her calmly that he would shoot her if she didn't keep quiet.
25. (a) He said, "Wow! India won the Sahara Cup.
26. (a) Mary asks Harry if he was ok.
27. (c) I said to him, "You are not working hard."
28. (b) was broken into
29. (d) is being done
30. (d) where he is going
31. (d) are being used
32. (a)

LEVEL - 2

1. (b) In case of present continuous verb+ing, being is used in passive voice.
2. (d) If a question word start with who change into by whom in voice
3. (c)
4. (a) Rule to make active voice of Simple present sentence :
        Passive subject + is/are/am + third form of verb + by + passive object.
5. (c)
6. (b) Apart from Rule to make active voice of Present Perfect Tense, which is
        Passive subject + has/have + been + third form of verb + by + passive object
        Please also note that words like, "someone", "somebody", "people", "police", "public" etc are dropped. But in rare cases we can use them if sentence meaning is not clear.
7. (b) 8. (d)
9. (d) Rule to make active voice of Simple Future Tense :
        Passive subject + shall/will + be + third form of verb + by + passive object
10. (c) Rule to make active voice of Future Perfect Tense :
        Passive subject + will/shall + have + been + third form of verb + by + passive object.
11. (d) S + modal + V1 + o (active)
        S + modal + be + V_3 + by + o (passive)
12. (a) 13. (c) 14. (c) 15. (d) 16. (a)
17. (b) 18. (c) 19. (a) 20. (b)

21. (a) When we use "we" with the universal truth, then "we" is not changed in Indirect speech.

22. (c) As in question we find word 'please' showing kind of request so, option c is right answer.

23. (c) When Reporting verb in past Tense and reported speech is having "was" after subject + First Verb.
    Then we change "was" to "had been" + First verb.

24. (a)

25. (d) Whenever some newspaper or magazine use "we", "our", "us" in direct speech , then it should be replaced by "it" or "its" in indirect speech.

26. (a)

27. (d) When Reporting verb in past Tense and reported speech is having "may" after subject + First Verb.
    Then we change "may" to "might" + First verb.

28. (a) If Reporting verb is in Past Tense and Reported Speech is a universal truth, then we do not change it in indirect speech.

29. (c) Note: while changing it to indirect speech, remove "Sir/Madam" with "respectfully" as we did in this question.

30. (d)   31. (c)

32. (b) The reported speech is beginning with wh-word, having interrogative sentence & present continous tense. So, the option (b) is the right choice.

33. (a) When Reporting verb in past Tense and reported speech is in "Past Perfect Continuous Tense", then we do not change the tense of the reported speech.

34. (a)   35. (d)   36. (c)

37. (d)

38. (d) In this type of imperative sentences, we do not use "if/whether", instead we use "to" to replace inverted commas.

39. (d)

40. (a)

41. (d) hasn't been

42. (b) told, in spite of

43. (b) can be interpreted

44. (c)

ONE WORD SUBSTITUTION

'One Word Substitution' as the phrase indicates itself is the word that replaces group of words or a full sentence effectively without creating any kind of ambiguity in the meaning of the sentences. Like the word-Autobiography, can be used in place of the sentence 'The life story of a man written by himself'. It is very important to write precisely and speak in a single word.

Generally, we speak or write in a verbose way. But, it is seen that precise words are always understood easily by all. At times we become garrulous which is not required and we are required to talk or speak precisely. This not only makes the language easily comprehensible but also makes it beautiful. The other way, we can say that these words are used to bring an effect of compression in any kind of writing. In English language, there are a lot of single words for a group of words that can be used effectively to make the writing to the point, that too without losing the meaning of the context.

To give up a throne voluntarily	Abdicate
Do away with	Abolish
The original inhabitants of a country	Aborigines
A condensed edition of a book	Abridged
To accustom oneself in new climate	Acclimatize
A substance that can stick or cause sticking	Adhesive
One who can use either hand with ease	Ambidextrous
Lack of feeling	Apathy
State of being unmarried	Bachelorhood
Cut the head of	Behead
Wishing good things for another	Benevolent
Using or knowing two languages	Bilingual

One who studies the science of plants	Botanist
One who pays too much attention to his clothes and appearance	Dandy
Become worse or disintegrate	Deteriorate
Continuous dry weather and lack of rain and water	Drought
A person who is slow in learning	Dunce
One who pretends to be what he is not	Hypocrite
Easily broken	Fragile
Irregular luminous band of stars	Galaxy
List of explanation	Glossary
Make-up room behind stage	Green room
Wicked to a high degree	Heinous
Thing of same nature	Homogeneous
A dumb show	Pantomime
Principles of teaching	Pedagogy
Study of sound	Phonetics, Acoustics
One who does something first	Pioneer
Fit to drink	Potable
A feather used as a pen	Quill
Too much official formalities	Red-Tapism
Witty, clever retort	Repartee
The art of elegant speech or writing	Rhetoric

PUNCTUATION RULES

There are fourteen punctuation marks commonly used in English grammar.

Period/ Full stop (.)	Question mark (?)
Exclamation mark (!)	Comma (,)
Semicolon (;)	Colon (:)
Dash (–)	Hyphen (-)
Parentheses (( ))	Brackets {}, (), [], < >
Braces ({})	Apostrophe (')
Quotation marks (" ")	Ellipsis (...)

SENTENCE ENDINGS

Three of the fourteen punctuation marks are appropriate for use as sentence endings. They are the period, question mark and exclamation mark.

The period (.) is placed at the end of declarative sentences, statements thought to be complete and after many abbreviations.

EXAMPLE

1.   As a sentence ender: Every summer we go to the camp.
2.   After an abbreviation: Mr. Kumar's son, Raul Jr., was born on Dec. 6, 2008.

Use a question mark (?) to indicate a direct question when placed at the end of a sentence.

EXAMPLE

When did you return from the market?

The exclamation mark (!) is used when a person wants to express a sudden outcry or add emphasis.

EXAMPLE

1.   Within dialogue: "Holy cow!" screamed Neha.
2.   To emphasize a point: My mother-in-law's rants make me furious!

COMMA, SEMICOLON AND COLON

The comma, semicolon and colon are often misused because they all can indicate a pause in a series.

The comma is used to show a separation of ideas or elements within the structure of a sentence. Additionally, it is used in numbers, dates and letter writing after the salutation and closing.

EXAMPLE

1.   Direct address: Thanks for all your help, Arjun.
2.   Separation of two complete sentences: We went to the movies, and then we went out to lunch.
3.   Separating lists or elements within sentences: Maria wanted the black, green and blue sarees.

The final comma, known as an Oxford or serial comma, is useful in a complex series of elements or phrases but is often considered unnecessary in a simple series such as in the example above. It usually comes down to a style choice by the writer.

The semicolon (;) is used to connect independent clauses. It shows a closer relationship between the clauses than a period would show.

EXAMPLE

Kiran was hurt; she knew he only said it to upset her.

A colon (:) has three main uses. The first is after a word introducing a quotation, an explanation, an example, or a series.

EXAMPLE

He was planning to study four subjects: Politics, Philosophy, Sociology and Economics.

The second is between independent clauses, when the second explains the first, similar to a semicolon.

I didn't have time to change: I was already late.

The third use of a colon is for emphasis.

There was one thing Lucy loved more than any other: her grandma.

A colon also has non-grammatical uses in time, ratio, business correspondence and references.

DASH AND THE HYPHEN

Two other common punctuation marks are the dash and hyphen. These marks are often confused with each other due to their appearance but they are very different.

A hyphen is used to join two or more words together into a compound term and is not separated by spaces.

EXAMPLE

part-time, back-to-back, well-known.

A dash is used to separate words into statements. There are two common types of dashes: en dash and em dash.

> *En dash*: Slightly wider than a hyphen, the en dash is a symbol (–) that is used in writing or printing to indicate a range or connections and differentiations, such as 1880–1945 or Delhi – Mumbai trains.

> *Em dash*: Twice as long as the en dash, the em dash can be used in place of a comma, parenthesis or colon to enhance readability or emphasise the conclusion of a sentence.

EXAMPLE

Sunaina gave him her answer — No!

Whether you put spaces around the em dash or not is, again, a style choice. Just be consistent.

BRACKETS, BRACES AND PARENTHESES

Brackets, braces and parentheses are symbols used to contain words that are a further explanation or are considered a group.

Parentheses (( )) are curved notations used to contain further thoughts or qualifying remarks. However, parentheses can be replaced by commas without changing the meaning in most cases.

EXAMPLE

Rajender and Shikha (who were actually cousins) both have brown hair.

Brackets are the squared off notations ([ ]) used for technical explanations or to clarify meaning. If you remove the information in the brackets, the sentence will still make sense.

He [Mr. Kumar] was the last person seen at the house.

Braces ({ }) are used to contain two or more lines of text or listed items to show that they are considered as a unit. They are not commonplace in most writing, but can be seen in computer programming to show what should be contained within the same lines. They can also be used in mathematical expressions.

EXAMPLE

$2\{1+[23-3]\} = x.$

APOSTROPHE, QUOTATION MARKS AND ELLIPSIS

The final three punctuation forms in English grammar are the apostrophe, quotation marks and ellipsis. Unlike previously mentioned grammatical marks, they are not related to each other in any form.

An apostrophe (') is used to indicate the omission of a letter or letters from a word, the possessive case, or the plurals of lowercase letters. Examples of the apostrophe in use include:

EXAMPLE

Omission of letters from a word:

I've seen that movie several times.

She wasn't the only one who knew the answer.

Possessive case: Sara's dog bit the neighbour.

Plural for lowercase letters: Six people were told to mind their p's and q's.

Quotations marks (" ") are a pair of punctuation marks used primarily to mark the beginning and end of a passage attributed to another and repeated word for word. They are also used to indicate meanings and to indicate the unusual or dubious status of a word.

EXAMPLE

"Don't go outside," she said.

Single quotation marks (') are used most frequently for quotes within quotes.

Marie told the teacher, "I saw Arav at the playground, and he said to me 'Daksh started the fight,' and I believed him."

The ellipsis is most commonly represented by three periods (. . .) although it is occasionally demonstrated with three asterisks (***). The ellipsis is used in writing or printing to indicate an omission, especially of letters or words. Ellipses are frequently used within quotations to jump from one phrase to another, omitting unnecessary words that do not interfere with the meaning. Students writing research papers or newspapers quoting parts of speeches will often employ ellipsis to avoid copying lengthy text that is not needed.

EXAMPLE

Omission of words: She began to count, "One, two, three, four…" until she got to 10, then went to find him.

Within a quotation: When Newton stated, "An object at rest stays at rest and an object in motion stays in motion…" he developed the law of motion.

BRITISH VS. AMERICAN ENGLISH

There are a few differences between punctuation in British and American English. The following chart details some of those differences.

	British English	**American English**
The " . " symbol is called	A full stop	a period
The " ! " symbol is called	an exclamation mark	an exclamation point
The " ( ) " symbols are called	brackets	parentheses
The " [ ] " symbols are called	square brackets	brackets
The position of quotation marks	Joy means "happiness".	Joy means "happiness."
The punctuation for abbreviations	Dr, Mr, Mrs, St, Rd, Ct	Dr., Mr., Mrs., St., Rd., Ct.

JUMBLED WORD

A word jumble is a word puzzle that gives you a group of scrambled letters and requires you to unscramble them to make a real word. For example, if you were given the letters "m-o-c-t-e-r-u-p" you could unscramble, or unjumble if you will, those letters to reveal the word computer.

Tips on Solving a Word Jumble

There are many hints, tips, and tricks that can help you to solve a jumbled word.

- The first trick is to look for any letters that appear frequently together. These include consonants such as "ch," "sh," or "ph." They can also include vowel consonant combinations like "qu."

- Another trick is to separate the consonants from the vowels and look at them separately. Sometimes looking at them away from one another makes the word become more obvious.

- You can also write the letters down like the numbers on the face of a clock. For some, displaying the letters in this way can help them to see the word clearly.

- Lastly, do a great deal of reading. Reading will help to improve your vocabulary. Therefore, make sure you read anytime you can.

Rearrangement of Jumbled Words

When solving jumbled sentences or "Sequence of Words" type questions, first determine the "Subject" and the "Predicate".

SUBJECT - The part which names the person or thing we are speaking about.

PREDICATE - The part that tells something about the subject.

After identifying the subject and predicate, identify the tense used and the verbs

Its always a good idea to read the answer options to figure out the most correct sentence, than to try solving the jumbled sentence yourself.

Tips for rearrangement of jumbled words.

1. By arranging words in order of subject +v+ object.

2. In interrogative sentences. The sentence begins with helping verb or wh- words.

3. Imperative sentence begins with main verb.

LEVEL 1

DIRECTIONS (Qs. 1-10) : *In questions given below out of four alternatives, choose the one which can be substituted for the given sentence.*

1. One who introduces performing artists on the stage programmes.   **(2012)**
   (a) curator   (b) choreographer
   (c) host   (d) compere

2. A place where water is collected and stored.
   (a) aquarium   (b) reservoir
   (c) waterbody   (d) scullery

3. A place to rest or a sleeping room in a college or public institution.   **(2013)**
   (a) dormitory   (b) cloakroom
   (c) creche   (d) elysium

4. A wooden box with a front of wire for rabbits.
   (a) hive   (b) burrow
   (c) hutch   (d) aviary

5. The period between two reigns.   **(2015)**
   (a) gap   (b) anachronism
   (c) stasis   (d) interregnum

6. An imaginary land with perfect social order.
   (a) zodiac   (b) sinecure
   (c) utopia   (d) elysium

7. A statement accepted as true without proof.
   (a) axiom   (b) anomaly   **(2014)**
   (c) abdication   (d) conscription

8. One who is a brilliant performer on stage (specially music)
   (a) musician   (b) vocalist
   (c) virtuoso   (d) veteran

9. One who is a habitual drunkard.   **(2016)**
   (a) teetotaller   (b) sot
   (c) uxorious   (c) sadist

10. A person considering himself to be superior in culture and intellect.   **(2015)**
    (a) highbrow   (b) honorary
    (c) pessimist   (d) connoisseur

DIRECTIONS (Qs. 11-15) : *In each sentence below, one word has been printed in bold type which is wrongly spelt. Choose the correctly spelt word for each.*

11. If you have an **acquintence** with someone, you have met them and you know them.   **(2015)**
    (a) acquaintance   (b) acquaintence
    (c) acquintance   (d) acquentence

12. Lata Mangeskhar has thousands of songs in her **repertoare**.   **(2013)**
    (a) repertoir   (b) rapertoir
    (c) repertoire   (d) repertare

13. Whatever the **vicisitudes** of her past life, Priya now seems to have come through.
    (a) visitudes   (b) vicissitudes
    (c) vicitudes   (d) viscitudes

14. The bank manager asked him to check his **superanuation** scheme.   **(2017)**
    (a) superannuation   (b) superenuation
    (c) superennuation   (d) superenation

15. If you give **succor** to someone who is suffering or in difficulties, it means you help them. **(2016)**
    (a) sucour   (b) succour
    (c) succuor   (d) succor

DIRECTIONS (Qs. 16-19) : *Find the correctly spelt words.*

16	(a) Foreign	(b) Foreine **(Tricky)**
	(c) Fariegn	(d) Forein
17	(a) Palete	(b) Palet **(2012)**
	(c) Palate	(d) Pelate
18.	(a) Bouquete	(b) Bouquette
	(c) Bouquet	(d) Boqquet
19.	(a) Excessive	(b) Exccessive
	(c) Exxcesive	(d) Excesive

DIRECTIONS (Qs. 20-29) : *Choose the correct option to punctuate the following sentences.*

20. How does television affect our lives   **(2013)**
    (a) How does television affect our lives?
    (b) How does television affect our lives!
    (c) How does television affect our lives.
    (d) How does television affect our lives;

21. Spring while we are writing is here
    (a) Spring, while we are writing, is here.
    (b) Spring! while we are writing is here!
    (c) Spring while we are writing, is here.
    (d) Spring, while we, are writing, is here.

22. The wind blows gently
    (a) The wind blows gently?
    (b) The wind blows gently.
    (c) The wind, blows, gently.
    (d) The wind blows gently

23. While the television was broken we played a lot of board games. **(2014)**
    (a) Broken, We   (b) broken we,
    (c) broken, we   (d) Broken We

24. My Father was born on June 16, 1949. **(2016)**
    (a) My father,
    (b) My father
    (c) my father
    (d) Correct as is

25. "why did you bring that stray dog home," my mama asked, "when you know your papa doesn't like animals in the house?" **(2012)**
    (a) why   (b) "Why,
    (c) "Why   (d) Why

26. "Are there enough pencils for everyone?" Radhika asked.
    (a) Everyone?" Radhika
    (b) everyone Radhika
    (c) everyone?" radhika
    (d) Correct as is

27. Many centuries ago most people thought the worlds' surface was flat, not round. **(2015)**
    (a) worlds
    (b) worl'ds
    (c) world's
    (d) Correct as is

28. Please put a Band-Aid on Ajay's cut. **(2013)**
    (a) ajay's
    (b) Ajays
    (c) Ajays'
    (d) Correct as is

29. We are going to the carnival in Dalhousie on Saturday afternoon?
    (a) Saturday, afternoon.
    (b) Saturday afternoon
    (c) Saturday afternoon?
    (d) Saturday, afternoon.

30. We have been off on an __________ for the past month which has been great fun. **(2018)**
    (a) adventure   (b) adventured
    (c) adventurous   (d) adventuring

DIRECTIONS (Qs. 31-33) : *Choose the option with correct spelling.*

31. What is the spelling of the word that means 'weak'? **(2019)**
    (a) Tenahus   (b) Tensious
    (c) Tenorous   (d) Tenuous

32. What is the spelling of the word that means 'to be able to see through'? **(2019)**
    (a) Transparent   (b) Trensperent
    (c) Transperant   (d) Trenparant

33. Someone who is in love with himself is a/an ______. **(2021)**
    (a) polyglot   (b) insolvent
    (c) narcissist   (d) lunatic

DIRECTIONS (Qs. 34-35): *Find the one word substitution for the following:* **(2022)**

34. One who is fond of delicious food
    (a) Edible
    (b) Epicure
    (c) Greedy
    (d) Espionage

35. One who is honourably discharged from service
    (a) Emeritus
    (b) Euphemism
    (c) Evanescent
    (d) Explicable

LEVEL 2

DIRECTIONS (Qs. 1-10) : *In questions given below, out of four alternatives, choose the word which can be substituted for the given sentence.*

1. A person who is indifferent to pain and pleasures of life.   **(2012)**
    (a) hermit   (b) stoic
    (c) hedonist   (d) recluse
2. A leader who sways his followers by his oratory.
    (a) debonair   (b) suave
    (c) demagogue   (d) cosmopolitan
3. One who often talks of his achievements.
    (a) egoist   (b) egotist
    (c) bigot   (d) optimist
4. A girl/woman who flirts with men.   **(Tricky)**
    (a) cynosure   (b) coquette
    (c) effeminate   (d) henpecked
5. One who is filled with excessive enthusiasm in religious matters.   **(2014)**
    (a) bigot   (b) apostate
    (c) bohemian   (d) ascetic
6. Official formality resulting in delay.
    (a) brevet   (b) red-tapism
    (c) provost   (d) probate
7. A remedy for all ills
    (a) panacea   (b) biopsy
    (c) vaccinations (d) ayurveda
8. One who does a thing for pleasure and not as profession.   **(2013)**
    (a) ambidexterous (b) agnostic
    (c) ascetic   (d) amateur
9. One who sneers at the beliefs of others
    (a) convalescent (b) dilettante
    (c) cynic   (d) fastidious
10. One who is inexperienced in anything **(2014)**
    (a) novice   (b) narcissist
    (c) misologist   (d) libertine

DIRECTIONS (Qs. 11-30) : *In each sentence below, one word has been printed in bold type which is wrongly spelt. Choose the correctly spelt word for each.*

11. His life is so hectic that he is prepared to be tolerant of trivial **pecadillos**.   **(2012)**

    (a) pecedillos   (b) pecedilos
    (c) peccadillos   (d) peccadilos
12. The weather is so hot that I am feeling full of **longour**.   **(2014)**
    (a) languor   (b) langur
    (c) langoor   (d) langour
13. It was an unexpected **denuement** in the play performed by the artists.   **(Tricky, 2016)**
    (a) denoument   (b) denuemant
    (c) denuement   (d) denouement
14. After World War II, all the network communication had gone **heywire**.   **(2015)**
    (a) hayvire   (b) heyvire
    (c) heivire   (d) haywire
15. I am reading various **hiroglyphics** of ancient Egypt.
    (a) hyroglyphics (b) hieroglyphics
    (c) hyrographics (d) hiroglyphics
16. To find a good theme for her play, she is searching **hetrogenous** collection of books from the library.
    (a) hetrogenius   (b) hetrogenius
    (c) heterogeneous (d) hectogenius
17. Everyone has a few **idiosyncracies**.
    (a) idiosyncrasies (b) idosyncrasies
    (c) idosyncracies (d) idiosincracies
18. In our society some people are **machiavelian** as they always seems to be secretive and dishonest.   **(Tricky, 2015)**
    (a) mechiavelian   (b) mechiavellion
    (c) machiavellian (d) machivellian
19. Perhaps I am too **acquisent**. To make myself comfortable. I have to be particular.
    (a) aquiscent   (b) acquescent
    (c) aquiescent   (d) acquiescent
20. After reconstruction, the flat has been **meteculously** cleaned.   **(2017)**
    (a) meticulously   (b) meticalusly
    (b) meticalously   (d) meticalosly
21. The **aperchur** of a camera is the size of the hole through which light passes to reach the film
    (a) aparchure   (b) aperture **(2016)**
    (c) apercher   (d) apertr

22. My neighbours have a **bourgois** and limited vision. **(2014)**
    (a) burgeois (b) bourgeus
    (c) burgeous (d) bourgeois

23. People usually complain about having to deal with too much **burocracy**. **(2017)**
    (a) bureaucracy (b) buraucracy
    (c) bureocracy (d) bureacracy

24. It was the **quintescence** of violence that has been shown in 'Julius Caesar'. **(Tricky)**
    (a) quentescence (b) quentessence
    (c) quintessence (d) quintesence

25. Pankaj has been served with a **subpoina** to answer the charges in court.
    (a) subpoina (b) subpoena
    (c) subpiona (d) subepoena

26. Chandigarh police is keeping track of the kidnapper using electronic **surveillance** equipment. **(2016)**
    (a) servillance (b) serviliance
    (c) surveillance (d) serveillance

27. His **uncorobrated** confessions were rejected by court. **(2015)**
    (a) uncoroborated (b) unicorrobrated
    (c) uncorrobrated (d) uncorroborated

28. Istanbul in Turkey is a very **slubrius** city.
    (a) sellubrius (b) sellubrious
    (c) salubrious (d) selibrious

29. The architect was **gesticulationing** at the paintings on the wall of the house. **(2013)**
    (a) gesticulating (b) gasteculating
    (c) gasticulating (d) gesteculating

30. Ishita's success is the result of a **fortitous** combination of circumstances.
    (a) fortituous (b) fortuitous
    (c) fortetuous (d) fortetous

DIRECTIONS (Qs. 31-40) : *Select the correctly punctuated sentence.*

---

31. The birds the flowers and the buds proclaim spring is here **(2012)**
    (a) The birds/the flowers/and the buds proclaim the spring is here.
    (b) The birds, the flowers, and the buds all proclaim the spring is here!
    (c) The birds, the flowers, and the buds all proclaim the spring is here.
    (d) The birds; the flowers; and the buds all proclaim the spring is here.

32. The sun set the moon has risen the stars have come out
    (a) The sun has set, the moon has risen, the stars have come out!
    (b) The sun has set the moon has risen, the stars have come out.
    (c) The sun has set, the moon has risen, the stars have come out.
    (d) The sun has set the moon has risen, the stars have come out.

33. O friend said Ashok will you help me in this hour of my need. **(2014)**
    (a) "O, friend," said Ashok, will you help me in this hour of my need.
    (b) "O, friend," said Ashok, will you help me in this hour of my need.
    (c) "O, friend," said Ashok, will you help me? in this hour of my need?
    (d) "O, friend," said Ashok, "will you help me in this hour of my need?"

34. He said to me please take your seat here **(2014)**
    (a) He said to me, "Please take your seat here."
    (b) He said, to me, "Please take your seat here."
    (c) He said to me, Please take your seat here.
    (d) He said to me, "Please, take, your seat, here."

35. (a) Sarah's uncle's car was found without its wheels in that old derelict warehouse. **(Tricky)**
    (b) Sarah's uncle's car was found without its wheels in that old, derelict warehouse.
    (c) Sarahs uncles car was found without its wheels in that old, derelict warehouse.
    (d) Sarah's uncle's car was found without it's wheels in that old, derelict warehouse.

36. (a) Spain is a beautiful country; the beache's are warm, sandy and spotlessly clean.
    (b) Spain is a beautiful country: the beaches are warm, sandy and spotlessly clean.
    (c) Spain is a beautiful country, the beaches are warm, sandy and spotlessly clean.
    (d) Spain is a beautiful country; the beaches are warm, sandy and spotlessly clean.

37. (a) She always enjoyed sweets, chocolate, marshmallows and toffee apples. **(2013)**
    (b) She always enjoyed: sweets, chocolate, marshmallows and toffee apples.
    (c) She always enjoyed sweets chocolate marshmallows and toffee apples.
    (d) She always enjoyed sweet's, chocolate, marshmallow's and toffee apple's.

38. (a) I can't see Tim's car, there must have been an accident. **(2015)**
    (b) I cant see Tim's car; there must have been an accident.
    (c) I can't see Tim's car there must have been an accident.
    (d) I can't see Tim's car; there must have been an accident.

39. (a) We decided to visit: Spain, Greece, Portugal and Italy's mountains.
    (b) We decided to visit Spain, Greece, Portugal and Italys mountains.
    (c) We decided to visit Spain, Greece, Portugal and Italy's mountains.
    (d) We decided to visit Spain Greece Portugal and Italy's mountains.

40. (a) The children's books were all left in the following places: Mrs Smith's room, Mr Powell's office and the caretaker's cupboard. **(2015)**
    (b) The children's books were all left in the following places; Mrs Smith's room, Mr Powell's office and the caretaker's cupboard.
    (c) The childrens books were all left in the following places: Mrs Smiths room, Mr Powells office and the caretakers cupboard.
    (d) The children's books were all left in the following places, Mrs Smith's room, Mr Powell's office and the caretaker's cupboard.

DIRECTIONS (Qs. 41-46) : *Arrange the jumbled words appropriately to form a meaningful sentence.*

41. our body/ carbohydrates/and/vitamins/proteins/ necessary/for/fats are **(Tricky, 2013)**
    (a) Proteins, vitamins, carbohydrates and fats are necessary for our body.
    (b) Proteins vitamins carbohydrates and fats are necessary for our body.
    (c) Necessary for our body are fats, proteins, carbohydrates and vitamins.
    (d) Proteins, fats, carbohydrates and vitamins are necessary our body for.

42. means of/fats/the body/provide/strong energy/a bad **(2014)**
    (a) Fats provide the body a bad means of strong energy.
    (b) Fats provide a bad means of strong energy the body.
    (c) The body fats provide a bad means of strong energy.
    (d) A bad means of strong energy provide the body fats.

43. as/cold/insulation/act/against/they
    (a) Insulation against cold they act as.
    (b) They act as insulation against cold.
    (c) Act as insulation against cold they.
    (d) Act as insulation they against cold.

44. is/reading/good/habit
    (a) Good reading is a habit.
    (b) A good habit is reading.
    (c) Reading is a good habit.
    (d) Habit is a good reading.

45. Problems/while/reading/face/you/can/many
    (a) You problems can face many reading while.
    (b) You can face many problems while reading.
    (c) While reading you can face problems many.
    (d) Many problems you can face reading while.

46. dictionary/you/should/for/words/consult/ difficult **(Critical Thinking)**
    (a) You should consult dictionary for difficult words.
    (c) You can face many problems while reading.
    (c) Consult dictionary you should for difficult words.
    (d) You consult should dictionary for words difficult.

47. You don't need to be particularly _______ for this task but it might help. **(2018)**
    (a) intelligent   (b) intelligence
    (c) intelligently   (d) intelligentsia

48. The activity of collecting coins is called ______. **(2018)**
    (a) congregation   (b) numismatics
    (c) omniscience   (d) philately

HINTS & EXPLANATIONS

LEVEL - 1

1. (d) A compere is a person who introduces the performers or contestants in a variety show.

2. (b) Reservoir is a large natural or artificial lake used as a source of water supply.

3. (a) Dormitory is large bedroom for a number of people in a school or institution.

4. (c) Hutch is a box or cage, typically with a wire mesh front, for keeping rabbits or other small domesticated animals.

5. (d) Interregnum is a box or cage, typically with a wire mesh front, for keeping rabbits or other small domesticated animals.

6. (c) Utopia is an imagined place or state of things in which everything is perfect.

7. (a)

8. (c) Virtuoso is a person highly skilled in music or another artistic pursuit.

9. (b) A habitual drunkard is called as a sot.

10. (a) Highbrow means an intellectual or rarefied in taste.

11. (a) Acquaintance means a person one knows slightly, but who is not a close friend.

12. (c) Repertoire means the whole list of items which are regularly performed.

13. (b) Vicissitudes are change of circumstances or fortune, typically one that is unwelcome or unpleasant.

14. (a) Superannuation means regular payment made into a fund by an employee towards a future pension.

15. (b) Succour means assistance and support in times of hardship and distress.

16. (a)　　　　17. (c)

18. (c) Bouquet - bunch of flowers, nosegay, fragrance of a wine, compliment.

19. (a)

20. (a) The right punctuation mark (?) is indicating a question.

21. (a) Here full stop is used to suggest that there is nothing more to say on the topic.

22. (b) This is a complete statement, indicated by a full stop.

23. (c)

24. (b) My father

25. (c)

26. (d)

27. (c)

28. (d)

29. (b)

30. (a)

31. (d) Tenuous

32. (a) Transparent

33. (c) narcissist

34. (b)

35. (a)

LEVEL - 2

1. (b) Stoic is a person who can endure pain or hardship without showing their feelings or complaining.

2. (c) Demagogue means a political leader who seeks support by appealing to popular desires and prejudices rather than by using rational argument.

3. (b) Egotist is a person who is excessively conceited or absorbed in themselves; self-seeker.

4. (b) Coquette is a playful woman.

5. (d) Ascetic person is characterized by severe self-discipline and abstention from all forms of indulgence, typically for religious reasons.

6. (b) Red-tapism means the practice of requiring excessive paperwork and tedious procedures before official action can be considered or completed.

7. (a) Panacea is a solution or remedy for all difficulties or diseases.

8. (d) Amateur is a person who engages in a pursuit, especially a sport, on an unpaid basis.

9. (c) Cynic is a person who questions whether something will happen or whether it is worthwhile.

10. (a) Novice is person new to and inexperienced in a job or situation.

11. (c) Peccadillos here means a relatively minor fault or sin.

12. (a) Languor means tiredness or inactivity, especially when pleasurable.

13. (d) The correct word denouement here means the final part of a play, film, or narrative in which the strands of the plot are drawn together and matters are explained or resolved.

14. (d) Haywire here means, erratic or out of control.

15. (b) The spelling hieroglyphics means here a stylized picture of an object representing a word, syllable, or sound, as found in ancient Egyptian and certain other writing systems is correct.

16. (c) The correct spelling is heterogeneous which means diverse in character or content.

17. (a) Idiosyncrasy is the correct spelling which here means a mode of behaviour or way of thought peculiar to an individual.

18. (c) Machiavellian is right spelling here means cunning, scheming, and unscrupulous, especially in politics.

19. (d) The correct spelling acquiescent here means, ready to accept something without protest, or to do what someone else wants.

20. (a) The correct spelling is meticulously which means in a way that shows great attention to detail or very thoroughly.

21. (b) The right spelling aperture in this sentence means a space through which light passes in an optical or photographic instrument, especially the variable opening by which light enters a camera.

22. (d) Bourgeois here means belonging to or characteristic of the middle class, typically with reference to its perceived materialistic values or conventional attitudes is the correct spelling.

23. (a) The word bureaucracy here means excessively complicated administrative procedure is the correct spelling.

24. (c) The correct spelling is quintessence which means essence or the intrinsic nature or indispensable quality of something, especially something abstract, which determines its character.

25. (b) The correct spelling is subpoena which means a writ ordering a person to attend a court.

26. (c) Surveillance is the correct spelling which means close observation, especially of a suspected spy or criminal in the given context.

27. (d) Uncorroborated is the correct spelling which means not confirmed or supported by other evidence or information.

28. (c) Here salubrious is the correct spelling that means health-giving or healthy.

29. (a) Gesticulating is the correct spelling which means using gestures, especially dramatic ones, instead of speaking or to emphasize one's words is the correct spelling here.

30. (b) Fortuitous means happening by chance rather than intention is the correct spelling in this sentence.

31. (c) The use of comma separating items is correct and the full stop gives a clear statement that is complete in its meaning.

32. (c) The use of comma indicating a pause between parts of a sentence or separating items is correct and the use of period is right.

33. (d) Use of double quotation mark is right as we are quoting someone's exact words.

34. (a) Here double inverted commas or quotation mark is required as we are quoting somebody's word.

35. (b)

36. (d)

37. (a)

38. (d)

39. (c)

40. (a)

41. (a) Proteins, vitamins, carbohydrates and fats are necessary for our body is the right order and uses proper punctuation marks.

42. (a) Fats provide the body a bad means of strong energy.

43. (b) They act as insulation against cold.

44. (c) Reading is a good habit.

45. (b) You can face many problems while reading.

46. (a) You should consult dictionary for difficult words.

47. (a)

48. (b) numismatics

CHAPTER 7

SYNONYMS & ANTONYMS/ HOMONYMS & HOMOPHONES

SYNONYMS & ANTONYMS

This is another very important area of the vocabulary section. This section tests widely and exhaustively one's knowledge of the language and word power, but goes beyond that to test your ability to remember words with similar meanings or opposite meanings. Or, alternately, to discover the similarity or proximity between the meaning of the given word with one of those in the options.

These exercises can get confusing sometimes because more than one option may appear as the right answer or none of them may look like the right answer. For such questions a student may consider the following strategies.

SYNONYM

A synonym is a word or phrase that means exactly or nearly the same as another word or phrase in the same language.

EXAMPLE

1. Enormous - Huge, gigantic, massive.
2. Injured - damaged, wounded, harmed.

	Words	**Synonyms**
1.	Absurd	ridiculous, silly, foolish
2.	Appalling	terrific, dreadful, horrible
3.	Arbitrary	despotic, wayward
4.	Allure	tempt, entice, fascinate
5.	Apparent	distinct, evident, obvious, perceptible
6.	Axiom	maxim, truth, saying, dictum
7.	Astute	clever, intelligent, wise, brilliant
9.	Abash	discourage, confound, embarrass, discompose
10.	Begin	commence, create, initiate
11.	Brutal	savage, beastly, cruel
12.	Bleak	dismal, gloomy, chilly, dreary
13.	Brittle	frail, fragile, breakable, delicate
14.	Benevolence	humanity, generosity, charity, liberality
15.	Barbarous	savage, uncivilized, untamed, brutal
16.	Bewitching	magical, fascinating, tantalising, spell binding

17.	Convict	felon, culprit, criminal
18.	Coy	modest, shy, reserved
19.	Cynical	incredulous, sarcastic, morose
20.	Corpulent	obese, ugly, fat, awkward
21.	Consternation	fear, disappointment, dismay, hopelessness
22.	Concede	yield, assent, permit, sanction
23.	Commodious	convenient, suitable, roomy, comfortable
24.	Chastise	punish, admonish, scold, reprove
25.	Deride	ridicule, mock, taunt
26.	Dexterity	adroitness, cleverness, skill
27	Diligence	care, effort
28.	Dwindle	shrink, diminish, decrease
29.	Despicable	contemptible, worthless, shameless, base
30.	Disdain	detest, despise, scorn, loathe

ANTONYM

Antonyms are the words with opposite meanings.

EXAMPLE

1. Ancient - Modern
2. Arrival - Departure

Words	**Antonyms**
1 Defray	decline, declaim, refuse, abjure
2. Dainty	clumsy, coarse, unpleasant, insipid
3. Deplore	cheer, rejoice, applaud, celebrate
4. Emanate	conceal, keep, hold
5. Enlighten	deceive, hide, harm
6. Exult	grieve, hide, mourn
7. Exult	lament, deplore, bemoan, grieve
8. Equivocal	lucid, obvious, clear, plain
9. Encumbrance	incentive, stimulant, patronize, vantage
10. Earnest	unheeding, frivolous, negligent, careless
11. Enjoin	prohibit, forbid, revolt, dissuade
12. Facile	arduous, difficult, hard
13. Felicitate	blame, censure, criticize
14. Fervour	apathy, indifference, lethargy
15. Frugal	spendthrift, lavish
16. Fabricate	destroy, wreck, dismantle, demolish
17. Frantic	subdued, gentle, lucid, coherent
18. Fleeting	enduring, perpetual, eternal, unceasing

19.	Fickle	resolute, determined, inalterable, invariable
20.	Feud	fraternity, harmony, reconciliation, recompose
21.	Genteel	uncivilized, boorish, rough
22.	Gloom	cheer, joy, hopefulness
23.	Gullible	astute, wise, knowledgeable
24.	Guile	honesty, frankness, sincerity integrity
25.	Grisly	pleasing, beautiful, attractive, alluring
26.	Gaudy	dull, faded, sober, solemn
27.	Genial	sullen, dismal, morose, melancholy
28.	Grudge	benevolence, affection, goodwill, kindness
29.	Heterogeneous	homogenous, identical, pure
30.	Humane	aloof, greedy, mean

STRATEGY-1

If you do not know the meaning of the given word, think of a context in which you might have used it, that may help you to figure out the meaning, for example, in the question find the word nearest in meaning to

MAGNIFY

(a) Forgive (b) diminish (c) swell (d) extract
Now if you do not know what magnify means think of a magnifying glass and what it does. It expands or makes a thing look bigger. So the right answer will be (c).

STRATEGY-2

If you are not able to find a correct antonym in the given option think of the antonyms you know of and subsequently check if there is any word in the given options which is synonymous to the antonyms in your mind. For example

INDUSTRIOUS

(a) stupid   (b) harsh (c) indolent (d) complex
If you don't know any of the words given as options think of antonyms you could think of, like lazy, idle. Now think of synonyms of lazy and you will know indolent is a synonym of lazy. So it will be the antonym to industrious. Formula   SYNONYM of ANTONYM is another ANTONYM.

STRATEGY-3

Look at the part of speech of the given verb. A word may exist in various parts of speech. For example precipitate exists as a verb which means send rapidly into a certain state and also as a noun, precipitate, which means a substance deposited from a solution.

POLISH

(a) ruthlessness (b) honesty (c) indolence (d) gaucheness
Now is this the verb polish or noun polish. Since all options are nouns, this cannot be the verb polish related to shoes but noun polish which means culture and sophistication and the antonym to this would be gaucheness.

HOMONYMS & HOMOPHONES

A homonym is a word that has different meanings. In the strict sense, words that share the same spelling and pronunciation but have different meanings. Homophones are words that sound like one another but have different meanings. Some homonyms are spelled the same, like, bark—the sound a dog makes and bark–the outer layer of a tree trunk. Some homonyms are spelled differently, like *one* (the number) and *won* (having been victorious). Homonym and homophone both include words that are pronounced alike and have different spellings, and also words that are spelled alike and have different meanings.

Homonyms, or multiple meaning words, are words that share the same spelling and the same pronunciation but have different meanings. For example, *bear*.

•   A bear (the animal) can bear (tolerate) very cold temperatures.

•   The driver turned left (opposite of right) and left (departed from) the main road.

Homophones, also known as sound-alike words, are words that are pronounced identically although they have different meanings and often have different spellings as well. These words are a very common source of confusion when writing.

Common examples of sets of homophones include: to, too, and two; they're and their; bee and be; sun and son; which and witch; and plain and plane.

Now, we can say:

Homonyms: Words with the same spelling, and pronunciation, but different meanings.

Homophones: Words with the same pronunciations but different spelling.

Few examples are given below.

1.   The farm was used to produce produce.

2.   He did not object to the object.

3.   They weren't close enough to close the door.

4.   The buck does funny things when does are present.

5.   The blue dress blew away in the wind.

6.   While picking up the bag of flour, she noticed fresh flowers in the jar.

LEVEL 1

DIRECTIONS (Qs. 1-15) : *Pick out the nearest correct meaning or synonym of the words given below.*

1. GERMINATE
   - (a) Decay
   - (b) Breed
   - (c) Produce
   - (d) Sprout

2. MAGNATE **(2014)**
   - (a) Tycoon
   - (b) Senior executive
   - (c) Non-magnetic
   - (d) Symbolic

3. FACET
   - (a) Sweet
   - (b) Tap
   - (c) Deceit
   - (d) Aspect

4. PERSUADE **(2012)**
   - (a) Assure
   - (b) Opinionated
   - (c) Convince
   - (d) Cheat

5. EXEMPT
   - (a) Duty
   - (b) Provide
   - (c) Relieve
   - (d) Forgive

6. FEMINITY
   - (a) Cowardice
   - (b) Manly
   - (c) Womanly
   - (d) Inheritant

7. CORDON **(Tricky)**
   - (a) Pile of logs
   - (b) Jeavy cloak
   - (c) Line of people placed as guard
   - (d) None of these

8. RECTIFY **(2015)**
   - (a) To command
   - (b) To correct
   - (c) To destroy
   - (d) To build

9. REVOKE
   - (a) Repudiate
   - (b) Repeal
   - (c) Impute
   - (d) Force

10. REDEEM **(2016)**
    - (a) Extend
    - (b) Fulfil
    - (c) Reconsider
    - (d) Recover

11. ADULT
    - (a) Infant
    - (b) Juvenile
    - (c) Mature
    - (d) Undeveloped

12. DILIGENT **(2013)**
    - (a) Fool
    - (b) Unhappy
    - (c) Hardworking
    - (d) Disappointed

13. FRAGILE
    - (a) Valid
    - (b) Strong
    - (c) Delicate
    - (d) Frank

14. GOODS
    - (a) Quality
    - (b) Transport
    - (c) Material
    - (d) Upright

15. SYNOPSIS
    - (a) Index
    - (b) Mixture
    - (c) Puzzle
    - (d) Summary

DIRECTIONS (Qs. 16-30) : *Pickout the farthest correct meaning or antonym of the words given below.*

16. ANCESTOR
    - (a) Descendant
    - (b) Forefather
    - (c) Precursor
    - (d) Grandparent

17. AUTHENTIC **(2013)**
    - (a) Factual
    - (b) Trustworthy
    - (c) Original
    - (d) Unreal

18. FURIOUS
    - (a) Calm
    - (b) Crazy
    - (c) Angry
    - (d) Violent

19. GENUINE
    - (a) Literal
    - (b) Exact
    - (c) Faithful
    - (d) Fake

20. RIGID **(2014)**
    - (a) Merciless
    - (b) Generous
    - (c) Lenient
    - (d) Tolerant

21. ABANDON
    - (a) Roost
    - (b) Forfeit
    - (c) Quit
    - (d) Forsake

22. HINDER
    - (a) Expedite
    - (b) Protect
    - (c) Devote
    - (d) Create

23. TRAIT **(2015)**
    - (a) Symbol
    - (b) Uncharacteristic
    - (c) Habit
    - (d) Identity

24. ORIGIN **(2016)**
    - (a) Ointment
    - (b) Detergent
    - (c) Remnant
    - (d) Comfort

25. PROVE
    - (a) Vapid
    - (b) Assume
    - (c) Disincline
    - (d) Atone

26. FRAIL **(2015)**
    - (a) Worried
    - (b) Strong
    - (c) Nervous
    - (d) Wily

27. PROCLAIM   **(2015)**
    (a) Denounce   (b) Pretend
    (c) Attend   (d) Distend
28. RADICAL   **(2013)**
    (a) Superficial   (b) Slow
    (c) Narrow   (d) Simple
29. HOLISTIC   **(2016)**
    (a) Negative   (b) Piecemeal
    (c) Impure   (d) Inadequate
30. DOMINATE
    (a) Defeat   (b) Succumb
    (c) Threaten   (d) Sheepish

DIRECTIONS (Qs. 31-40) : *Choose the right word from the options given below:*

31. Can I go _____ the party?   **(2016)**
    (a) to   (b) too
    (c) two   (d) tuu
32. This is my favourite _____ of jeans.   **(2013)**
    (a) pare   (b) pair
    (c) pear   (d) pyre
33. The merchant wants to _____ as many TVs as possible.   **(2017)**
    (a) sell   (b) cell
    (c) shell   (d) sale
34. No body _____ what you are thinking. **(2014)**
    (a) knows   (b) knose
    (c) nose   (d) nows
35. Humans have hands. Dogs have _____ .
                                                (2015)
    (a) paws   (b) pause
    (c) puse   (d) pawse
36. I don't want to talk about the _____ anymore. (past/passed)
37. I _____ (sent/scent) a letter to my aunt in Vietnam.
38. The children got _____ during the lecture. (bored/board)
39. I have _____ (fore/four) rupee in my pocket.
40. I need to take a _____ (break/brake) from this exercise.

DIRECTIONS (Qs. 41-45) : *Choose the correct answer from the given options.*

41. He gave a **vivid** description of the movie he had seen a week before.   **(2012)**

(a) Simple   (b) Dull
(c) Clear   (d) Confused
42. **Brevity** is suggested for expressing yourself.
                                              (Tricky)
    (a) Conciseness   (b) sharpness
    (c) intelligence   (d) confidence
43. Because of a family **feud,** the whole family was wiped out.   **(2016)**
    (a) Problem   (b) Quarrel
    (c) Crisis   (d) Trouble
44. His style is quite **transparent.**
    (a) Witty   (b) Funny
    (c) Lucid   (d) Involed
45. The merchant was **renowned** for his simple way of living.
    (a) Notorious
    (b) Famous
    (c) Unknown
    (d) Notable

DIRECTIONS (Qs. 46-50) : *Choose the antonym of the underlined word from the given options.*

46. He is extremely <u>intelligent</u> but proud.
    (a) Simple   (b) stupid
    (c) Weak   (d) dull
47. In ancient days, a <u>fragile</u> glass jar was considered to be more valuable than a human slave.
    (a) Broad   (b) Tall   **(2014)**
    (c) Strong   (d) Heavy
48. One can <u>acquire</u> fame only by being truthful, honest and faithful.   **(2012)**
    (a) Lose   (b) Deprive
    (c) Forsake   (d) Surrender
49. Always <u>avoid</u> late night jobs.   **(2015)**
    (a) Inspire
    (b) Compel
    (c) Confront
    (d) Take
50. Many people try to <u>resist</u> reforms in society.
    (a) Repel   (b) Welcome **(2016)**
    (c) Accept   (d) Fight

DIRECTIONS (Qs. 51-52) : *Choose correct synonym of the give word*

51. Odorous **(2019)**

    (a) Misshapen　　(b) Similar

    (c) Awry　　(d) Balmy

52. Pontificate **(2019)**

    (a) Decide　　(b) Address

    (c) Deprecate　　(d) Repair

DIRECTIONS (Qs. 53-54) : *Choose correct synonym of the give word*

53. Magnificent **(2020)**

    (a) Grandiose　　(b) Offensive

    (c) Lowly　　(d) Ignoble

54. Retaliate **(2020)**

    (a) Recompense　　(b) Pardon

    (c) Depart　　(d) Excuse

DIRECTIONS (Qs. 55-56) : *Choose correct synonym of the give word* **(2021)**

55. Encourage

    (a) Dampen　　(b) Embolden

    (c) Confound　　(d) Perturb

56. Exuberance

    (a) Disinterest　　(b) Inactivity

    (c) Lack　　(d) Eagerness

DIRECTIONS (Qs. 57-58) : *Choose the correct antonym for the given word.* **(2022)**

57. Terse

    (a) Expensive　　(b) Brief

    (c) Concise　　(d) Detailed

58. Grant

    (a) Award

    (b) Refusal

    (c) Hire

    (d) Pawn

DIRECTIONS (Qs. 59-61) : *Find the antonyms of the words given in the questions:* **(2022)**

59. Abdicate

    (a) Resign

    (b) Forget

    (c) Continue

    (d) Forgive

60. Reminisce

    (a) Recall

    (b) Ignore

    (c) Cite

    (d) Retain

61. Deterrent

    (a) Discouragement

    (b) Encouragement

    (c) Bridle

    (d) None of these

LEVEL 2

DIRECTIONS (Qs. 1-20) : *Choose the correct word that best completes each sentence.*

1. The plaster cast will help _____ the broken bone.
   - (a) heal
   - (b) heel
   - (c) hale
   - (d) hele

2. The _____ is the specialised part of a plant that contains reproductive organs. **(2014)**
   - (a) cede
   - (b) seed
   - (c) sced
   - (d) sead

3. Dr. Venketesh built his castle on a dreary deserted _____ located far away from the mainland. **(2016)**
   - (a) aisle
   - (b) I'll
   - (c) isla
   - (d) isle

4. Dasha's piano _____ is at 3:30 every week.
   - (a) lessen
   - (b) lesson
   - (c) laison
   - (d) lession

5. Would you _____ the cheese for the pizza?
   - (a) grate
   - (b) great
   - (c) gratee
   - (d) greeat

6. After Ravi's surgery, she looked _____ and tired for several weeks. **(2015)**
   - (a) pail
   - (b) pale
   - (c) piel
   - (d) peel

7. Mrs. Sharma's voice was _____ by the time she finished reading all the test items. **(2013)**
   - (a) hoarse
   - (b) horse
   - (c) hours
   - (d) hour

8. If there is a monopoly, there is only one _____ for the commodity. **(2014)**
   - (a) cellar
   - (b) seller
   - (c) sailor
   - (d) sailer

9. _____ desk has been moved to the corner of the room. **(Tricky)**
   - (a) You're
   - (b) Your
   - (c) your
   - (d) none

10. I can _____ away many pleasant hours in the Museum of Natural History. **(Tricky, 2017)**
    - (a) idle
    - (b) idol
    - (c) ideal
    - (d) None

11. You _____ to have said it long ago.
    - (a) ought
    - (b) aught
    - (c) oat
    - (d) None

12. _____ float on the sea to warn ships of danger.
    - (a) Buoys
    - (b) Boys
    - (c) bouse
    - (d) bounce

13. We must try our best to _____ away all prejudices. **(2012)**
    - (a) caste
    - (b) cast
    - (c) caast
    - (d) cost

14. The travellers had a terrible journey through the _____ road.
    - (a) torturous
    - (b) tortuous
    - (c) tortious
    - (d) tortous

15. We _____ the orange with a knife. **(2013)**
    - (a) peel
    - (b) peal
    - (c) pill
    - (d) none

16. _____ is used to row the boat.
    - (a) Ore
    - (b) Oar
    - (c) Or
    - (d) None

17. Every airport has a _____. **(2015)**
    - (a) hanger
    - (b) hangar
    - (c) hunger
    - (d) hungar

18. If you want to reach God you have to _____ worldly pleasures. **(2016)**
    - (a) forgo
    - (b) forego
    - (c) forge
    - (d) none

19. _____ bird does not fly in the air.
    - (a) Fowl
    - (b) Foul
    - (c) Fail
    - (d) Foal

20. She narrated the series of _____ events.
    - (a) discrete
    - (b) descreet
    - (c) discrit
    - (d) descrit

DIRECTIONS (Qs. 21-30) : *Choose the correct synonym of the words given below.*

21. ALIEN **(2014)**
    - (a) Proper
    - (b) Stranger
    - (c) Different
    - (d) Freak

22. BITTERNESS
    - (a) Mildness
    - (b) Kindness
    - (c) Acrimony
    - (d) Sweetness

23. FRIGHT
   (a) Calmness   (b) Disappoint
   (c) Scare   (d) Thrill
24. GRAPHIC   **(Tricky)**
   (a) Obscure   (b) Implicit
   (c) Visual   (d) Vague
25. INITIATIVE   **(2012)**
   (a) Apathy   (b) Inventiveness
   (c) Confidence   (d) Desire
26. LIBERAL   **(Critical Thinking)**
   (a) Miserly   (b) Generous
   (c) Visionary   (d) Imaginative
27. PROHIBIT
   (a) Prescribe   (b) Allow
   (c) Forbid   (d) Provide
28. RESCUE   **(2013)**
   (a) Peril   (b) Danger
   (c) Pitfall   (d) Save
29. SWIFT
   (a) Move   (b) Speedy
   (c) Leisurely   (d) Sluggish
30. VALOUR   **(2015)**
   (a) Cowardice   (b) Wise
   (c) Courage   (d) Beautiful

DIRECTIONS (Qs. 31-40) : *Choose the correct antonym of the words given below.*

31. AFFIRM   **(Tricky, 2015)**
   (a) Accept   (b) Deny
   (c) Allow   (d) Welcome
32. BOLD   **(Critical Thinking)**
   (a) Brave   (b) Timid
   (c) Incredible   (d) Courageous
33. CONFIDENT
   (a) Diffident   (b) Wise
   (c) Intelligent   (d) Invincible
34. EFFECTIVE   **(2017)**
   (a) Affective
   (b) Impressive
   (c) Suitable
   (d) Incapable
35. GALLANT
   (a) Fun   (b) Bold
   (c) Coward   (d) Frolic

36. KNOWLEDGE   **(2014)**
   (a) Awareness   (b) Ignorance
   (c) Wisdom   (d) Learning
37. MOISTURE   **(2016)**
   (a) Wetness   (b) Dryness
   (c) Dampness   (d) Roughness
38. QUIT
   (a) Remain   (b) Depart
   (c) Leave   (d) Abandon
39. SHARP   **(2012)**
   (a) Fast   (b) Quick
   (c) Fine   (d) Blunt
40. WORRIED
   (a) Untroubled   (b) Upset
   (c) Afraid   (d) Anxious

DIRECTIONS (Qs. 41-42) : *Choose the correct antonym of the given word*   **(2019)**

41. Regress
   (a) Develop   (b) Truncate
   (c) Slide   (d) Patrol
42. Taunt
   (a) Dislike   (b) Blame
   (c) Flatter   (d) Confuse

DIRECTIONS (Qs. 43-46) : *Choose the correct antonym of the given word.*   **(2020)**

43. Accomplished
   (a) Adept   (b) Cultivated
   (c) Inept   (d) Hep
44. Turmoil
   (a) Flurry   (b) Agitation
   (c) Mayhem   (d) Harmony
45. Choose the correct synonym of the given word. Clairvoyant   **(2020)**
   (a) Oracular
   (b) Unprophetic
   (c) Conformist
   (a) Demagogue
46. Choose the correct antonym of the given word. Perfidious   **(2020)**
   (a) Treacherous   (b) Insidious
   (c) Mendacious   (d) Veracious

DIRECTIONS (Qs. 47-50) : *Choose the correct antonym of the given word.*   **(2021)**

47. Feud
    (a) Run-in   (b) Hostility
    (c) Bickering   (d) Harmony

48. Oration
    (a) Writing   (b) Homily
    (c) Sermon   (d) Speech

49. Choose the correct synonym of the given word.
    Covetous   **(2021)**
    (a) Benign   (b) Expensive
    (c) Envious   (d) Altruistic

50. Choose the correct antonym of the given word.
    Abundance   **(2021)**
    (a) Dearth   (b) Excess
    (c) Ardor   (d) Zest

DIRECTIONS (Qs. 51-54) : *Choose the correct synonym for the given word.*   **(2022)**

51. Extraneous
    (a) Irrelevant   (b) Broadening
    (c) Essential   (d) Pertinent

52. Vindicate
    (a) Convict   (b) Fault
    (c) Judge   (d) Justify

53. Choose the correct synonym of the given word.
    Parity
    (a) Equivocal   (b) Originality
    (c) Vicinity   (d) Similarity

54. Choose the correct antonym of the given word.
    Punctilious
    (a) Careless   (b) Curious
    (c) Damage   (d) Furious

DIRECTIONS (Qs. 55-57): *Find the synonyms of the words given in the questions:*   **(2022)**

55. Humdrum
    (a) Busy
    (b) Monotonous
    (c) Rare
    (d) Different

56. Robust
    (a) Weak
    (b) Legal
    (c) Engrossed
    (d) Vigorous

57. Find the word which is neither the synonym nor the antonym of the given word.   **(2022)**
    Decrepit
    (a) Feeble
    (b) Strong
    (c) Dilapidated
    (d) Ludicrous

HINTS & EXPLANATIONS

LEVEL - 1

1. (d) When a seed germinates, it puts forth shoots. In other words, it sprouts.

2. (a) John D Rockefeller was an oil magnate. Onassis was a shipping tycoon. Both Rockefeller and Onassis were big businessmen, their spheres being oil (petroleum) and shipping respectively. Both magnate and tycoon refer to businessmen who have made it big, their success making them rich and powerful.

3. (d) A facet of something is a single part or aspect of it.

4. (c) If you persuade me to do something, you try to convince me that it should be done.

5. (c) Certain categories of companies have been exempted from paying tax. That is, they do not have to shoulder the burden of tax-paying. In other words, their burden has been relieved.

6. (c) The quality of being female; womanly

7. (c) Cordon means a line of people, policemen or soldiers which guards or prevents people entering or leaving an area.

8. (b) Rectify is to correct.

9. (b) When a law is revoked, it stands cancelled. We can also say that the law has been repealed.

10. (d) I have lost my reputation and nothing can redeem it. That is, much though I may try, no good action on my part can bring my lost reputation back. In other words, I cannot recover my reputation.

11. (c) Adult means a person who is fully grown or developed that is mature.

12. (c) Diligent as an adjective means having or showing care and conscientiousness in one's work or duties. So the word 'Hardworking' is the correct synonym.

13. (c) Fragile is the object which is easily broken or damaged and therefore, delicate is the correct option.

14. (c) Goods is inherently useful and relatively scarce tangible item; article, commodity, material, merchandise, supply, produced from ↔ agricultural ↔ construction, manufacturing, or mining activities. Material is the right option.

15. (d) Synopsis means brief summary or general survey of something. So, summary is the right option.

16. (a) Ancestor refers to a person, typically one more remote than a grandparent, from whom one is descended. Descendant means the opposite that is a person, plant, or animal that is descended from a particular ancestor.

17. (d) Authentic means something of undisputed origin and not a copy or genuine. The word unreal is the correct antonym as it means something imaginary or illusory.

18. (a) Furious means extremely angry therefore calm is the right antonym.

19. (d) Genuine means something authentic and fake means not genuine; imitation or counterfeit.

20. (d) Rigid means unable to bend or be forced out of shape; not flexible. Tolerant broadly means showing willingness to allow the existence of opinions or behaviour that one does not necessarily agree with.

21. (a) Roost-to settle

22. (a) Hinder means to prevent the growth or progress of something while expedite is to

make fast the process or facilitate. Vindicate means to justify.

23. (b) Trait means characteristic.

24. (c) Origin means the starting point and remnant is what is left after finishing or distrubution.

25. (b) Prove means to state that a statement or theory is correct after giving valid and logical reasons while assumption is something which is believed without any proofs or evidence.

26. (b) Frail means something or someone very weak, usually due to illness.

27. (a) Proclaim is to announce usually in favour of, denounce means to speak against.

28. (a) Radical comes from Latin radix (= root). If you make a radical change in something, the change goes to its very roots, thus affecting the entire thing. On the other hand, there are changes which do not disturb the entire thing; the changes take place only on the surface. In other words, they are superficial changes.

29. (b) Holistic medicine treats the whole person, not just the diseased part. That which is holistic is based on the principles of holism. Holism is the belief that everything in nature is connected in some way. A piecemeal approach, on the other hand, deals with only one part at a time.

30. (b) Having piled a huge total, the Sri Lankan cricket team was in a dominating position. That is, the Sri Lankans were in control of the match (the Independence Cup final). The Pakistani succumbed to the pressure. That is, they were affected by the Sri Lankan domination.

31. (a) The preposition to expressing motion in the direction of a particular location.

32. (b) Pair here means a set of two things used together or regarded as a unit.

33. (a)

34. (a) knows

35. (a) paws

36. past

37. sent

38. bored

39. four

40. break

41. (c)

42. (a)

43. (b)

44. (c)

45. (b)

46. (b)

47. (c)

48. (a)

49. (c)

50. (b)

51. (d) Balmy

52. (b) Address

53. (a) Synonym of magnificent is grandiose.

54. (a) Synonym of retaliate is recompense.

55. (b) Synonym of encourage is embolden.

56. (d) Synonym of exuberance is eagerness.

57. (d) Antonym of terse is detailed.

58. (b) Antonym of grant is refusal.

59. (c)

60. (b)

61. (b)

LEVEL - 2

1. (a) Here heal means to become sound or healthy again.

2. (b) Here seed in the context means a mature plant ovule containing an embryo.

3. (d) In the context of the sentence, Isle means an island or peninsula, especially a small one

4. (b) Lesson means a task as assigned signed for learning or teaching

5.   (a)   Reduce (food) to small shreds by rubbing it on a grater.

6.   (b)   Pale here means having less colour than usual, typically as a result of shock, fear or ill health.

7.   (a)   Hoarse means of a person's voice sounding rough and harsh, typically as the result of a sore throat or of shouting

8.   (b)   In the context of the sentence it means an economic situation in which goods or shares are scarce and sellers can keep prices high.

9.   (b)   Belonging to or associated with the person or people that the speaker is addressing.

10.   (a)   To pass time doing nothing often followed by away.

11.   (a)   Here the modal ought is expressing logical expectation

12.   (a)   A distinctively shaped and marked float, sometimes carrying a signal or signals, anchored to mark a channel, anchorage, navigational hazard, etc., or to provide a mooring place away from the shore.

13.   (b)   Here the word cast means to throw off or away

14.   (b)   Tortuous is the right option because it means full of twists, turns, or bends; twisting, winding or crooked.

15.   (a)   To strip something of its skin, rind, bark, etc.

16.   (b)   This means a long shaft with a broad blade at one end, used as a lever for rowing or otherwise propelling or steering a boat.

17.   (b)   A shoulder shaped frame with a hook at the top, usually of wire, wood,or plastic, for draping and hanging a garment when not in use.

18.   (a)   Forgo means to give up, renounce, or resign.

19.   (a)   The domestic or barnyard hen or rooster; chicken.

20.   (a)   Apart or detached from others; separate; distinct

21.   (b)   Belonging to a foreign country

22.   (c)   Bitterness means sharpness of taste; lack of sweetness therefore acrimony is the correct synonym.

23.   (c)   Fright means a sudden intense feeling of fear

24.   (c)   Relating to visual art, especially involving drawing, engraving, or lettering

25.   (b)   Initiative means the ability to assess and initiate things independently.

26.   (b)   Here liberal means of a person giving generously.

27.   (c)   Prohibit means to forbid something by law, rule, or other authority.

28.   (d)   Rescue means to save someone from a dangerous or difficult situation.

29.   (b)   Swift means moving or capable of moving at high speed.

30.   (c)   Valour means great courage in the face of danger, especially in battle.

31.   (b)   To express agreement with or commitment to; uphold; support.

32.   (b)   Timid means showing a lack of courage or confidence; easily frightened.

33.   (a)   Diffident means modest or shy because of a lack of self-confidence.

34.   (d)   Effective means successful in producing a desired or intended result.

35.   (c)   Gallant in the case of a person refers to or the behaviour that is brave or heroic. So coward is the correct antonym.

36.   (b)   Knowledge refers to awareness or familiarity gained by experience of a fact or situation. So ignorance is the correct antonym.

37.   (b)   Moisture means water or other liquid diffused in a small quantity as vapour, within a solid, or condensed on a surface, so dryness is the correct antonym.

38. (a) Quit means to leave (a place), usually permanently, so remain is the correct antonym.

39. (d) Blunt means not having a sharp edge or point therefore it is the right antonym of sharpness.

40. (a) Worried means anxious or troubled about actual or potential problems. Untroubled is the right option.

41. (a) Develop

42. (c) Flatter

43. (c) Antonym of accomplished is inept.

44. (d) Antonym of turmoil is harmony.

45. (a) Synonym of clairvoyant is oracular.

46. (d) Antonym of perfidious is veracious.

47. (d) Antonym of feud is harmony.

48. (a) Antonym of oration is writing.

49. (c) Synonym of covetous is envious.

50. (a) Antonym of abundance is dearth.

51. (a) Synonym of extraneous is irrelevant.

52. (d) Synonym of vindicate is justify.

53. (d) Synonym of parity is similarity.

54. (a) Antonym of punctilious is careless.

55. (b)

56. (d)

57. (d)

IDIOMS AND PHRASES/PROVERBS

IDIOM

The term refers to a set expression or a phrase comprising two or more words. An interesting fact regarding the device is that the expression is not interpreted literally. The phrase is understood as to mean something quite different from what individual words of the phrase would imply. Alternatively, it can be said that the phrase is interpreted in a figurative sense.

We can say that idiom is a word or phrase which means different from its literal meaning. These are common phrases or terms whose meaning are not real, but can be understood by their popular use.

It is very necessary to use idioms properly; otherwise it will bring no sense. Some idioms are only used by some groups of people or at certain times. The idiom *shape up* or *ship out*, which is like saying improve your behaviour or leave if you don't, might be said by an employer or supervisor to an employee, but not to other people.

Idioms are made of normal words that have a special meaning known by almost everyone. To learn a language a person needs to learn the words in that language, and how and when to use them. But people also need to learn idioms separately because certain words together or at certain times can have different meanings.

To know the history of an idiom can be useful and interesting, but is not necessary to be able to use the idiom properly. For example most native British English speakers know that "No room to swing a cat" means "there was not a lot of space" and can use the idiom properly, but few know it.

A better understanding of an idiom is that it is a phrase whose meaning cannot be understood from the dictionary definitions of each word taken separately.

EXAMPLE

"Every cloud has its silver lining but it is sometimes a little difficult to get it to the mint."

The statement quoted above uses "silver lining" as an idiom which means some auspicious moment is lurking behind the cloud or the difficult time.

FUNCTIONS OF IDIOM

The purpose behind this vast use of idioms is to ornate language, make it richer and spicier and help in conveying subtle meanings to intended audience.

Not only do idioms help in making the language beautiful, they also make things better or worse through making the expression good or bad. They are at times work exact and more correct than the literal words and sometimes a few words are enough to replace a full sentence. They help the writer make his sense clearer than it is, so that he could convey maximum meanings through minimum words and also keep the multiplicity of the meanings in the text intact.

It has also been seen that idioms not only convey subtle meanings but also convey a phenomenon that is not being conveyed through normal and everyday language and also they keep the balance in the communication. Furthermore, they provide textual coherence, so that the reader could be able to piece together a text that he has gone through and extract meanings the writer has conveyed.

EXAMPLE

He cried crocodile tears because he wanted his dad to buy him something.

Just as a crocodile cannot cry, the boy was not crying at all! He was just acting!

People use idioms to make their language richer and more colourful. Idioms and idiomatic expressions can be more precise than the literal words, often using fewer words but saying more.

Some commonly used Idioms :

Beat back (to compel to retire) : The firemen were *beaten back* by angry flames and the building was reduced to ashes.

Boil down to (to amount to) : His entire argument *boiled down* to this that he would not join the movement unless he saw some monetary gain in it.

Cast aside (to reject, to throw aside) : Men will *cast aside* truth and honesty for immediate gains.

Cry down (to deprecate) : Some of the Western powers did their best to *cry down* India's success in the war.

To cut off with a shilling (to give someone a mere trifle in the will) : The father was so angry with the son over his marriage that *he cut him off with a shilling.*

Egg on (to urge on) : Who *egged* you on to fight a professional boxer and get your nose knocked off?

Gloss over (explain away) : Even if you are an important person your faults cannot be *glossed over.*

To laugh in one's sleeves (to be secretly amused) : While I was solemnly reading my research paper to the audience, my friends were *laughing in their sleeves* for they knew what it was worth.

Play off (to set one party against another for one's own advantage) : It best serves the interests of the super powers to *play off* one poor nation against another.

Pull one through (to recover, to help one recover) : Armed with the latest medicines, the doctor *will pull him through.*

Cost a slur upon (by word or act to cast a slight reproach on someone) : Many a man casts a *slur* on his own good name with some mean act.

To catch a Tartar (to encounter a strong adversary) : When Hitler marched in to Russia he little knew that he would *catch a Tartar* in the tough people of that country.

To come off with flying colours (to come out of a conflict with brilliant success) : The 1971 election outcome was uncertain but finally the Congress *came off with flying colours.*

To come off second best (to be defeated in every contest) : Be it an election or a tambola, I have always come off the second best.

To cut the Gordian knot (to remove a difficulty by bold or unusual measures) : The Parliament threw out the Bill for Abolition of Privy Purses. The Government cut the Gordian knot by abolishing the privy purses through an ordinance.

To fall to one's lot (to become one's fate): It fell to the lot of Mujib and his colleagues to reconstruct the shattered economy of their nation.

To get into hot water (to get into difficulty): The businessman *got into hot water* with the Income-tax authorities for concealing his income from ancestral property.

To give someone the slip (to dodge someone who is looking for you): The police had nearly got the dacoits when the *latter gave* them the *slip* in the Chambal ravines.

To go on a fool's errand (to go on an expedition which leads to a foolish end): Many people earlier believed that going to the moon was like *going on a fool's errand*

To go to the wall (to get the worst in a competition): In the struggle of life, the weakest *goes to the wall.*

To go to rack and ruin, to go to the dogs (to be ruined): If a big war comes, our economy will *go to the dogs.*

To have one's hands full (to be very busy): Pakistan could hardly expect active help from the U.S.A. *as her hands were already full with Vietnam*, Laos and West Asia problems.

To have a bone to pick with one (to have a difference with a person which has not yet been fully expressed). The extreme leftists *have a bone to pick* with the police and if ever they come to power there may be unpleasantness between the two.

To have the whip hand of (to have mastery over): After the split in the party Mrs. *Gandhi* has *the whip hand of* the Congress.

To have too many irons in the fire (to have so much work in hand that some part of it is left undone or is done very badly): Let the Government not go in for nationalisation so fast. If they *have too many irons in the fire* they are bound to fare badly.

To have the tree or right ring (To be genuine): Nixon's pronouncements on world peace do not *have the right ring.*

*To have two strings to one's bow (*to have an alternative means of achieving one's purpose): A wife always has *two strings to her bow* if coaxing fails to achieve the desired end; tears succeed.

To have an axe to grind (have personal interests to serve): Bigger nations supply arms to the smaller ones primarily because they (the bigger nations) *have their own axe to grind.*

To keep the wolf from the door (to keep away extreme poverty and hunger): Lakhs in India have to struggle everyday to *keep the wolf from the door.*

To make short work of (to bring to sudden end): The locusts *made short work* of the ripe standing corn.

To make amends for (to compensate for damage): By his kindness today he has made *amends pr* his past insolence.

To make common cause with (to unite, to co-operate with): During the last elections the princes *made a common cause with* the rightist parties. Both went down.

To make a virtue of necessity (to do a very disagreeable thing as though from duty but really because you must do it): When a minister knows that he is going to be booted out of the cabinet he *makes a virtue of necessity* and resigns on health grounds.

To make much ado about nothing (make a great fuss about a trifle): Demonstrations and protests over the change in the timing of news bulletins over AIR was *making much ado about nothing*

To make a cat's paw or a tool of someone (to use someone as a means of attaining your object): The super-powers have *made a cat's paw* of the smaller nations of Asia in their game of power politics.

To play into the hands of someone (to act as to be of advantage to another) By raising the slogan 'Indira Hatao' the opposition *played into her hands* and Mrs. Gandhi won the elections hands down (easily).

To play second fiddle' (to take a subordinate part) : With Mrs. Gandhi as the undisputed leader of the Congress and the nation, everyone else was content to *play second fiddle to her.*

To put the cart before the horse (to begin at the wrong end to do a thing): Preparing the blue print of a project without the provision of funds is like *putting the cart before the horse.*

To put one's shoulder to the wheel (to make great efforts) : No amount of foreign aid will pull us out of the economic morass; we have to *put our own shoulders to the wheel.*

To set store by (to value highly): India, *surely sets much store by* the Indo Soviet Treaty of Friendship.

To set the Thames on fire (to do something extraordinary): He is a steady worker but never likely *to set the Thames on fire.*

To set one's house in *order* (to arrange one's affairs): Let Pakistan *set her own house in order* before talking of the welfare of the Kashmiris.

To take into one's head (to occur to someone): The Manager *look it into his head* that by shutting off the electricity for a few hours daily he could save on refrigeration costs.

To take the bull by the horns (to grapple with a problem courageously instead of avoiding it): There is no short cut to prosperity. We have *to take the bull by the horns* and make people work like slaves.

To take a leap in the dark (to do a hazardous thing without any idea of what it may result in): You *took a leap in the dark* in going into partnership with that man.

To throw cold water upon (to discourage something): The doctor *threw cold water upon* my plans for a world tour by declaring that I could never stand the strain of it.

To throw up the sponge (to give up a contest): Faced with stiff competition from big companies, many a small company will *throw up the sponge.*

To turn over a *new leaf (to* change one's course of action completely): After a long career of crime the convict suddenly *turned over a new leaf* and became a model citizen.

To turn tail (to retreat ignominiously): The enemy *turned tail* in the face of heavy onslaughts on its key positions.

To turn the tables (to reverse someone's success or superiority): Pakistan started war with a blitz on our positions but the superior tactics of our Armed Forces soon *turned the tables* on them.

To cook or doctor an account (to tamper with or falsify the account): From the balance sheet presented to the shareholders, the company seemed to be flourishing, but it afterwards turned out that the Secretary had *cooked the accounts.*

To bear the *brunt* of (to endure the main force or shock of): The infantry has to *bear the brunt of a* battle.

To beard the lion in his den (to oppose someone, in his stronghold): The Indian Army broke through strong Pakistani fortifications, and in the Shakargarh area *bearded the lion in his own den.*

To bid fair to (to give fair prospect of): His health is so good that he *bids fair to* live till he is sixty.

To blow one's own trumpet (to parade one's own good deeds): Modesty does not pay. Only if you *blow your own trumpet,* you can succeed.

To blunt the edge of (to make something less effective): Time *blunts the edge* of grief.

To build castles in the air (to indulge in reveries or visionary schemes): There is nothing wrong if you *build castles in the air;* now put foundations under them.

To burn the candle at both ends (to use too much energy): Our resources are limited. Let us use them judiciously and not *burn the candle at both ends.*

To buy a pig in a poke (to purchase a thing without previously examining it): Buying shares in a new Company started by unknown entrepreneurs is like buying a *pig in a poke.*

To cross or pass the Rubicon (to take a decisive step forward): The Government will have to think of many things before nationalising the textile industry for once they *cross the Rubicon* there will be no going back.

To cry over spilt milk (to nurse unnecessary regrets): We have failed to build up a sizeable total against England's meagre first innings total. It is no use crying *over spilt milk* now.

To err on the safe side (to choose a course which may in fact be inaccurate, but which will keep you safe from risk or harm): In going *in* for mixed economy rather than wholesale nationalisation the Government were *erring on the safe side.*

To flog a *dead horse* (waste one's energies): We *are flogging* a *dead horse* if we are trying to make Sanskrit the national language of India.

To feather one's nest (to provide for oneself through dishonest means): Many tax collectors make a point of *feathering their* own *nests* well while they have opportunity.

To Eat one's heart out (to brood over one's sorrows or disappointments): Don't *eat your heart out* over failure in this competition.

To eat humble pie (to have to humiliate oneself): Since none came to his support he had to eat *humble pie* and give in to their demands.

To eat one's words (*to* retract one's assertions under compulsion): It is hard for a haughty man to have to *eat his words.*

To throw down the gauntlet, to take up the gauntlet (to offer or give a challenge, to accept a challenge): It is not for a small country to throw down the gauntlet to the right and the left.

PHRASES

In our everyday life, we use several words that don't necessarily carry a literal meaning. They are infact synonymous with expressions. These expressions are termed as phrases.

These phrases could be a euphemism, a saying or a proverb. It is merely a figure of speech.

EXAMPLE

> All rights reserved
> economical with the truth
> A knight in shining armour
> A see change

PROVERBS

Every culture has a collection of wise sayings that offer advice about how to live your life. These sayings are called "proverbs".

It's good to know the really common English proverbs because you hear them come up in conversation all the time. Sometimes people say the entire proverb to give advice to a friend. More often, someone will say just part of a proverb like this:

You know what they say: when the going gets tough...

Proverbs can also give you good example sentences which you can memorise and use as models for building your own sentences.

GRAMMATICAL STRUCTURES OF PROVERBS

Proverbs in various languages are found with a wide variety of grammatical structures. In English, for example, we find the following structures (in addition to others).

- Imperative, negative - Don't beat a dead horse.
- Imperative, positive - Look before you leap.
- Parallel phrases - Garbage in, garbage out.
- Rhetorical question - Is the Pope Catholic?
- Declarative sentence - Birds of a feather flock together.

However, people will often quote only a fraction of a proverb to invoke an entire proverb, e.g., "All is fair" instead of "All is fair in love and war", and "A rolling stone" for "A rolling stone gathers no moss." The grammar of proverbs is not always the typical grammar of the spoken language, often elements are moved around, to achieve rhyme or focus.

USE IN CONVERSATION

Proverbs are used in conversation by adults more than children, partially because adults have learned more proverbs than children. Also, using proverbs well is a skill that is developed over years. Additionally, children have not mastered the patterns of metaphorical expression that are invoked in proverb use. Proverbs, because they are indirect, allow a speaker to disagree or give advice in a way that may be less offensive.

EXAMPLE

A bad tree does not yield good apples.	A bad parent does not raise good children.
A bad workman blames his tools.	Blaming the tools for bad workmanship is an excuse for lack of skill.
A bird in hand is worth two in a bush.	It is better to keep what you have rather than to risk losing it by searching for something better.
A broken friendship may be soldered but will never be sound.	Friendships can be rebuilt after a dispute but will never be as strong as before.
A burden of one's own choice is not felt.	Something difficult seems easier when it is done voluntarily.
A burnt child dreads the fire.	A bad experience will make people stay away from certain things.
A cat has nine lives.	(1) Cats can survive many accidents because they land on their feet without injury.

(2)   Nine lives = 3 years to play, 3 years to stray, 3 years to stay.

A chain is no stronger than its weakest link.	The strength of a group depends on each individual member.
A change is as good as a rest.	A change in routine is often as refreshing as a break or a holiday.
A dry March, a wet April and a cool May fill barn and cellar and bring much hay.	Harvest predictions are made according to the weather.
A fault confessed is half redressed.	Confession is the beginning of forgiveness.
A flower blooms more than once.	If you miss an occasion, you can avail yourself of it another time.
A fool and his money are (soon) easily parted.	A foolish person usually spends money carelessly.
A fool at forty is a fool forever.	If a person hasn't matured by the age of 40, they never will.
A friend in need is a friend indeed.	Someone who helps you when you are in trouble is a real friend.
A friend to all is a friend to none.	Someone who is a friend to everyone makes none of them feel special.
A friend's eye is a good mirror.	A real friend will tell you the truth.
A good example is the best sermon.	Giving a good example is better than giving advice.
A good beginning makes a good end.	If a task is carefully planned, there's a better chance that it will be well done.
A good conscience is a soft pillow.	You sleep well when you have nothing to be guilty about.
A guilty conscience needs no accuser.	If you know that you have done something wrong, you don't need anyone to tell you that you're guilty.
A hungry belly has no ears.	A hungry person is totally concentrated on their need for food and nothing else interests them.
A hungry wolf is fixed to no place.	A desperate person will go from place to place in order to satisfy their needs.
Early to bed, and early to rise, makes a man healthy, wealthy and wise.	It is much better for you to go to bed early and to get up early in the morning;
(The) early bird catches the worm.	Act early, or before anyone else, if you want to have an advantage or be successful.
Easier said than done.	What is suggested sounds easy, but it is more difficult to actually do it.
Facts speak louder than words	People show what they are really like by what they do, rather than by what they say.
Failure teaches success.	People can learn from their failures and be successful later on.
Fair exchange is no robbery	Swapping two items of equal value is an honest deal.
False friends are worse than open enemies.	It's better to know who your real enemies are rather than trust someone who pretends to be a friend but is capable of stabbing you in the back.
Half a loaf is better than none	You should be grateful for something, even if it is not as much as you wanted.
(A) handful of patience is worth more than a bushel of brains.	Patience is more precious than intelligence.
Handsome is what handsome does.	Behaviour is more important than appearance.
(A) happy heart is better than a full purse.	Happiness is better than wealth.
Hard words breaks no bones.	Criticism or verbal attacks may be unpleasant but will not kill anyone.

LEVEL 1

DIRECTIONS (Qs. 1-10) : *Choose the correct meaning of the following.*

1. To bite the dust   **(Tricky, 2013)**
    (a) To be defeated in battle
    (b) To learn a lesson
    (c) To be ashamed of
    (d) To work very hard
2. Between the devil and the deep sea
    (a) in a dilemma   **(Critical Thinking)**
    (b) a man who is drowning
    (c) to be evil-tempered
    (d) a deep sea diver
3. He cannot make both ends meet.
    (a) control affairs
    (b) earn enough
    (c) work hard
    (d) manage the business
4. At close quarters   **(2014)**
    (a) close examinations
    (b) live near to each other
    (c) live far to each other
    (d) in love
5. An apple of discord   **(2011)**
    (a) cause of wealth
    (b) cause of illness
    (c) cause of happiness
    (d) cause of quarrel
6. At sixes and sevens
    (a) in perfect order   (b) very happy
    (c) in disorder   (d) very sad
7. A load of cobblers   **(Tricky)**
    (a) Good news
    (b) Very famous
    (c) Rubbish
    (d) None of above
8. Break the ice
    (a) To do something with courage
    (b) To win a prize
    (c) To speak first after long silence
    (d) To win some one heart

9. Black and Blue   **(2015)**
    (a) To put things in order
    (b) To put things in disorder
    (c) To trust someone
    (d) To beat very badly
10. Bring to book   **(2016)**
    (a) To punish   (b) To serve
    (c) To praise   (d) To write a story

DIRECTIONS (Qs. 11-20) : *Choose the right meaning of idioms in bold letters.*

11. He will go **to any length** to achieve success.
    (a) lose her sanity   **(2012)**
    (b) do all that is possible
    (c) can do all misdeeds
    (d) can humiliate
12. My family needs to **tighten the belt** in this time of scarcity.
    (a) be more careful
    (b) be attentive
    (c) make economies in expenditure
    (d) revive itself
13. The director **took him to task** for this misconduct.   **(2013)**
    (a) reprimanded him
    (b) forced him to resign
    (c) give him additional work
    (d) suspended his assignment
14. There was criticism to the new policy of the Government **by the rank and file**.   **(2015)**
    (a) the ordinary members
    (b) the majority
    (c) the official machinery
    (d) the ministers
15. It is not good to **add fuel to the fire**.   **(2014)**
    (a) humiliate
    (b) aggravate trouble
    (c) become aggressive
    (d) lighten

16. Shekhar was **left high and dry** by his friends when he spent all his money.   **(2013)**
    (a) depressed   (b) very alone
    (c) without help   (d) isolated
17. I will **leave no stone unturned** to satisfy my superiors.   **(2016)**
    (a) take no pains
    (b) resort to illegitimate
    (c) do very irrelevant things
    (d) use all available means
18. When she would say anything about herself, she is inclined **to draw the longbrow.**   **(2014)**
    (a) understate   (b) get excited
    (c) get emotional   (d) exaggerate
19. He is **a great hand** at organising public events.   **(2016)**
    (a) well qualified for
    (b) very fond of
    (c) expert at
    (d) accustomed to
20. It will be wise for her to let the **bygones be bygones.**   **(2014)**
    (a) ignore the past
    (b) resist the past
    (c) revive the past
    (d) recollect the past

DIRECTIONS (Qs. 21-30) : *Match the following proverbs with their meaning.*   **(Tricky)**

	A		B
21.	A tree is known by its fruit	(a)	It's not good to do too many things at the same time.
22.	Beauty lies in the eyes of the beholder	(b)	A person's character is more important than their appearance.
23.	He who is everywhere is nowhere	(c)	A person shows their competence or ability when difficulties arise.
24.	Beauty is only skin deep	(d)	It takes time to do a job properly. You should not expect to do it quickly
25.	Calm sea does not make a skilled sailor	(e)	A man is judged by his actions
26.	Learn to walk before you run	(f)	Trying to obtain everything will often result in gaining nothing.
27.	Rome was not built in a day	(g)	Different people have different tastes
28.	Grasp all, lose all	(h)	Behaviour is more important than appearance
29.	Honesty is the best policy	(i)	Don't rush into doing something before you know how to do it
30.	Handsome is what handsome does	(j)	It's always better to be honest

DIRECTIONS (Qs. 31-39) : *Choose the right meaning of the given proverb.*

31. All's well that ends well.
    (a) Once a decision has been made, it cannot be reversed.
    (b) Everything that is attractive on the face need not be really valuable inside.
    (c) It is preferable to be cautious than be rash and get into trouble.
    (d) A satisfactory conclusion makes up for earlier disappointments.
32. The child is father of the man.   **(2013)**
    (a) People who talk a lot or threaten may not be actually harmful.
    (b) One's actions whether good or bad determine one's rewards or punishments.
    (c) The character of a child shows the kind of man he will grow up to be.
    (d) What pleases the sight varies from one person to another.
33. Slow but sure wins the race.
    (a) A satisfactory conclusion makes up for earlier disappointments.
    (b) If one arrives early, one gets a better choice
    (c) The character of a child shows the kind of man he will grow up to be.
    (d) Steady progress is better in the long run than inconsistent speed.

34. Birds of a feather flock together.
    (a) It is better to accept the little we have than reject it hoping to get a lot later.
    (b) People with similar interests and tastes tend to group.
    (c) The character of a child shows the kind of man he will grow up to be.
    (d) There are often early indications of future happenings.

35. A burnt child dreads the fire.   **(2015)**
    (a) It is not good to only toil and have no recreation.
    (b) Family ties are stronger than other relationships.
    (c) A mistake can be a great teacher.
    (d) What pleases the sight varies from one person to another.

36. Left-handed compliment   **(2018)**
    (a) An insincere compliment
    (b) A flattering
    (c) An honest compliment
    (d) A well-deserved compliment

37. I don't want to blow my own _______, but I do think I single-handelly won the match for us.
    (2019)
    (a) Flute   (b) Mind
    (c) Whistle   (d) Trumpet

38. I think if we had thought about it more carefully the solution would have _______ on us earlier.
    (2019)
    (a) come   (b) though
    (c) dawned   (d) arrived

39. Murphy struggled _______ to complete his university studies.   **(2020)**
    (a) for all ends
    (b) to all parts
    (c) against all odds
    (d) to all odds and ends

DIRECTIONS (Qs. 40-41) : *Choose the part of the sentence that has an error.*   **(2022)**

40. 'Bone to pick' means _______.
    (a) to feed dogs
    (b) to have a grievance that needs to be talked out
    (c) to buy some food
    (d) to clean a particular place

41. 'Feather in one's cap ' means _______.
    (a) to solve a notoriously difficult problem
    (b) to brag about oneself
    (c) to set a limit
    (d) an accomplishment a person can be proud of

LEVEL 2

DIRECTIONS (Qs. 1-32) : *Choose the right meaning of the idioms in bold letters.*

1. Whenever we went out to dinner, I had to **foot the bill**.
   - (a) beyond control
   - (b) pay for it
   - (c) finds favour with
   - (d) lower than expectation

2. You have **hit the nail on the head.**   **(2013)**
   - (a) said/ done the right thing
   - (b) ran away fast
   - (c) scolded him for
   - (d) to inflict severe punishment

3. When the politician raised hate slogans, the crowd got **out of hand**.   **(2014)**
   - (a) pay for it
   - (b) beyond control
   - (c) finds favour with
   - (d) ran away

4. She is **in the good books** of the teacher.
   - (a) said/ done the right thing
   - (b) finds favour with
   - (c) ran away fast
   - (d) good relations

5. He is working **against time** on this project
   - (a) at great speed
   - (b) beyond control
   - (c) finds favour with
   - (d) a great delay

6. The headmaster **took him to task for** his unpunctuality.
   - (a) scolded him
   - (b) beyond control
   - (c) finds favour with
   - (d) punished severely

7. They wanted the agreement **in black and white**.
   - (a) finds favour with
   - (b) in writing **(2014)**
   - (c) beyond control
   - (d) in a simple way

8. The boys **took to their heels** on seeing the hive.
   - (a) beyond control
   - (b) ran away fast
   - (c) scolded him for
   - (d) throw away shoes

9. Pinky and Rosy are very **hard of hearing**.
   - (a) disinterested
   - (b) deaf   **(2013)**
   - (c) inaudible
   - (d) insensitive

10. Ashok's family is really **a broken reed**.   **(Tricky, 2012)**
    - (a) Frustrated
    - (b) Unsupportive
    - (c) unsuccessful
    - (d) unhealthy one

11. We do not like to **rake up** old issues and create troubles.
    - (a) revive
    - (b) end
    - (c) forget
    - (d) blame

12. He is a **queer fish**, we could not understand him.   **(Critical Thinking, 2015)**
    - (a) sensitive person
    - (b) funny person
    - (c) contemplating
    - (d) strange person

13. Prakash used to **chew the cud** in every situation.   **(2012)**
    - (a) forget others
    - (b) get disturbed
    - (c) muse on
    - (d) accuse others

14. Despite having a lot of money and stamina, yet all his plans are **built on sand**.
    - (a) unstable
    - (b) inexperienced
    - (c) immature
    - (d) cheap

15. Rohan is always **picking holes** in every assignment.   **(Tricky)**
    - (a) suggesting improvements
    - (b) finding faults
    - (c) creating problems
    - (d) asking irrelevant questions

16. His blaming attitude **gets on my nerves.**
    - (a) pierces my eardrums
    - (b) shivers me
    - (c) makes me ill
    - (d) irritates me

17. The supervisor dominates his employees with **a high hand.**   **(2016)**
    - (a) democratically
    - (b) oppressively
    - (c) sympathetically
    - (d) kindly

18. Can you please **bury the hatchet** and make up with your sister?
    (a) work in garden
    (b) stay together
    (c) make peace with someone
    (d) to come to a conclusion
19. I met him after a long time, but he gave me **the cold shoulder**
    (a) scolded me
    (b) insulted me
    (c) abused me
    (d) ignorned me
20. I warned him not to indulge in any **monkey business.**   **(2015)**
    (a) dishonest schemes
    (b) funny tasks
    (c) futile tasks
    (d) underhanded business
21. The officer played **ducks and drakes** with his job.   **(Tricky)**
    (a) took unjustifiable risk
    (b) tried to improve
    (c) tried to popularise
    (d) tried to make extra money
22. Her attempt to flying the helicopter was like trying to **square a circle.**   **(2014)**
    (a) train oneself
    (b) do the impossible
    (c) drive in a round about manner
    (d) try to show off
23. Rohit has a **stick-in-the-mud** attitude to life.
    (a) slow and unprogressive   **(2012)**
    (b) from attitude
    (c) disagreeable and unacceptable
    (d) non-yielding
24. There is simply **no royal road** to be successful.
    (a) strife-filled route
    (b) cheap manner
    (c) quickest and easiest way
    (d) luxurious way
25. **Words failed** the victim when she was accused of the forgery.
    (a) Unable to utter sounds
    (b) Tried to speak glibly
    (c) Shocked and angered and unable to speak
    (d) Threatened by words

26. Why don't you believe me, I am **all at sea.**
    (a) puzzled   (b) drowning
    (c) out of reach   (d) disheartened
27. Our school is **within a stone's throw** of our house.   **(2015)**
    (a) at a short distance
    (b) within certain circumference
    (c) within the place
    (d) resembles
28. I **made no bones** about such conducts and thus faced a tough opposition.   **(Tricky, 2013)**
    (a) made no plans
    (b) done without hesitation
    (c) not invited any comments
    (d) wasted no time
29. All the political leaders are **tarred with the same brush.**   **(2014)**
    (a) have the same merits
    (b) profess the same policies
    (c) possess the same defects
    (d) treated equally
30. **By and large,** the papers he presented were quite impressive.
    (a) Inspite of many mistakes
    (b) In addition to
    (c) Mostly
    (d) In a big amount
31. Rajat and I have remained friends through **thick and thin.**   **(2017)**
    (a) In all good and bad conditions
    (b) through the days of struggle
    (c) inspite of all difficulties
    (d) narrow escape
32. Discipline is **on the wane** among students these days.
    (a) Increasing   (b) spiralling
    (c) declining   (d) spreading

DIRECTIONS (Qs. 33-41) : *Complete the following proverbs.*

---

33. The apple doesn't fall far from the _________.
    (a) river   (b) farm
    (c) tree   (d) sky
34. A bad man is better than a bad _________.
    (a) name   (b) cloth   **(2016)**
    (c) woman   (d) boy

35. A bird in hand is worth __________.
    (a) one in the sky
    (b) two in the bush
    (c) two in the pocket
    (d) two in the table
36. A little learning is a __________ thing.   **(2015)**
    (a) sweet   (b) profitable
    (c) good   (d) dangerous
37. An empty mind is the __________.
    (a) God's house
    (b) giant's office
    (c) devil's workshop
    (d) man's office
38. A wise foe is better than __________.
    (a) a foolish relative   **(Tricky, 2014)**
    (b) a foolish friend
    (c) a wise son
    (d) an intelligent father
39. Practice makes a man __________.
    (a) perfect   (b) idle
    (c) angry   (d) handsome
40. First deserve then __________.
                                (Critical Thinking)
    (a) snatch   (b) rob
    (c) desire   (d) give

41. Bring matters to a head   **(2018)**
    (a) To take matters seriously
    (b) To make matters to a decisive point
    (c) To create an atmosphere of confrontation
    (d) To make matters serious

DIRECTIONS (Qs. 42-44): *Choose the options which best express the meanings of the idiom/phrase given in the questions:*   **(2022)**

42. Hit the jackpot
    (a) To gamble
    (b) To worry about the future
    (c) To lose wealth
    (d) Be highly successful, especially unexpectedly
43. Itsy bitsy
    (a) Very educated
    (b) Very large
    (c) Very small
    (d) Very happy
44. Knit one's brow
    (a) To laugh
    (b) To pacify
    (c) To smile
    (d) To frown

HINTS & EXPLANATIONS

LEVEL - 1

1. (a) Suffer defeat or death is related with battle.

2. (a) In a difficult situation where there are two equally unpleasant choices.

3. (b) Manage so that one's financial means are enough for one's needs

4. (b) In close proximity; very near together

5. (d) Something attractive that causes envy and quarrels among people who think they deserve it.

6. (c) In complete disorder

7. (c) Nonsense, rubbish

8. (c) Do or say something to relieve tension or get conversation going in a strained situation or when strangers meet.

9. (d) Bruised, physically or emotionally.

10. (a) To punish someone

11. (b) Go to any length means—do absolutely anything, go to any extreme, go to any limits, observe no limits

12. (c) Tighten one's belt means cut one's expenditure; live more frugally.

13. (a) Take someone to task means reprimand or criticise someone severely for a fault or mistake.

14. (a) Rank and file means the ordinary members of an organization as opposed to its leaders.

15. (b) Add fuel to the fire means cause a situation or conflict to become more intense.

16. (c) Left high and dry means without resources or help.

17. (d) Leave no stone unturned means try every possible course of action in order to achieve something.

18. (d) To draw the longbrow means to exaggerate in telling stories; overstate something.

19. (c) A great hand here suggests expert man in his profession.

20. (a) Let bygones be bygones means forget past offences or causes of conflict and be reconciled.

21. (e) This proverb means, people judge your character by what you do.

22. (g) This proverb means, different people have different ideas about what is beautiful otherwise saying something that you say which means that each person has their own opinion about what or who is beautiful.

23. (a) This proverb means it's not good to do too many things at the same time.

24. (b) This proverb means a pleasing appearance is not a guide to character.

25. (c) This African proverb means calm times do not show anything; it's the tough times that make you what you are.

26. (i) This proverb means you must master a basic skill before you are able to learn more complex things.

27. (d) The proverb means a complex task is bound to take a long time and should not be rushed.

28. (f) This proverb means one who wants everything, may lose it all.

29. (j) This proverb means there are often practical as well as moral reasons for being honest.

30. (h) It is more important to treat people well than to be good- looking; Just because you are good-looking does not mean you are a good person

31. (d)

32. (c)

33. (d)

34. (b)

35. (c)

36. (a) An insincere compliment

37. (d) trumpet

38. (c) dawned

39. (c) "against all odds" which means "to achieve something despite a lot of difficulty or challenges".

40. (b) "bone to pick" idiom means "to have a grievance that needs to be talked out".

41. (d) "feather in one's cap" idiom means "an accomplishment a person can be proud of".

LEVEL - 2

1. (b) This idiom means to pay all the costs for something.

2. (a) The idiom means find exactly the right answer.

3. (b) This idiom means not under control

4. (b) This idiom means among those he likes, on his list of good people

5. (a) This idiom means with utmost speed, so as to finish by a specified time.

6. (a) This idiom means reprimand or criticize someone severely for a fault or mistake.

7. (b) This idiom means in writing or print.

8. (b) This idiom means to run away.

9. (b) This idiomatic use means to be deaf.

10. (b) This idiomatic expression means an unreliable or unsupportive person.

11. (a) Rake up means to revive the memory of an incident or period that is best forgotten.

12. (d) The idiom means a person whose behaviour seems strange or unusual.

13. (c) Chew the cud means to think about something carefully and for a long time.

14. (a) This phrase means without reliable foundations or any real substance.

15. (b) This phrase means to find mistakes in something someone has done or said, to show that it is not good or not correct

16. (d) This idiom means to annoy someone, especially by doing something again and again.

17. (b) This idiom means with power; in force; triumphantly or arbitrarily.

18. (c) People who agree to bury the hatchet means they agree to forget their argument.

19. (d) This idiomatic use means to show ignorance towards someone.

20. (a) This phrase means mischievous or deceitful behaviour.

21. (a) The phrase means to behave recklessly.

22. (b) This phrase means to find a good solution to a problem when that seems impossible, especially because the people involved have very different needs or opinions about it.

23. (a) This idiomatic phrase refers to a person who is dull and unadventurous and who resists change.

24. (c) The idiomatic use here means a way of attaining or reaching something without trouble.

25. (c) This phase is used to express one's disbelief or dismay.

26. (a) The phrase means in a state of confusion and disorder.

27. (a) This phrase means very close to something.

28. (b) To be frank about something without any hesitation is the meaning of this phrase.

29. (c) This phrase means to consider certain people to have the same faults.

30. (c) This idiomatic expression means on the whole; everything considered.

31. (a) This idiomatic use means under all circumstances, no matter how difficult.

32. (c) This idiomatic phrase means becoming weaker or less extensive.

33. (c) This proverbial saying means children are not different from their parents.

34. (a) Ill reputation is worse than ill-deeds.

35. (b) A small but sure gain is better than a doubtful double gain.

36. (d) The implication is that a small amount of knowledge can lead to overconfidence, leaping to invalid conclusions based on what you do know without taking into account the things that you don't know.

37. (c) People who have nothing worthwhile to think about will usually think of something bad to do.

38. (b) One of the meanings of this proverb could be... Foolish friends are more dangerous than an enemy who is intelligent.

39. (a) Doing something over and over again is the only way to learn to do it well.

40. (c) In order to get almost any earthly thing on your own, you must first deserve it before it is healthy to desire it. You deserve something - in the only sense that ultimately satisfies - only when you work for it.

41. (b) to take matters to a decisive point

42. (d)

43. (c)

44. (d)

CONTEXTUAL USAGE

One of the difficulties in learning English language is the vocabulary. Although the words may seem simple enough to memorize, the contextual use of these words proves to be quiet challenging at times.

Did you ever find yourself in a conversation where you have no idea what the other person is saying? May be it's the person at the car repair place using words like 'carburetor' or 'camshaft,' and you just nod your head and wait for the price. Or may be you're taking a test, and you're supposed to analyze a passage. But there are certain words in the passage you are unable to understand. You have no access to a dictionary. What do you do?

Well, we're not going to teach you car terminology. It's all about determining the meaning of the word by using context. Context refers to the other words and sentences around the word in question.

There are several methods for using context to figure out what words mean. The first is to look and see if the definition of the word is right there. This can also be a restating of the word.

Consider this sentence: 'While planning the party, Reshma was prudent with the guest list, acting with great caution and care not to invite anyone with whom she wouldn't want to jump around in a bounce house.'

What does 'prudent' mean? In this sentence, the definition of the word is right there. Who is being prudent? Reshma. With what? The guest list. You don't need to know what prudent means to figure that out. And how else is Reshma's behaviour with the guest list described? She's acting with great caution and care. So what's the definition of prudent? Acting with great caution and care.

Other times, you'll see examples that help explain the word in question. This is very similar to finding the definition. Look at this sentence: 'Ravi procrastinated to avoid his homework all day, watching TV, playing video games and even writing thank you cards to his grandparents.'

What does 'procrastinate' mean? This time, it's not defined elsewhere in the sentence. But we do have examples of what it means. We know that watching TV, playing video games and writing thank you cards are all forms of procrastination. If Ravi should be doing his homework, but he's doing these other things instead, then procrastination must mean delaying or putting off. Now, those examples helped us figure it out.

WHAT IS CONTEXTUAL PASSAGE?

The contextual passage test in problem solving assessment (PSA) is aimed to assess children's different aspects of written communication of English language that include word spelling, grammar, idioms and phrases, spot the error, one word substitution, sentence improvement, English comprehension etc.

The contextual passage tests evaluate basic understanding of language. Literacy knowledge and skills are essential to effective communication across all learning areas.

These passage tests focus on the use and knowledge of vocabulary in written Standard British English. These skills are essential for the development of reading and writing. The content of the contextual passage tests particularly complements the writing tests where spelling, grammar and punctuation are explicitly assessed in context. However, students' understanding of contextual passage is also necessary for reading.

Content clues are hints found within a sentence, paragraph or passage that a reader can use to understand the meanings of new or unfamiliar words. Learning the meaning of a word through its use in a sentence or paragraph is the most practical way to build vocabulary, since a dictionary is not always available when a reader encounters an unknown word.

By being sensitive to the circumstances in which a word is used, we can decide upon an appropriate definition to fit the context.

The clues can be found in any of the following ways.

- Definition or description
- Antonym
- mood/tone

EXAMPLE

- Fluoroscopy, examination with a fluorscope, has become a common practice. (definition)
- When the light brightens, the pupils of the eyes contract; however, when it grows darker they dilate. (Antonym)
- The lugubrious wails of the gypsies matched the dreary whistling of the wind in all but deserted cemetry (mood).

In order to keep you updated, we are providing with some exercises which may prove to be a perfect guide that will help score well in the test. The examples given here will also provide deep insight into the critical elements of the test - Language Conventions. These exercises will also provide theoretical inputs along with practice exercises. These practice exercises will help students in developing the right temperament to crack this exam. The detailed solutions to the exercises are also provided at the end of the exercises.

(Examples 1 - 8) : Read the following passage carefully and select the most suitable option from each list.

There is hardly a thing or commodity whose price has not gone up in the recent times. Rise in prices has become a common feature in India and the people are reconciled to this fact. Rise in prices is called inflation. There are various factors that contribute to this rise in prices. Some are natural factors like unfavourable weather conditions which affect the food production and lead to the shortage of commodities in the market. With more money chasing fewer goods, the prices take to the wings.

1.   Which of the following could replace 'hardly' as used in the passage above?

    (a)   and   (b)   also

    (c)   scarcely   (d)   never

2.   Which of the following is the correct spelling of 'commoddity'?

    (a)   commoddity   (b)   commudity

    (c)   commodety   (d)   commodity

3.   Which of the following could replace 'reconciled to' as used in the passage above?

    (a)   come in handy   (b)   gone with the wind

    (c)   come to terms   (d)   come forward

4.   Which of the following is the opposite in meaning to 'inflation' as used in the passage above?

    (a)   deflation   (b)   rising prices

    (c)   pomposity   (d)   pretentiousness

5.   Which of the following could replace 'various' as used in the passage above?

    (a)   little   (b)   several

    (c)   few   (d)   a few

6.   Which of the following could replace 'contribute' as used in the passage above?

    (a)   deter   (b)   warn

    (c)   dissuade   (d)   add

7. Which of the following could replace 'unfavourable' as used in the passage above?

    (a) popular   (b) settled

    (c) liveable   (d) not favourable

8. Which of the following could replace 'take to the wings' as used in the passage above?

    (a) rise   (b) decrease

    (c) fall   (d) grow

While solving this problem, let's take question 1 and you have to find out a replacement to the word 'hardly'. If you use a bit of common sense, you'll see that all the three options 'and', 'also' and 'never' are nowhere near the meaning of 'hardly'. Hence, only 'scarcely' fits in here which means 'almost not' and even 'hardly' expresses the same meaning which is 'almost not'.

Now take the question 2. The word 'commodity' is wrongly spelt here and if you check all the four spellings you will find that the spelling of option no. 4 is not unusual, not strange and so, that can be your correct answer. Now come to the question 3, if you go through each option one by one you'll notice that 'come in handy' means be useful for a certain purpose, 'gone with the wind' is just a 1939 Hollywood movie which has no relevance here. Option no. 4 'come forward' means to offer help to someone or offer to do something. So, you are left with only one option which is 'come to terms' which means 'to accept an unpleasant or sad situation and no longer feel upset or angry about it' and that's the right answer. In the same manner, you can solve rest of the problems with accuracy and correctness.

Key to questions:

1. **(c)** Scarcely   2. **(d)** commodity
3. **(c)** come to terms   4. **(a)** deflation
5. **(b)** several   6. **(d)** add
7. **(d)** not favourable   8. **(a)** rise

EXAMPLES

(Questions 1 - 8) : Read the following passage carefully and select the most suitable option from each list.)

For Kaku, Mathematics was extremely hard to understand. In order to keep his results high enough to succeed and to satisfy his parents, Kaku attempted a number of strategies. The answer though was simple. He had to work constantly and diligently at applying the different formulas to a range of contexts. Often he was envious of his peers to whom comprehension came easily. However, at the end of the year, it seemed his relentless work was rewarded when his results put him amongst the leading scholars of his class.

1. Which of these would be the best word to use to replace the word 'extremely' as it is used in the passage above?

    (a) vastly   (b) mostly

    (c) especially   (d) massively

2. Which of these is closest in meaning to 'strategies' as used in the passage above?

    (a) rules   (b) questions

    (c) approaches   (d) instructions

3. Which of the following could replace 'answer' as used in the passage above?

    (a) reply   (b) puzzle

    (c) solution   (d) explanation

4. Which of the following could replace 'though' as used in the passage above?

    (a) yet   (b) even so

    (c) however   (d) all the same

5. Which of the following is the correct way to spell 'dilajentley'?

    (a) dilajently   (b) diligently

    (c) dilejently   (d) dilegently

6. Which of these is closest in meaning to 'contexts' as used in the passage above?

    (a) ways   (b) settings

    (c) numbers   (d) situations

7. Which of the following is closest in meaning to 'was envious of' as used in the passage above?

    (a) was jealous of   (b) was resentful of

    (c) was bitter towards   (d) was hostile towards

8. Which of the following is the opposite in meaning to 'rewarded' as used in the passage above?

    (a) forfeited   (b) punished

    (c) penalised   (d) disadvantaged

Key to questions:

1.	**(c)** especially	2.	**(c)** approaches
3.	**(c)** solution	4.	**(c)** however
5.	**(b)** diligently	6.	**(d)** situations
7.	**(a)** was jealous of	8.	**(b)** punished

Tips on how to do the language conventions test

- Students will go through the text slowly without using any of the options. Read it two or three times until you have a clear perspective of what the passage is all about.

- Next students are advised to go through all the 4 options one by one. Just identify which optional words are the most misleading, out of context and irrelevant to the passage. Go through the text once again and try to choose the correct word from the rest of options that are left after eliminating two or three options.

- While finalizing the correct word, you will be able to eliminate all the three obvious false words and now you zero in on the correct answer.

LEVEL 1

PASSAGE-1

The French-Egyptian **archiological** mission discovered the oldest harbour of the world in Egypt. It is believed that it dates back to 4500 years. The harbour was **discovered** on Red Sea coast, which is said to be that of Pharaoh Khufu (Cheops) in the Fourth Dynasty.

This oldest known commercial habour was discovered at Wadi Al-Jarf area, which is 180 km south of Sueze, Egypt. The team **in the meanwhile** also discovered the oldest **papyri** in Egypt.

Pierre Tallet, Egyptologist at the University of Paris-Sorbonne and director of the mission explained that the **evidences** from the site indicate towards the fact that it dates back to over 1000 years any other harbour was known in the world.

The harbour is said to be most important **commercial** ports. From this port, trading trips to export important minerals as well as copper from Sinai were launched. **(2013)**

1. Which word can best replace the word "discovered" as used in the passage?
   (a) Researched   (b) Found
   (c) Looked for   (d) None of these

2. What is the correct spelling of the word 'archiological'?
   (a) Archieological   (b) Acheological
   (c) Archaeological   (d) Archiologiecal

3. What is the synonymn of the word 'evidences' as used in the passage?
   (a) Facts   (b) Assumptions
   (c) Guess   (d) Proofs

4. The meaning of the phrase ' in the meanwhile' as given in the passage is
   (a) around the same time
   (b) all the time around
   (c) perenially
   (d) temporarily

5. The opposite of the word 'commercial' is
   (a) discommercial   (b) uncommercial
   (c) non-commercial   (d) incommercial

6. 'Ancient writing material' is the meaning of the word
   (a) pharoah   (b) khufu
   (c) dynasty   (d) papyri

7. The meaning of the phrase 'indicate towards the fact' in the context of the passage is
   (a) show that   (b) displays them
   (c) offers is   (d) none of these

8. 'Oldest' is the ____________ degree of comparison of the adjective old.
   (a) comparative   (b) superlative
   (c) lowest   (d) none of these

PASSAGE-2

In 1893, Lokmanya Tilak converted the Ganpati Festival into a public ceremony. He campaigned **towards** the wide **circulasion** of this public celebration throughout Maharashtra. It was **from** this festival that he could **control** public **places** to the national movement. The desired **impact** of this festival was further **decided** by Shivaji festival. It was inaugurated in honour of Chhatarpati Shivaji, the greatest Maratha king, in the **service** of several thousand people. **(2014)**

9. Which of the following could replace 'towards' as used in the passage above?
   (a) with   (b) with standing
   (c) for   (d) against

10. Which of the following is correct spelling of 'circulasion'?
    (a) Circulation   (b) Circulassion
    (c) Circulason   (d) Circulashion

11. Which of the following could replace 'from' as used in the passage above?
    (a) before   (b) indeed
    (c) exactly   (d) through

12. Which of the following could replace 'control' as used in the passage above?
    (a) advise   (b) demand
    (c) mobilise   (d) enhance

13. Which of the following could replace 'places' as used in the passage above?
    - (a) festivals
    - (b) support
    - (c) grievances
    - (d) celebrations

14. Which of the following is the opposite in meaning to 'impact' as used in the passage above?
    - (a) outcome
    - (b) meeting
    - (c) uproot
    - (d) results

15. Which of the following could replace 'decided' as used in the passage above?
    - (a) displayed
    - (b) generated
    - (c) manifested
    - (d) reinforced

16. Which of the following could replace 'service' as used in the passage above?
    - (a) protest
    - (b) honour
    - (c) memory
    - (d) presence

PASSAGE-3

Scientists have developed **a new technique** that could be applied **worldwide** to create an early warning system for **massive** tsunamis **trigered** by earthquakes.

Scientists from Stanford University have identified key **acoustic** characteristics of the 2011 Japan earthquake that **indicated** it would cause a large tsunami. The same technique could be used to create an **early warning system** for tsunamis, they believe.

(2014)

17. Which of the following could replace the phrase 'a new technique' as used in the passage above?
    - (a) a departed method
    - (b) a novel method
    - (c) an unskill method
    - (d) lack method

18. Which of the following could replace the word "worldwide" as used in the passage above?
    - (a) local
    - (b) limited
    - (c) globally
    - (d) rural

19. Which of the following is the correct spelling of 'trigered"?
    - (a) trigeared
    - (b) tregired
    - (c) triggered
    - (d) None of these

20. Which of the following is the opposite of "massive" as used in the passage?
    - (a) wonderful
    - (b) huge
    - (c) large
    - (d) miniature

21. What is the meaning of the phrase "early warning systems" as used in the passage?
    - (a) a system giving a problem
    - (b) a process of great use
    - (c) a condition indicating an impending problem
    - (d) None of these

22. Both character and characteristics are
    - (a) verbs
    - (b) adverbs
    - (c) nouns
    - (d) adjectives

23. Which of the following best replaces the word "acoustics" as used in the passage?
    - (a) sound
    - (b) echo
    - (c) reverbation
    - (d) none of these

24. The word "indicated" as used in the passage can be best replaced with
    - (a) shared
    - (b) cleared
    - (c) pondered
    - (d) pointed out

LEVEL 2

DIRECTIONS (Qs. 1-24) : *Read the following passages and answer the questions that follow.*

PASSAGE-1

Patients suffering liver failure may not have to **wait without end** to get a matching donor anymore.

Transplant surgeons claim those with **mismatched** donors can also undergo the life-saving procedure under a **novel** technique involving **supresion** of antibodies responsible for **rejection** of incompatible organs with the help of plasma exchange and drug **therapy**.

It has been used successfully to treat three patients at Medanta Medicity, Gurgoan. Now that all the three patients are doing fine, many others in the hospital want **to follow suit**.   **(2012)**

1. Which of the following could replace 'mismatched' as used in the passage above?
   - (a) Suitable
   - (b) Unsuited
   - (c) Colorful
   - (d) Colorless
2. Which of the following is the correct spelling of 'supresion'?
   - (a) Suppresion
   - (b) Supression
   - (c) Suppression
   - (d) Suipression
3. Which of the following could replace the phrase 'wait without end' as used in the passage above?
   - (a) Wait eternally
   - (b) To stand forever
   - (c) To rest without end
   - (d) None of these
4. Which of the following is opposite in meaning to 'rejection' as used in the passage above?
   - (a) Absorbtion
   - (b) Objection
   - (c) Retention
   - (d) Acceptance
5. 'Treatment to heal a disorder is the meaning of the word
   - (a) technique
   - (b) procedure
   - (c) antibodies
   - (d) therapy
6. The adverb of the word 'success' is
   - (a) successful
   - (b) successfulness
   - (c) successfully
   - (d) successive
7. Which of the following can replace the phrase 'to follow suit'?   **(Tricky)**
   - (a) To over do something
   - (b) To do something repeatedly
   - (c) To do the same as
   - (d) None of these
8. Which of the following is the meaning of the word 'Novel' as used in the passage ?   **(Tricky)**
   - (a) Innovative
   - (b) Wonderful
   - (c) Beautific
   - (d) Fantastic

PASSAGE-2

There may be a **growing demand** for new multilevel parking lots in the city but the existing ones are underutilized. The reasons are not far to seek: poor **maintenance** and **indifferent** management by the civic agencies.

Of the five multilevel parking lots in Delhi, two – Asaf Ali Road and Gandhi Maidan – are in a **deplorable** condition. These are dimly lit and stink. And they have hundreds of **abndoned** vehicles. **Despite repeated complaints**, North Delhi Municipal Corporation, has **done little to address** this problem.   **(2015)**

9. Which of the following could replace 'deplorable' as used in the passage above?
   - (a) Perishable
   - (b) Miserable
   - (c) Tenable
   - (d) Viable
10. Which of the following is the correct spelling of 'abndoned'?
    - (a) 'abandoned'
    - (b) 'abanndoned'
    - (c) 'abbndoned'
    - (d) 'abbndoneed'
11. Which of the following could replace the phrase 'growing demand' as used in the passage above?
    - (a) Increasing needs
    - (b) Decreasing levels
    - (c) Lengthening ways
    - (d) None of these
12. Which of the following is opposite in meaning to 'abandoned' as used in the passage above?
    - (a) Inhabited
    - (b) Decorated
    - (c) Visited
    - (d) Recovered
13. Apathetic is the meaning of the word
    - (a) Concerned
    - (b) Indifferent
    - (c) responsive
    - (d) caring

14. 'Maintain' is the 'verb' of the word
    (a) Maintained   (b) Maintenance
    (c) Maintainer   (d) Maintainable

15. Which of the following can replace the phrase "done little to address."?
    (a) Done nothing
    (b) Take too much task
    (c) Taken hardly any steps to solve
    (d) Go to some address

16. What is the meaning of the phrase "despite repeated complaints" as used in the passage ?
    (a) Inspite of complaning again and again
    (b) Not complaning
    (c) Very few complaints
    (d) None of these

PASSAGE-3

The Delhi Sikh Gurdwara Management Committee will build a **memorial** at Gurdwara Rakabganj in Delhi for the anti-Sikh riot victims of 1984.

DSGMC president Manjit Singh GK said that he had **convened** a special **general** house session of the **comitee** members on Wednesday at the gurdwara to give the formal **approval**. In the 51-member house, SAD (B) has 43 members.

He **alleged** that instead of helping and **extending support** for the memorial, Delhi's Congress government has been **causing hurdles** in their way.

(2013)

17. Which of the following can replace the phrase "extending support" as used in the passage above?
    (a) lowering   (b) favouring
    (c) demoralizing   (d) moralizing

18. Which of the following could replace the phrase "causing hurdles" as used in the passage above?
    (a) creating work
    (b) playing well
    (c) placing obstacles
    (d) None of these

19. Which of the following is the correct spelling of "comtee"?   **(Tricky)**
    (a) committee
    (b) comittea
    (c) commette
    (d) None of these

20. Which of the following is opposite in meaning to 'general' as used in the passage above?
    (a) wonderful   (b) creative
    (c) all over   (d) particular

21. What is the meaning of the word "memorial" as used in the passage above?
    (a) rhetoric
    (b) monument
    (c) building
    (d) palace

22. The 'Noun' form of the word approve is
    (a) approving
    (b) approved
    (c) approval
    (d) approbation

23. The meaning of the word 'convened' in the context of the passage is
    (a) summoned   (b) screened
    (c) verified   (d) None of these

24. The meaning of the word 'alleged' as used in the passage above is
    (a) connected   (b) withstood
    (c) complained   (d) supported

HINTS & EXPLANATIONS

LEVEL - 1

1. (b) The word 'discovered' here means found.
2. (c)
3. (d) The meaning of the word evidences as used in the passage is proofs.
4. (a) The phrase "in the meanwhile" as given in the passage means simultaneously or around the same time.
5. (c) Commercial means something related to money or finance. Non-commercial is the opposite of commercial.
6. (d) Papyri is a type of tree from which the ancient writing material in Egypt etc. were made.
7. (a) 'Indicate towards the fact' in this context means show that .
8. (b) Old, Older, Oldest, old is the adjective, older is the comparative degree and oldest is the superlative degree.
9. (c)   10. (a)   11. (d)   12. (c)
13. (b)   14. (c)   15. (d)   16. (d)
17. (b) The phrase "a new technique" means a novel method. New stands for novel or fresh, and technique stands for method.
18. (c) The term "worldwide" here means all over the world or globally.
19. (c) triggered
20. (d) The opposite of massive is little or miniature.
21. (c) The technical definition of early warning systems is a condition indicating an impending problem.
22. (c) The word character is a noun, characteristics is also a noun.
23. (a) The word acoustics means the sound or the quality of the sound.
24. (d) The word indicated here means pointed out.

LEVEL - 2

1. (b) The word 'mismatched' means that which is not suitable that is unsuited.
2. (c)
3. (a) 'Wait without end' simply means to wait for a very long time that is eternally.
4. (d) The opposite of rejection meaning to throw off is acceptance.
5. (d) The word therapy refers to some treatment to heal a disease.
6. (c) The successful is an adjective of the noun success. Successfully is the adverb of success.
7. (c) To follow suit means to do the same thing with reference to a particular action or deed.
8. (a) The word 'novel' means innovative, the context of this passage.
9. (b) The word 'deplorable' as used in the passage means in a bad or miserable condition.
10. (a)
11. (a) The words 'growing demand' in the context of the passage means 'increasing'.
12. (a)   13. (b)
14. (b) Maintenance is the noun of the word maintain which is a verb.
15. (c) Done little to address means taken hardly any steps to solve. Address is similar to solve, and done little to is similar to hardly any steps.
16. (a) Repeated means again and again despite can be replaced with inspite of .
17. (b) 'Extending support' means giving approval or favouring a certain proposal.
18. (c) 'Causing hurdles' means creating problem or placing obstacles in the way of some work.
19. (a)
20. (d) The word general refers to all. The opposite of general is particular or any one.
21. (b) Here the word 'memorial' means a monument built in the memory of someone or something.
22. (c) The word approve is a verb, approval is its noun. Here it means sanction.
23. (a) Here convened a special session of members means to summon a meeting of the members.
24. (c) Here the word alleged means complained or accused about the other party.

CHAPTER 10

COLLOCATIONS

The knowledge of Collocations is very important for proper use of English Language. If we cannot use right collocations, a grammatically correct sentence will stand out awkward.

English Collocations fall into the category of Phraseology which means a particular mode of expression, especially one characteristic of a particular speaker or subject area. It is the study of set or fixed expressions, such as idioms, phrasal verbs, and other types of multi-word lexical units (often collectively referred to as phrasemes).

In this type of use the component parts of the expression take on a meaning more specific than or otherwise not predictable from the sum of their meanings when used independently.

We can say Collocation is the way words are habitually used together to produce a specific meaning. This includes, among others, verbal phrases, verbs compounds, noun compounds, compounds with particles and adjective-noun collocates.

In addition to producing specific meaning, collocations or its initiatory parts, increase the predictability of the message and anchor it in the context of communication by signaling to the listener or reader that a specific meaning is about to be proved.

There are several different types of collocations. Collocations can be:
- Adjective Collocations
- Adverbial Collocations
- Verbal Collocations
- Genitive Collocations

Example of seven main types of collocations:
1. adverb + adjective
   - Invading that country was an **utterly stupid** thing to do.
   - We entered a **richly decorated** room.
   - Are you **fully aware** of the implications of your action?
2. adjective + noun
   - The doctor advised him to take **regular exercise**.
   - The Titanic sank on its **maiden voyage**.
   - He was writhing on the ground in **excruciating pain**.
3. noun + noun
   - Let's give Mr. Sharma a **round of applause**.
   - The **ceasefire agreement** came into effect at 11am.
   - I'd like to buy two **bars of soap,** please.
4. noun + verb
   - The **lion** started **to roar** when it heard the **dog barking**.
   - **Snow was falling** as our **plane took off**.
   - The **bomb went off** when he started the car engine.

5. verb + noun
   - The prisoner was hanged for **committing murder**.
   - I always try to **do my homework** in the morning, after making my bed.
   - He has been asked **to give a presentation** about his work.
6. verb + expression with preposition
   - We had to return home because we **had run out of money**.
   - At first her eyes **filled with horror**, and then she **burst into tears**.
   - Their behaviour was enough to **drive anybody to crime**.
7. verb + adverb
   - She **placed** her keys **gently** on the table and sat down.
   - Sweety **whispered softly** in Raj's ear.
   - I **vaguely remember** that it was growing dark when we left.

SOME EXAMPLES OF COMMON COLLOCATIONS

VERB COLLOCATIONS

Have	do	make
have a bath	do business	make a difference
have a drink	do nothing	make a mess
have a good time	do someone a favour	make a mistake
have a haircut	do the cooking	make a noise
have a holiday	do the housework	make an effort
have a problem	do the shopping	make furniture
have a relationship	do the washing up	make money
have a rest	do your best	make progress
have lunch	do your hair	make room
have sympathy	do your homework	make trouble
Take	**break**	**catch**
take a break	break a habit	catch a ball
take a chance	break a leg	catch a bus
take a look	break a promise	catch a chill
take a rest	break a record	catch a cold
take a seat	break a window	catch a thief
take a taxi	break someone's heart	catch fire
take an exam	break the ice	catch sight of
take notes	break the law	catch someone's attention
take someone's place	break the news to someone	catch someone's eye
take someone's temperature	break the rules	catch the flu
Pay	**save**	**keep**
pay a fine	save electricity	keep a diary
pay attention	save energy	keep a promise
pay by credit card	save money	keep a secret
pay cash	save one's strength	keep an appointment
pay interest	save someone a seat	keep calm

pay someone a compliment	save someone's life	keep control
pay someone a visit	save something to a disk	keep in touch
pay the bill	save space	keep quiet
pay the price	save time	keep someone's place
pay your respects	save yourself the trouble	keep the change
Come	**go**	**get**
come close	go abroad	get a job
come complete with	go astray	get a shock
come direct	go bad	get angry
come early	go bald	get divorced
come first	go bankrupt	get drunk
come into view	go blind	get frightened
come last	go crazy	get home
come late	go dark	get lost
come on time	go deaf	get married
come prepared	go fishing	get nowhere
come right back	go mad	get permission
come second	go missing	get pregnant
come to a compromise	go on foot	get ready
come to a decision	go online	get started
come to an agreement	go out of business	get the impression
come to an end	go overseas	get the message
come to a standstill	go quiet	get the sack
come to terms with	go sailing	get upset
come to a total of	go to war	get wet
come under attack	go yellow	get worried

MISCELLANEOUS

Time	Business English	Classifiers
bang on time	annual turnover	a ball of string
dead on time	bear in mind	
early 12th century	break off negotiations	a bar of chocolate
free time	cease trading	
from dawn till dusk	chair a meeting	a bottle of water
great deal of time	close a deal	
late 20th century	close a meeting	a bunch of carrots
make time for	come to the point	
next few days	dismiss an offer	a cube of sugar
past few weeks	draw a conclusion	
right on time	draw your attention to	a pack of cards
run out of time	launch a new product	

save time	lay off staff	a pad of paper
spare time	go bankrupt	
spend some time	go into partnership	
take your time	make a loss	
tell someone the time	make a profit	
time goes by	market forces	
time passes	sales figures	
waste time	take on staff	

We can now say that Collocation refers to how words go together or form fixed relationships.

Examples : heavy rain, high temperature, scenic view, have an experience etc.

Collocations may be strong or weak. Strong collocations are where the link between the two words is quite fixed and restricted. Weak collocations are where a word can collocate with many other words.

Compare

Strong make express + a wish fulfil	Very few words can collocate with the noun wish. This makes wish a strong collocator.
Weak apartment, beach, car, camera, chance, big + disappointment, fight, gun, lamp, moon, news, ocean, pain, pity, price, queue, table, umbrella, upset, wait, window	big can collocate with hundreds of words, therefore it's a weak collocator.
Strong Collocations whisk an egg winding road	curly hair blissfully ignorant

WEAK COLLOCATIONS

1. big/enormous/large + house/lorry/cup
2. fast/shiny/expensive + car/motorbike/aeroplane
3. very/really/extremely + interesting/hot/generous
4. brown/straight/long + fence/hair/line

LEVEL 1

1. Money Laundering **(2013)**
    (a) the crime of processing stolen money through a legitimate business or sending it abroad to a foreign bank, to hide the fact that the money was illegally obtained.
    (b) storing money
    (c) stealing money
    (d) spending money
2. A Round of Applause
    (a) praising somebody
    (b) the noise made by a group of people clapping their hands to show approval
    (c) a token of gratitude
    (d) a note of appreciation
3. Make Coffee **(2014)**
    (a) preparing coffee
    (b) serving coffee
    (c) put on a pot of coffee to serve to drink yourself or serve others
    (d) taking coffee
4. Flesh and blood
    (a) human beings
    (b) severe bloody fighting
    (c) matter of common concern
    (d) member of your family
5. Frenetic competition **(2017)**
    (a) friendly contest
    (b) serious and energetic effort to defeat a person, group or organisation in a contest
    (c) old rivalry
    (d) open fighting
6. Do one's nails **(2012)**
    (a) to paint one's finger or toe nails
    (b) to bite one's nail
    (c) trimming nails
    (d) pain in one's nail
7. Life expectancy **(2015)**
    (a) supposed length of life
    (b) the length of time one wants to live
    (c) length of time that living beings normally likely to live
    (d) calculated life span
8. Wide awake
    (a) suddenly leave bed
    (b) short sleep
    (c) fully awake
    (d) awaken but drowsy
9. Leisure time
    (a) the time when you are not working and you can relax and do things that you enjoy
    (b) play time
    (c) holidays
    (d) with no work to do
10. Loud and clear
    (a) Resounding
    (b) Audible
    (c) strong and determined
    (d) your voice is very clear and you express yourself very clearly

11. I don't like either of the alternatives. We're faced with an awkward ______ .
    (a) choice   (b) climate
    (c) collection   (d) coincidence
12. He electrified the packed ______ with his presentation. **(2016)**
    (a) crowd   (b) attitude
    (c) authorities   (d) audience
13. I'm afraid I've developed a deep ______ to this topic.
    (a) awareness   (b) aversion
    (c) attitude   (d) barriers
14. What we need to do is to raise consumer ______ of our product. **(2014)**
    (a) consciousness   (b) forum
    (c) awareness   (d) bank
15. She has done well to get to her present job. She comes from a deprived ______
    (a) background   (b) family
    (c) state   (d) mentality
16. I only have a rough idea of the problem. Perhaps you could sketch in the ______ ? **(2016)**
    (a) picture   (b) idea
    (c) background   (d) scene

17. We've got too far away from our key goals. We need to get back to ______ .
    (a) originals   (b) basics
    (c) elementary   (d) fundamentals
18. He was elected in a secret ______ .   **(2016)**
    (a) ballot   (b) vote
    (c) election   (d) campaign
19. We need to maintain the delicate ______ between the need for quality and the need for quantity.
    (a) coordination   **(2013)**
    (b) relation
    (c) equality
    (d) balance
20. I need to get away from everything and lie back and relax on an unspoilt ______ somewhere
    (a) beach   (b) belief
    (c) blunder   (d) blame

DIRECTIONS (Qs. 21-30) : *Choose the right collocations from the given options.*

21. I'm an ______ admirer of your work. **(Tricky)**
    (a) ardent   (b) triumphant
    (c) stale   (d) considerable
22. I wouldn't upset him. He can be a ______ adversary.   **(2013)**
    (a) ardent   (b) significant
    (c) unfair   (d) dangerous
23. He gave me some ______ advice and I took it.
    (a) ardent   (b) significant
    (c) dangerous   (d) blunt
24. They don't always agree but I think there is a bond of ______ affection between them.
    (a) ugly   (b) everyday **(2015)**
    (c) deep   (d) blunt

25. It seems no time at all since I started work and here I am at ______ age.
    (a) retirement   (b) old
    (c) young   (d) proper
26. That type of behaviour was possible in a ______ age but we are more tightly regulated these days.
    (a) retirement   (b) bygone **(2012)**
    (c) proper   (d) old
27. I don't trust him. I think he has a ______ agenda.
    (a) top   (b) angry
    (c) hidden   (d) quick
28. We cannot tolerate this sort of ______ aggression from a competitor in one of our key markets.
    (a) deceit   (b) wrap   **(2014)**
    (c) calm   (d) naked
29. We have a ______ agreement with them and we must respect it.
    (a) binding   (b) hidden
    (c) valid   (d) severe
30. I think they must be providing them with some kind of ______ aid. But I don't know what.
    (a) open   (b) covert **(2015)**
    (c) blunt   (d) desired
31. Complete the collocation: "I was getting late So I only had ______ shower."   **(2019)**
    (a) short   (b) quick   (c) fast
    (d) deep
32. Complete with a verb + adverb collocation: "You can achieve it if you ______". **(2019)**
    (a) work hard   (b) really work
    (c) work to   (d) work hardly

LEVEL 2

DIRECTIONS (Qs. 1-10) : *Choose the best answer to fill the gap in each of the following:*

1. He burst _______ laughter when he realised his mistake.

   (a) explored in   (b) into

   (c) broke in   (d) broke into

2. He assured me he was _______ sure where the house was.

   (a) a bit   (b) rather

   (c) very   (d) quite

3. We didn't arrange to meet. It was _______ coincidence that I saw him.   **(2014)**

   (a) clear   (b) clean

   (c) great   (d) pure

4. Please! I'm trying to work here. Don't _______ my time with stupid questions!   **(2013)**

   (a) waste   (b) loose

   (c) abuse   (d) break

5. He had to go to the hospital because it was a very _______ cut.   **(2012)**

   (a) hard   (b) heavy

   (c) deep   (d) wide

6. Our neighbour is a very _______ smoker and smokes two packets a day.   **(2014)**

   (a) hard   (b) heavy

   (c) tough   (d) strong

7. We managed to get up the steep hill only because our car is very _______.

   (a) powerful   (b) hard

   (c) strong   (d) aggressive

8. I don't know him that well. He's only a _______ acquaintance.   **(2017)**

   (a) loose   (b) casual

   (c) weak   (d) poor

9. I'm an honest and _______ citizen.   **(2015)**

   (a) lawful   (b) law-abiding

   (c) law   (d) law-watching

10. Do you know where we are? If you ask me, we are _______ lost.   **(Tricky)**

    (a) very   (b) totally

    (c) rather   (d) extremely

DIRECTIONS (Qs. 11-17) : *Each sentence given below contains an incomplete collocation. Complete the collocation by supplying a suitable word. Choose your answers from the options given below.*

11. My grandfather liked to have _______ coffee.

    (a) serial   (b) black

    (c) big   (d) frequent

12. She was a/an _______ wife who loved her husband more than anything else in the whole universe.

    (a) devoted   (b) sincere

    (c) intelligent   (d) loving

13. I always avoid his company because he is a crashing _______.   **(Tricky, 2012)**

    (a) bore   (b) nuisance

    (c) guy   (d) wicked

14. It is a golden _______. If you miss it, you will regret it.

    (a) chance   (b) opportunity

    (c) offer   (d) scope

15. She seemed quite interested in buying that house, but at the last moment, she changed her _______.

    (a) mind   (b) thoughts   **(2015)**

    (c) offer   (d) decision

16. Although I was _______ annoyed by her attitude, I said nothing.   **(2016)**

    (a) moderately   (b) lightly

    (c) slightly   (d) simply

17. Could you _______ the oil?   **(2014)**

    (a) inspect   (b) check

    (c) test   (d) see

18. He spoke English with a ________ French accent.
    (a) average   (b) careless   **(2013)**
    (c) widespread   (d) pronounced

19. His new novel has met with ________ acclaim.
    (a) careless   (b) dreadful
    (c) great   (d) wholehearted

20. We need to make sure that there is enough ________ accommodation to house all the delegates.   **(Tricky)**
    (a) careless   (b) dreadful
    (c) luxury   (d) space

21. He gave us a ________ account of all that you had achieved over there.
    (a) glowing   (b) luxury
    (c) careless   (d) yellow

22. Could you please give me an ________ account?
    (a) itemised   (b) dreadful   **(2015)**
    (c) great   (d) glowing

23. We need to crack down hard on the ________ abuse of drugs.
    (a) average   (b) outright
    (c) widespread   (d) frenetic

24. He was able to predict what was going to happen with ________ accuracy.   **(2014)**
    (a) itemised   (b) uncanny
    (c) careless   (d) luxury

25. They've made some highly ________ accusations about us.
    (a) clean   (b) lightly
    (c) damaging   (d) economic

26. We need to find a new site with ________ access to the Nepal motorway network.   **(2013)**
    (a) ready   (b) outright
    (c) widespread   (d) pronounced

27. This will probably be the ________ achievement of her career.
    (a) uncanny   (b) damaging
    (c) crowning   (d) glowing

28. I did all the groundwork on this project but he only gave me a ________ acknowledgement in his report.   **(2016)**
    (a) grudging   (b) crowning
    (c) damaging   (d) uncanny

29. Later we all realized that it was a/ an ________ stupid idea.   **(2017)**
    (a) utterly   (b) casually
    (c) honestly   (d) damaging

30. We're fighting for the ________ abolition of the death penalty.   **(2012)**
    (a) average   (b) outright
    (c) decisive   (d) chronic

31. I'm afraid he was involved in a ________ accident.   **(2015)**
    (a) ready   (b) dreadful
    (c) widespread   (d) mild

32. He invited me around to see his ________ acquisition, a new car.
    (a) casual   (b) latest
    (c) damaging   (d) crowning

33. We need to take some ________ action before it is too late.
    (a) casual   (b) latest
    (c) decisive   (d) random

34. He wasn't particularly good. He was of about ________ ability.
    (a) average   (b) latest
    (c) decisive   (d) wild

35. I don't think we can succeed without the ________ acceptance of the unions.   **(2012)**
    (a) Average   (b) wholehearted
    (c) polite   (d) careless

36. There is always a lot of ________ activity going on but nothing much seems to get done!
    (a) careless   (b) latest
    (c) frenetic   (d) growing

37. I'm afraid her husband has got a ________ addiction to gambling.   **(Tricky)**
    (a) chronic   (b) furious
    (c) regular   (d) interesting

38. We know very little about this. We need to bring in an ________ adviser to help us.
    (a) outside   (b) significant
    (c) unfair   (d) blunt

39. I don't like this at all. It's a really ________ affair.
    (a) outside   (b) ugly
    (c) fair   (d) unfair

40. It's not a very challenging job. I only have to deal with _________ affairs.

    (Critical Thinking)

    (a) manic (b) everday

    (c) stiff (d) dangerous

DIRECTIONS (Qs. 41-50) : *Choose the word from the options that goes best with the word given.*

41. Cloudy

    (a) day (b) beautiful

    (c) end (d) mind

42. Alphabetical

    (a) music (b) row

    (c) order (d) none

43. Loud

    (a) noise (b) drink

    (c) hair (d) none

44. Chocolate

    (a) biscuit (b) cake

    (c) ice-cream (d) all

45. Curly

    (a) comb (b) dress

    (c) hair (d) cap

46. Soft

    (a) pen (b) drink

    (c) back (d) none

47. Major　　　　　　　　　　**(2014)**

    (a) disaster (b) flight

    (c) mind (d) none

48. Vivid　　　　　　　　　　**(2016)**

    (a) expanding

    (b) calling

    (c) coming

    (d) imagination

49. Hugely

    (a) coffee (b) popular

    (c) read (d) order

50. Narrowly　　　　　　　　　**(2015)**

    (a) hair (b) flight

    (c) avoided (d) daylight

51. Family planning is essential for curbing the rapid _______ in population.　　**(2019)**

    (a) spurt (b) augment

    (c) spread (d) increase

HINTS & EXPLANATIONS

LEVEL - 1

1. (a) Nouns collocated after 'money' are management, problems, laundering, market, box

2. (b) Verb + Applause be greeted with, draw, earn, get, receive, win. Example. The speech drew loud applause.

3. (c) Common collocations before 'coffee'

4. (a) Phrase flesh and blood means human being

5. (b) Frentic collocates with competition which means a competition involving a lot of excitement and activity

6. (a) We often use do to refer to work of any kind. Examples: ... your work, homework, housework, your job, business, your hair, your nails

7. (c) Life + Noun, history, story, membership, imprisonment, sentence, expectancy, span (also lifespan)

8. (c) Collocation pattern: adverb + adjective, Meaning: completely awake or fully alert

9. (a) Common collocations before 'leisure' time.

10. (d) Phrases means expressing yourself very clearly, loud and clear.

11. (a) The described situation implies that the choice was awkward and this is rightly collocated.

12. (d) Adjectives collocated with 'audience' ---- big, capacity, large, Mass, packed, vast, wide, select, small, appreciative, enthusiastic, receptive, sympathetic, hostile, captive, potential, target, cinema, live, radio, studio, television, private.

13. (b) Aversion in noun form means (a person or thing that causes) a feeling of strong dislike or of not wishing to do something collocates with deep which means strong aversion.

14. (c) Nouns collocated after 'consumer' --- durables, electronics, goods, products, services, attitudes, awareness, behaviour, choice, confidence, demand, expenditure, needs, preferences, spending, tastes, protection, rights, group, organisation, watchdog, society, market, prices, boom, boycott.

15. (a) Adjectives collocated with 'background': broad, narrow, mixed, privileged, Wealthy, deprived, disadvantaged, poor, middle class, upper class, working class, academic, class, cultural, educational, ethnic, family.

16. (c) The verb sketch collocates with in the background which implies an imagery idea.

17. (b) Verb + Basics means to return, esp. to a former position or activity

18. (a) A secret ballot (the system of voting in writing and usually in secret; an occasion on which a vote is held) is a strong collocation

19. (d) Adj+noun, Delicate collocates with balance means even combination/ distribution.

20. (a) Adj+noun is rightly collocated to mean something fresh and attracting.

21. (a) Adj+noun--- Admirer noun collocates with adjectives like--- ardent, devoted, fervent, great, keen, secret

22. (d) Adj+noun--- Here dangerous collocates with adversary that means the opponent is dangerous

23. (d) This idiomatic expression is a strong collocation

24. (c) Affection noun collocates with adjectives like--- deep, genuine, great, real, special, strong, warm, mutual

25. (a) Age (noun) collocates with childbearing, pensionable, retirement, school, school-leaving, voting, working

26. (b) Bygone (adj.) collocates with these nouns like age, era

27. (c) Agenda (noun) collocates with hidden and secret (Adj.)

28. (d) Aggression (noun) collocates with adjectives like--- extreme, intense, controlled, mild, naked, open.

29. (a) Agreement (noun) collocates with adjectives like---formal, written, legal, (legally) binding.

30. (b) The sense of the two sentences suggests something concealed or secret. Therefore the adj. covert collocates with the noun aid appropriately.

31. (a) short

32. (a) work hard

LEVEL - 2

1. (b) Verbs collocated before 'laughter' are burst into, dissolve into/with, explode with, bellow with, cackle with, hoot with, howl with, roar with, scream with, shriek with, snort with, whoop with, yell with, rock with, shake with.

2. (d) Collocation pattern: adverb + adjective, Meaning: completely sure

    For example: 1. Are you quite sure you don't want to come?

    2. I'm quite sure she'll be late. She's never on time.

3. (d) Adjectives collocated with 'coincidence': complete, pure, sheer, mere, happy, unfortunate, unhappy, amazing, curious, extraordinary, funny, incredible, odd, remarkable, strange, wonderful

4. (a) You can spend time doing something, which is positive, but if you feel that the time passes in a negative, unproductive manner, then you're wasting your time. The first sentence gives the idea of wasting time better collocates.

5. (c) Here in the adjective form deep properly collocates with noun cut.

6. (b) Common collocations with heavy: heavy smoker, heavy schedule, heavy losses etc., are used as a rule.

7. (a) Common collocations before 'powerful' are used: most, very, even, how, such, something, has, rich, big, only, will, make, look, much

    Here, we managed to get up the steep hill implies a powerful car.

8. (b) When the two persons are well known the word casual collocates with acquaintance which means occasional.

9. (b) Law-abiding in its adj. form means obeying or keeping the law; obedient to law i.e., law-abiding citizens.

10. (b) Adverbs collocated with 'lost' are--- completely, completely, totally, very, a bit, a little, rather.

    In this sentence the collocations means the speaker has no idea about his where about.

11. (b) Common collocations before coffee include - get, make black, want, made, etc. The collocation is perfect.

12. (a) The wife who loved her husband more than anything else in the whole universe collocates properly with devoted.

13. (a) Crashing gives a kind of exaggeration to the word bore, in this case. So it means like an idiot a really boring person, which one has nothing to say.

14. (b) According to conventional word combination we collocate a golden opportunity.

15. (a) Change one's mind (but not change one's thoughts) is the right collocation.

16. (c) The collocation here suggests a way of suggesting something in a slightly annoyed way, especially when you think someone has been silly or has done something wrong.

17. (b) One can check the oil not inspect. Check the engine oil level regularly. Here the verb check rightly collocates with oil.

18. (d) Accented should collocate with pronounced.

19. (c) Acclaim means to praise enthusiastically and often publicly. The book met with great acclaim. Therefore great is the right collocation.

20. (c) To house the delegates luxury accommodation is the desired collocation.

21. (a) Here the correct collocation means giving enthusiastic praise e.g., glowing account.

22. (a) Itemised account means to place or include account on a list of items. The collocation is right.

23. (c) Here the adjective widespread rightly collocates with abuse that means wrong/ bad use of something like alcohol, drug, solvent, substance (= drugs or solvents).

24. (b) Uncannily is used with these adjectives: accurate, similar also used the verb resemble as collocation.

25. (c) Here the collocation means to dampen someone's image.

26. (a) Here the Adjective ready collocates with access in a right way.

27. (c) Here the adjective crowning is rightly collocated with achievement

28. (a) Here the word grudging in its adjective form which means an action or feeling one that you do unwillingly collocates with acknowledgement.

29. (a)

30. (b) Here the adjective outright means open and direct collocates with abolition.

31. (b) Here the adjective dreadful collocates with accident the noun. Adjectives like, horrific, major, nasty, serious, terrible, tragic etc., can also collocate with accident.

32. (b) Adjectives collocated with 'acquisition' are latest, new, recent, data, language and property. Here the latest acquisition that is a new car is perfectly collocated.

33. (c) Here the sentence means it is too late and a final and drastic action is required which is rightly collocated.

34. (a) Adjectives collocated with 'ability' are exceptional, extraordinary, great, outstanding, remarkable, uncanny, inherent, innate, natural, proven, academic, acting, artistic, athletic, creative, intellectual, linguistic, mathematical, musical, Reading, technical, mental, physical, high, limited, Low, average, mixed

35. (b) Acceptance noun collocates with adjectives like complete, full, total, unconditional, wholehearted, conditional, grudging, reluctant, gradual, greater, growing, and increasing etc. Here in this sentence, I don't think we can succeed without the wholehearted acceptance of the unions is perfectly collocated.

36. (c) 'Activity' in its noun form collocates with the adjectives like frantic, frenetic, heightened, increased, intense etc. Frentic activity means fast and energetic action in a rather wild and uncontrolled way.

37. (a) Chronic the adjective means habitual or continuing for a long time collocates with addiction.

38. (a) The implication given in the first sentence requires this collocation 'outside advisor'.

39. (b) Here the adjective 'ugly' collocates with affair which means something obscene or unpleasant.

40. (b) The word affair collocates with everday which means somthing usual.

41. (a) Cloudy day

42. (c) Alphabetical order

43. (a) Loud noise

44. (d) All options can collocate

45. (c) Curly hair

46. (b) Soft-drink

47. (a) Major disaster

48. (d) Vivid imagination

49. (b) Hugely popular

50. (c) Narrowly avoided

51. (d) increase

CHAPTER 11
COMPREHENSION (PROSE & POETRY)

READING COMPREHENSION

Being an area that tests a candidate's understanding of the language, comprehension consists of questions based on given text (a passage, one or more paragraphs). Questions may even be based on certain real-life situations to test how good a candidate is at fact-finding, sifting through information, interpreting text, concluding from given information and discerning between stated and implied meanings of the given information. Understanding of vocabulary, rhetorical tools, hunting for the required information while keeping the holistic picture in mind, etc., are essential comprehension skills at play in this area.

Poetry comprehension requires deeper understanding of the poetic devices and literary expressions. You have to be acquainted with these areas practising small passages first.

TIPS FOR POETRY COMPREHENSION

1. Realize complete understanding, as with any poem, will not come after one reading.
2. Use clues from the poem's title to identify the topic. Often the topic will not be stated explicitly in the poem.
3. Read through the poem once to get a general idea of what the poem's about. Don't try to figure it out the first time through.
4. Pay attention to punctuation and the physical structure of the poem.
5. Consider, first, the literal meaning of the poem; that is, what is the concrete object or idea being discussed. Once that is identified, concern yourself with analysis and symbolic meaning.
6. Analyze imagery and figurative language. What is the author's purpose?
7. Identify parts of the poem that confuse you. Can you use the poem's context to interpret confusing parts?
8. Consider multiple ways of interpreting the poem. There may be more than one correct interpretation.
9. Read the poem aloud. Sound devices are often clues to the poem's meaning.
10. The role of vocabulary development and instruction play an important role in helping students to understand the complex cognitive process of reading.
11. The reader must be actively involved with the text by intentionally thinking about what he or she is reading.

To comprehend means 'to understand and grasp'. A comprehension exercise is , therefore, meant to test a candidate's ability to understand and retain the contents of a given passage.

TREND OF QUESTIONS

In this type of questions, generally a long passage consisting of certain paragraphs is given, followed by 10-15 questions based on it. The questions may be based on :

(i) Theme of the passage
(ii) Choosing the correct or wrong statement on the basis of the given passage
(iii) View of the author regarding the main point discussed in the passage
(iv) Synonyms or Antonyms of some selected words in the passage

Technique of Solving

1. Read the passage carefully once and detect its theme.
2. Note what the questions are about.
3. Answer the questions.

"In Questions on Synonyms & Antonyms, what is to be remembered is that the answer is to be given according to the sense in which the word has been used in the passage, not just on the basis of its literal meaning.

Example: *Read the following passage and answer the questions that follow:*

Nature is like business. Business sense dictates that we guard our capital and live from the interest. Nature's capital is the enormous diversity of living things. Without it, we cannot feed ourselves, cure ourselves of illness or provide industry with the raw materials of wealth creation. Professor Edward Wilson, of Harvard University says, "The folly our descendants are least likely to forgive us is the ongoing loss of genetic and species diversity. This will take millions of years to correct."

Only 150 plant species have ever been widely cultivated. Yet over 75,000 edible plants are known in the wild . In a hungry world , with a population growing by 90 million each year, so much wasted potential is tragic.

Medicines from the wild are worth around 40 billion dollars a year. over 5000 species are known to yield chemical with cancer fighting potential. Scientists currently estimate that the total number of species in the world is between 10-30 million with only around 1.4 million identified.

The web of life is torn when mankind exploits natural resources in short-sighted ways.

The trade in tropical hardwoods can destroy whole forests to extract just a few commercially attractive specimens. Bad agricultural practice triggers 24 billion tonnes of top soil erosion a year losing the equivalent of 9 million tonnes of grain output. Cutting this kind of unsuitable exploitation and instituting "sustainable utilisation" will help turn the environmental crisis around.

1. Why does the author compare 'nature' to business?
   (a) Because of the capital depletion in nature and business
   (b) Because of the similarity with which one should use both
   (c) Because of the same interest level yield
   (d) Because of the diversity of the various capital inputs

2. "The folly our descendants are least likely to forgive us." What is the business equivalent of the folly the author is referring to?
   (a) Reducing the profit margin
   (b) Not pumping some money out of profits into the business.
   (c) Eroding the capital lease of the business
   (d) Putting interest on capital back into the business

3. Which of the following statements is false in context of the given passage?
   (a) The diversity of plant life is essential for human existence.
   (b) Scientists know the usefulness of most plant species .
   (c) Chemicals for cancer treatment are available from plants .
   (d) There are a round ten times the plant species undiscovered as compared to the discovered ones.

4. Which of the following correctly reflects the opinion of the author to take care of hunger in the world?
   (a) In crease the number of edible plants being cultivated.
   (b) Increase cultivation of the 150 species presently under cultivation ,
   (c) Increase the cultivation of medical plants ,
   (d) Increase the potential of the uncultivated edible plants?

5. Which of the following is mentioned as the immediate cause for the destruction of plant species?
   (a) Soil Erosion
   (b) Destruction of habitat
   (c) Cultivation
   (d) Agricultural practices

DIRECTIONS (Qs. 6 - 8) : *Choose the word which is nearly same in meaning to the given word as used in the passage.*

6. WASTED
   (a) Consumed   (b) Squandered
   (e) Unutilised   (d) Unprofitable
7. TRIGGERS
   (a) Starts   (b) Makes
   (c) Results   (d) Causes

8. WORTH
   - (a) Cost
   - (b) Purchase
   - (c) Deserving
   - (d) Sell

DIRECTIONS (Qs. 9 - 10) : *Choose the word which is nearly opposite in meaning to the given word as used in the passage.*

---

9. CUTTING
   - (a) Uniting
   - (d) Increasing
   - (c) Joining
   - (d) Combining

10. GUARD
   - (a) Demolish
   - (b) Relieve
   - (c) Consume
   - (d) Release

Solution:

1. (b) According to the author, just as in business, capital is kept safe and its interest is utilised, similarly man should increase the potential of available diversity for his benefit and not destroy the bounties of nature.

2. (c) Same clue as Q. 1.

3. (b) The author's statement that some plant varieties are edible, some have medicinal uses, some varieties yield cancer fighting drugs, uses, some varieties yield cancer fighting drugs etc. Confirms (a).

The author's statement that over 5000 species are known to yield chemical with cancer fighting potential verifies (c). According to the passage, the total number of plant species is 10-30 million and that of those identified is 1.4 million. Thus, (d) is correct,

4. (d) The author says that out of 75,000 edible plant species. only 150 are cultivated . So, to take care of hunger in the world, the potential of uncultivated edible species should be increased .

5. (b) The last paragraph of the passage gives us the answer

6. (c) The author talks about cultivating only 150 species out of 75,000 as 'wasted potential'. Thus, 'wasted' means 'untilised'.

7. (d) 'Triggers' as used in third paragraph means 'causes'

8. (c) 'worth' as used in second paragraph means 'deserving'.

9. (b) 'Cutting' as used in last sentence means 'reducing', So, opposite of it is 'increasing'.

10. (a) 'Guard' as used in first paragraph means 'protect'.
    So, opposite of it is 'demolish'.

LEVEL 1

DIRECTIONS (Qs. 1-24) : *Read the following passages and answer the questions that follow.*

PASSAGE-1

The National Festivals, like the Independence Day, the Republic Day and the Gandhi Jayanti play a great part in promoting national integration. In these festivals, people belonging to all religions, castes, creeds, colours and sexes take part equally and commonly. As such they are swayed by the common feeling of unity.

Similarly, the National Symbols like the National Flag, the National Anthem and the National Emblem act as a great binding force. They bind us as one nation and one country. In times of rejoicing as well as in times of crises they act as strong bonds to unite people belonging to different corners of the country. Any disrespect shown to them is regarded as disrespect to the entire nation.   **(2012)**

1. What is the main characteristic about India?
   (a) Its constitution is very rigid
   (b) People belonging to minorities are not given rights
   (c) Unity in Diversity
   (d) Dictator type of Government

2. Why do people belonging to all different religions celebrate National Festivals?
   (a) they get common feeling of unity.
   (b) it is compulsory for all to celebrate National Festivals.
   (c) Only cabinet ministers celebrate National Festivals.
   (d) None of the above

3. Three different colours of our National Flag symbolizes about
   (a) sacrifices, truth and prosperity
   (b) education, health and religion
   (c) movement, independence and republic
   (d) None of the above

4. Gandhi Jayanti is celebrated on
   (a) 8th January   (b) 2nd October
   (c) 24th August   (d) 27th December

5. Should everyone respect our National Flag?
   (a) No, it is not necessary to respect our National Flag
   (b) Yes, everyone should respect our National Flag
   (c) Yes, only people belonging to political background should respect National Flag
   (d) None of the above

6. The word 'creed' has been used in the above passage which stands for
   (a) covered with glue
   (b) figure of speech
   (c) sad and disappointed
   (d) a set of principles or religious beliefs, people of all races.

PASSAGE-2

The Indian women won the inaugural Asian Cricket Council's Women T-20 Asia Cup beating Pakistan by 18 runs in the final on October 31, 2012 in Guangzhou. India's decision to bat first seemed to have misfired when the team was restricted to 81 runs. India's Poonam Raut scored 25 runs and helped for take team to a modest score. But Indian bowlers did a great job and dismissed Pakistan to 63 in 19.1 overs. India's Achana Das and N. Niranjana took two wickets each to set up India's title win.   **(2014)**

7. The word 'inaugural' has been used in the above passage which describes about
   (a) to show anger
   (b) making the beginning of important thing
   (c) to insult in the presence of others
   (d) to regard with contempt

8. Final match of women's T-20 Asia Cup was played between
   (a) Bangladesh and England
   (b) Sri Lanka and India
   (c) West Indies and Australia
   (d) India and Pakistan

9. Name the Indian batsman who contributed highest runs during final match?
    (a) Poonam Raut
    (b) Jasleen Arora
    (c) Vineeta Khanna
    (d) Katyayani Sachdeva

10. Name the Indian bowlers who took two wickets each during final Watch?
    (a) Archana Das and N.Niranjana
    (b) Shivangi Tanwar and Sonakshi
    (c) Puneet Sethi and Geetika Suneja
    (d) Sangeeta and Vandana

11. In which city the final match between these two teams was played?
    (a) Lahore
    (b) Rawalpindi
    (c) Guangzhou
    (d) Bhopal

12. Who played very significant role in beating Pakistan in the final match?
    (a) Indian batsman
    (b) Indian bowlers
    (c) Indian wicketkeeper
    (d) Indian captain

PASSAGE-3

Mohandas Karamchand Gandhi was the greatest leader of modern India. He was a great political worker. He was born on October 2, 1869 at Porbandar in Kathiawar. His father, Karamchand Gandhi, was the Diwan of the Kathiawar state. The young Gandhi was an ordinary boy. He was married at the age of thirteen. After passing the matriculation examination in India, he went to England for higher studies and came back as a barrister.

Gandhiji started his public life in Africa where he went as a lawyer to plead the case of a Parsi firm. There he started *Satyagraha* against the policy of racial discrimination followed by the South African government. He succeeded in his mission there. He returned India in 1915 and joined the National Congress and soon became one of its greatest leaders. He dominated the Indian politics from 1919 to 1947. This period is rightly called the *'Gandhian Era'* in the history of India. He led the national movement during this period, gave it a new turn, character and meaning *of a movement.*   **(2013)**

13. Mahatma Gandhi was born on –
    (a) October 22, 1869
    (b) October 12, 1869
    (c) October 2, 1869
    (d) October 2, 1870

14. After getting higher studies, Mahatma Gandhi became a –
    (a) barrister
    (b) doctor
    (c) engineer
    (d) professor of physics

15. For the first time, where did Mahatma Gandhi start his Satyagraha movement?
    (a) China   (b) Britain
    (c) India   (d) S. Africa

16. What do you mean by the term 'racial discrimination'?
    (a) to treat people on the basis of their religion
    (b) to treat people on the basis of their economic status
    (c) to treat people on the basis of their qualification
    (d) to treat people on the basis of colour of their skin

17. Gandhian era is called from the period to
    (a) 1919, 1947   (b) 1930, 1950
    (c) 1920, 1947   (d) 1935, 1955

18. After spending a long period in Africa, Mahatma Gandhi came to India in
    (a) 1928   (b) 1923
    (c) 1931   (d) 1915

PASSAGE-4

Early religion of the Aryans was very simple—both to understand and to practice. But gradually, it became quite complex. The inherent truth vanished, giving place to empty rituals in place of the purity of heart and conduct.

Religious practices had become not only complex but also very costly. The introduction of animal sacrifice in the *yajnas* further alienated the people. They craved for a simple religion devoid of high expenses and animal sacrifice.

Not only this, the early Vedic religion lost its purity and simplicity and common people began to believe in charms, spells and magic. People lost faith in such a religion and yearned for a simple religion.

Sanskrit, the language of the Vedic texts, was now no longer within the comprehension of the common people. Hence a revolt was simmering against the use of Sanskrit and for the adoption of simple language. The simple Varna system had degenerated into a rigid caste system. The high caste Hindus developed hatred for the low caste people, most of whom were branded as Shudras or untouchables who were subjected to abject humiliation, suffering and misery. They were even not allowed to draw water from the public wells or to visit temples.

It was during this period of religious degeneration and social persecution of the common people, that two great teachers, Mahavira Vardhamana and Gautama, the Buddha, preached them the path of love, kindness and piety. They denounced the rigidity of the caste system and condemned the practice of untouchability. **(2015)**

19. In which language, the Vedic texts were written?
    (a) Prakrit   (b) Pali
    (c) Sanskrit   (d) Hindi

20. Why did people become against Sanskrit?
    (a) Common people were not in a position to understand Sanskrit
    (b) Books based on Sanskrit were not available
    (c) Because kings of different provinces used to oppose Sanskrit as a language
    (d) None of the above

21. What was Varna system?
    (a) Equal respect for all religion
    (b) Women should be given more rights
    (c) Religious educational programmes for girls
    (d) Under this system treatment of people was based on their community.

22. The word 'denounce' has been used in the above passage which stands for-
    (a) to strongly criticize
    (b) the state of being the highest authority
    (c) policy of undue interference and attack
    (d) A gang of robbers and dacoits

23. How Shudras were treated during Vedic period?
    (a) They had to bear insult throughout their life.
    (b) They had to perform *yajnas* during Vedic Age

    (c) It was compulsory for Shudras to get proper education.
    (d) None of the above

24. Practice of 'untouchability' was condemned by-
    (a) Babur and Akbar
    (b) Mahavira and Gautam Buddha
    (c) Brahmanas and Kshatriyas
    (d) None of the above

DIRECTIONS (Qs. 25-29) : *Read the poem given below and answer the questions that follow by selecting the most appropriate option.*

The sun descending in the west,
    The evening star does shine;
The birds are silent in their nest.
    And I must seek for mine.

The moon, like a flower
    In heaven's high bower,
With silent delight
    Sits and smiles on the night.

Farewell, green fields and happy grove,
    Where flocks have took delight:
Where lambs have nibbled, silent move
    The feet of angels bright;

Unseen they pour blessing
    And joy without ceasing
On each bud and blossom,
    And each sleeping bosom.

They look in every thoughtless nest
    Where birds are cover'd warm;
They visit caves of every beast,
    To keep them all from harm:

If they see any weeping
    That should have been sleeping,
They pour sleep on their head,
    And sit down by their bed.

25. The evening star rises when
    (a) the birds leave their nests
    (b) it is midnight
    (c) it is dawn
    (d) the sun descends in the west

26. Here, 'bower' represents
    (a) a potted plant
    (b) a frame that supports climbing plants
    (c) a bouquet of flowers
    (d) a flower vase
27. The poet compares moon to
    (a) a flower
    (b) a bird in the nest
    (c) An evening star
    (d) an angel
28. The angels come down on earth to
    (a) spread moon light
    (b) give blessing and joy
    (c) make people, dance and have fun
    (d) take blessing and joy
29. Birds' nest described as 'thoughtless' because
    (a) the angels are blessing the birds to be happy
    (b) the birds are covered in the warmth of their nest
    (c) it is made without any thought
    (d) the occupants are asleep without any care

DIRECTIONS (Qs. 30-34) : *Read the passage and answer the question that follow.*   **(2019)**

Few countries can garner as much funny news in a single year as Russia. This was exemplified when a Russian branch of a famous pizza company sorely underestimated their consumers when they released a free pizza for life promotion in August.

The officer promised 100 free pizzas yearly for 100 years to anyone who got the company's logo tattooed on their body. They were ultimately forced to end the promotion early because to many people took them up on their officer. The officer proved too simple a challenge for Russians, as the promise of free pizza for life could be achieved in just three steps.

First, pizza fans were required to get a tattoo of the company's logo "in a prominent place:. Then, that participant was to post a picture of the tatoo on Instagram, Facebook or VKontakte (Russias version of Facebook), along with the hashtag that roughly translates to "#dominance". Finally, the participant could go to any location to receive their official free pizza certificate.

The promotion was initially intended to run for two month, through October. But after just five days, more than 300 post of tattoos with the promotional hashtag went up on Instagram alone. The pizza shop was subsequently forced to shut the operation down as profit losses posed a very legitimate threat.

The company seemed to believe that only a few people would be crazy enough to get tattoos of their logo for free food.

Seemed like paying a couple of people in pizza for permanent ad space was a pretty even exchange. Perhaps they simply underestimated just how good their pizza really is. Meanwhile, tattoo shops all over Russia probably reaped some benefits from this deal.

30. Choose the best title or heading for the passage.
    (a) Pizza for Everyone
    (b) Daredevil Russians
    (c) Tattoo Love
    (d) Simple and Savoury
31. What does the company want its customers to do?
    (a) Post pictures on Instagram
    (b) Have free pizzas
    (c) Get a tattoo of the company's logo
    (d) Challenge each other
32. The company's offer promised __________.
    (a) 100 pizzas
    (b) 100 free pizzas yearly for 100 years
    (c) cash prize
    (d) free publicity
33. How many people posted on Instagram?
    (a) 100
    (b) 300+
    (c) 1000
    (d) 5
34. What does the word 'subsequently' mean in the second last paragraph?
    (a) Luckily
    (b) Unfortunately
    (c) Formerly
    (d) Eventually

DIRECTIONS (Qs. 35-39): *Read the passage and answer the questions that follow.*

1. With the New Year just weeks away, you are probably looking forward to watching the dazzling fireworks shows that will usher in 2018 worldwide. Unfortunately, the over ten million visually impaired and blind Americans, and scores more around the globe, have never been able to experience this joyful celebration. Thanks to Feeling Fireworks, a tactile fireworks experience invented by the masterminds at the Disney Research Lab in Switzerland.

2. To experience the show, users stand in front of a large, 2.9 by 2.9 feet, flexible latex screen. They then place their hands at the base of the screen and move them around to feel the fireworks. Alternatively, their hands can be situated in the centre of the screen, where the initial explosions happen, and then moved across to explore other fireworks on the edges.

3. As the fireworks begin to explode, one of five nozzles situated at the back of the screen starts to spurt water, creating vibrations mimicking the show. According to the inventors, Feeling Fireworks allows users to experience "tactile fireworks that are directly linked to physical fireworks happening in the sky."

4. A screen displaying the vivid images created by the water jets makes the tactile experience fun for everyone. Paul Beardsley, who led the research team, says, "We want blind, visually impaired, and sighted people to all try Feeling Fireworks and have enjoyable memory."

5. Unveiled at the User Interface Software and Technology conference held in Quebec City, Canada for all to see in 2017, the low-cost technology is still in its early stage, with only a 66 percent success rate. However, the team plans to continue improving the experience and believes the day when everyone will be able to enjoy the thrill of fireworks shows is not far. When ready, Feeling Fireworks will initially be available only at the Disney theme parks, and then hopefully, at fireworks shows worldwide.

(2020)

35. Choose the best title or heading for the passage.
    (a) Fireworks for the Visually Impaired
    (b) Biggest Fireworks Ever
    (c) New Year Without Fireworks
    (d) Being Safe When Using Fireworks

36. What is the name of the tactile fireworks invented in Switzerland?
    (a) Touching Fireworks
    (b) Fireworks at Fingers
    (c) Feeling Fireworks
    (d) Sparkling Fireworks

37. Where was the conference held?
    (a) America
    (b) Canada
    (c) Switzerland
    (d) Germany

38. According to the User Interface Software and Technology conference, the low-cost technology has only _______ percent of success rate.
    (a) seventy six   (b) fifty
    (c) sixty six   (d) eighty six

39. What is the meaning of the word 'dazzling' in the first paragraph?
    (a) Shining
    (b) Explosive
    (c) Dull
    (d) Inventing

DIRECTIONS (Qs. 40-44) : *Read the passage and answer the questions that follow.*   **(2021)**

A school library is a structure within the school that houses a collection of books, audio-visual material and other content that serves common use to meet the educational, informative and recreational needs of the users. The chief objective of libraries is to meet the academic needs of the particular educational institution which it serves. Besides serving students in their studies and teachers in their research school, libraries aim at creating interest in reading amongst the students who get the best of resources and environment here.

It provides us with quality fiction and nonfiction books that encourage us to read more for pleasure and enrich our intellectual, artistic, cultural, social and emotional growth. The ambiance of the school library is perfect for learning without getting disturbed.

This ma kes it easy for us to learn and grasp faster. It provides teachers the access to professional development, relevant information and reference material to plan and implement effective learning programs. While the role of the school library remains constant, its design, digital platform, strategies and tools could change as technology changes.

School libraries help to:

i.   Impact positively on the academic achievements of the students. Students can perform better during examination by reading various books.

ii. Facilitate the work of the classroom teacher and ensure each student has equitable access to resources, irrespective of home opportunities or constraints.

iii. Run independent learning programs, which integrate information resources and technologies.

iv. Equip students with the skills necessary to succeed in a constantly changing technological, social and economic environment.

v.   Collaborate with classroom teachers to plan, implement and evaluate inquiry-based programs that will ensure students acquire skills to collect, critically analyse and organize information, solve problems and communicate their findings.

vi. Provide and promote quality fiction to develop and sustain in students the habit of reading for pleasure and to enrich students' intellectual, aesthetic, cultural and emotional growth.

40. Choose the best title or heading for the passage.

   (a) Fiction and Non-Fiction

   (b) Importance of School Library

   (c) Reading Books

   (d) Students' Achievement

41. Which of the following sentence is not correct?

   (a) A school library positively impacts the academic achievements of the students.

   (b) It facilitates the work of the classroom teacher.

   (c) It helps the school to run independent learning programs.

   (d) It provides a place to have recreational activities during classes.

42. Choose the correct synonym of the given word.
     Enrich

   (a) Take   (b) Slash

   (c) Endow   (d) Trim

43. Along with other intellectual purposes, library also generates _________ interest in students.

   (a) sports

   (b) union

   (c) reading

   (d) leadership

44. A library helps in the _______ development of the student.

   (a) intellectual, artistic and social

   (b) artistic

   (c) just social

   (d) fictitious

DIRECTIONS (Qs. 45-47) : *Read the passage carefully and answer the questions that follow:* **(2022)**

The interview may be conducted by letter and by telephone, as well as in person. Letter and telephone interviews are less satisfactory. Direct contact with an individual and a face-to-face relationship often provide a stimulating situation for both interviewer and interviewee. Personal reaction and interaction aid not only in rapport but also in obtaining nuances and additional information by the reactions which are more fully observed in a face-toface relationship. Adequate preparation for the interview is a "must". Careful planning saves not only time but also energy of both parties concerned. The interview is used to obtain facts or subjective data such as individual opinions, attitudes, and preferences. Interviews are used to check on questionnaires which may have been used to obtain data, or when a problem being investigated is complex, or when the information needed to solve it cannot be secured easily in any other way. People will often give information orally but will not put it in writing.

45. The intention of the writer of this passage is to:

(a) warn the readers against conducting interviews.

(b) instruct people on the best means of conducting interviews.

(c) tell people how to make friends with interviewers.

(d) advise people on the use of letters and telephone.

46. According to the author, the best way to conduct interviews is:

(a) to talk to the interviewees over telephone.

(b) to write letters to the interviewees.

(c) to observe the interviewees from a distance.

(d) to have a direct conversation with the interviewees.

47. Face-to-face interaction with the interviewees enables the interviewer to:

(a) understand shades of meaning not readily available in written responses.

(b) see physical stature.

(c) listen to the voice of the interviewee.

(d) None of these

LEVEL 2

DIRECTIONS (Qs. 1-17) : *Read the following poems carefully and choose the correct option to answer the questions that follow.*

POEM-1

I lay in sorrow, deep distressed:
My grief a proud man heard;
His looks were cold, he gave me gold
But not a kindly word.

My sorrow passed—I paid him back
The gold he gave to me;
Then stood erect and spoke my thanks
And blessed his Charity.

I lay in want, in grief and pain:
A poor man passed my way;
He bound my head he gave me bread
He watched me night and day.

How shall I pay him back again,
For all he did to me
Oh, gold is great, but greater far

Is heavenly Sympathy!   **(Critical Thinking)**

1. How did the proud man help the poet when he was 'in deep distresses'?
    (a) He gave him jewels
    (b) He took him home
    (c) He gave some money
    (d) He pitied the poet.
2. What was it he did not give the poet?
    (a) money   (b) gold
    (c) food   (d) sympathy
3. How did the poor man take care of the poet?
    (a) The poor man gave him some money and food
    (b) The poor man gave gold and kind words
    (c) The poor man gave food to the poet and took care of him day and night
    (d) He took the poet home and bound his head which was hurt.

4. Which of the following statements is not true?
    (a) The poet repaid his debt to the proud man by taking care of him.
    (b) The poor man blessed the charity of the poet.
    (c) The poor man gave food to the poet and took care of him day and night.
    (d) He took the poet home and bound his head which was hurt
5. Which word in the poem means "giving money to a person who is in need"?
    (a) charity   (b) sympathy
    (c) kindness   (d) distress

POEM-2

The grass so little has to do,
—A sphere of simple green,
With only butterflies to brood,
And bees to entertain,

And stir all day to pretty tunes
The breezes fetch along,
And hold the sunshine in its lap
And bow to everything;
And thread the dews all night, like pearls,
And make itself so fine, —
A duchess were too common
For such a noticing.
And even when it dies,
to pass In odors so divine,
As lowly spices gone to sleep,
Or amulets of pine.
And then to dwell in sovereign barns,
 And dream the days away, —
The grass so little has to do,

I wish I were the hay!   **(2015)**

6. What does the speaker of the poem say the grass does with sunshine?
    (a) holds it in its lap
    (b) threads it all night
    (c) stirs it
    (d) bows to it

7. What does the grass do at night?
    (a) entertain the bees
    (b) hold the sunshine in its lap
    (c) thread the dews like pearls
    (d) bow to everything
8. What do the breezes bring to the grasses?
    (a) thread
    (b) pearls
    (c) pretty tunes
    (d) bees to entertain
9. Why does the speaker say she wants to be the hay (or grass)?
    (a) It has so little to do.
    (b) It is a simple green colour.
    (c) It can dream.
    (d) It smells divine.
10. Which is the best summary of this poem?
    (a) The green grass has a lot to do.
    (b) The grass does few things, so the poet wishes she were the grass (the hay).
    (c) When the grass (the hay) dies, it has a wonderful smell like spices or pines.
    (d) Hay dreams each day away, and so does the poet.
11. To what does the speaker compare the odor of dead grasses?
    (a) sunshine
    (b) butterflies
    (c) spheres of simple green
    (d) spices gone to sleep
12. Why does the speaker probably compare the dews to pearls?
    (a) because both are small and round
    (b) because both can be found in barns
    (c) because both can be worn
    (d) because both are green
13. Why does the speaker probably wish she were the hay?
    (a) She is a duchess.
    (b) She likes the smell of grass.
    (c) She has many things to do.
    (d) She had a dream about the grass.
14. The speaker writes that the grasses stir in the breezes. What is the meaning of stir here?

    (a) to mix
    (b) to move
    (c) to make a lot of noise
    (d) to notice
15. What is the main reason that Dickinson wrote this poem?
    (a) to teach readers facts about grass
    (b) to persuade readers to think about grass
    (c) to explain what happens to grass when it dies
    (d) to entertain readers with her thoughts about grass
16. What tells you that this is a poem?
    (a) It is about grass.
    (b) It has a title.
    (c) It has some rhyming lines.
    (d) It has end punctuation.
17. How many stanzas are in this poem?
    (a) 4   (b) 5
    (c) 20   (d) 22

DIRECTIONS (Qs. 18-30) : *Read the following passages and choose the correct answers from the given options.*

PASSAGE-1

For fourteen and half months I lived in my little cell or room in Dehradun jail, and I began to feel as if I was almost a part of it. I was familiar with every bit of it, I knew every mark and dent on the whitewashed walls and on the uneven floors and on the ceiling with the moth eaten rafters. In the little yard outside I greeted little tufts of grass and odd bits of stone as old friends. I was not alone in my cell, for several colonies of wasp and hornets lived there, and many lizards found the home behind the rafters, emerging in the evening in the search of prey.

18. Which of the following explains best the sentence in the passage "I was almost a part of it"?
    (a) I was not alone in the cell
    (b) I was familiar with every bit of the cell
    (c) I greeted little tufts of grass like old friends.
    (d) I felt quite at home in the cell

19. The passage attempts to describe:

    (a) The general conditions of the country's jail

    (b) The prisoner's capacity to notice the minute details of his surroundings

    (c) The prisoner's conscious efforts to overcome the loneliness

    (d) The prisoner's ability to live happily with other creatures

20. The author of the passage seems to suggest that

    (a) It is possible to adjust oneself to uncongenial surroundings.

    (b) The conditions in Indian prisons are not bad

    (c) It is not difficult to spend one's time in prison

    (d) There is a need to improve the conditions in our jails.

PASSAGE-2

We started pitching the highest camp that has been ever made. Everything took five times as long as it would have taken in the place where there was enough air to breathe; but at last we got the tent up, and when we crawled in, it was not too bad. There was only a light wind and inside it was not too cold for us to take off our gloves. At night most climbers took off their boots; but I preferred to keep them on. Hilary, on the other hand took his off and lain them next to his sleeping bag.   **(Critical Thinking)**

21. What does the expression "pitching the highest camp" imply?

    (a) They reached the summit of the highest mountain in the world.

    (b) Those who climbed that far earlier did not pitch any camp.

    (c) So far nobody climbed that high.

    (d) They were too many climbers and needed to pitch a big camp

22. They took a long time to finish the work because:

    (a) They were very tired.

    (b) There was not enough air to breathe

    (c) It was very cold

    (d) It was very dark

23. When they crawled into the tent

    (a) They took off their gloves because it was not very cold

    (b) They could not take off their gloves because it was very cold.

    (c) They took of their gloves though it was very cold.

    (d) They did not take off their gloves though it was not very cold.

PASSAGE-3

A local man, staying on the top of the floor of an old wooden house, was awakened at midnight by fire. Losing his way in the smoke-filled passage, he missed the stairway and went into another room. He picked a bundle to protect his face from fire and immediately fell through the floor below where he managed to escape through a clear doorway. The "bundle" proved to be the baby of the Mayor's wife. The "hero" was congratulated.

24. The man went to another room because

    (a) He did not know where the stairway was

    (b) The passage was full of smoke

    (c) He was extremely nervous

    (d) He stumbled on bundle

25. The man was called hero because he

    (a) Expressed his willingness to risk his life to save others

    (b) Managed to escape from fire

    (c) Showed great courage in fighting the fire.

    (d) Saved a life

PASSAGE-4

There is a famous expression in English: "Stop the world, I want to get off!" This expression refers to a feeling of panic, or stress, that makes a person want to stop whatever they are doing, try to relax, and become calm again. 'Stress' means pressure or tension. It is one of the most common causes of health problems in modern life. Too much stress results in physical, emotional, and mental health problems.

There are numerous physical effects of stress. Stress can affect the heart. It can increase the pulse rate, make the heart miss beats, and can cause high blood pressure. Stress can affect the respiratory system. It can lead to asthma. It can cause a person to breathe too fast, resulting in a loss of important carbon dioxide. Stress can affect the stomach. It can cause stomach aches and problems digesting food. These are only a few examples of the wide range of illnesses and symptoms resulting from stress.

Emotions are also easily affected by stress. People suffering from stress often feel anxious. They may have panic attacks. They may feel tired all the time. When people are under stress, they often overreact to little problems. For example, a normally gentle parent under a lot of stress at work may yell at a child for dropping a glass of juice. Stress can make people angry, moody, or nervous.

Long-term stress can lead to a variety of serious mental illnesses. Depression, an extreme feeling of sadness and hopelessness, can be the result of continued and increasing stress. Alcoholism and other addictions often develop as a result of overuse of alcohol or drugs to try to relieve stress. Eating disorders, such as anorexia, are sometimes caused by stress and are often made worse by stress. If stress is allowed to continue, then one's mental health is put at risk.

It is obvious that stress is a serious problem. It attacks the body. It affects the emotions. Untreated, it may eventually result in mental illness. Stress has a great influence on the health and well-being of our bodies, our feelings, and our minds. So, reduce stress: stop the world and rest for a while. **(Tricky, 2014)**

26. Which of the following is not a common problem caused by stress?
    (a) physical problems
    (b) anecdotal problems
    (c) mental problems
    (d) emotional problems
27. According to the passage, which of the following parts of the body does not have physical problems caused by stress?
    (a) the arms
    (b) the stomach
    (c) the lungs
    (d) the heart
28. Which of the following shows that stress can affect the emotions?
    (a) it can make people feel nervous
    (b) it can cause panic attacks
    (c) it can make people feel angry
    (d) all of the above
29. Which of the following cannot result from long-term stress?
    (a) anger   (b) depression
    (c) alcoholism   (d) whimsy
30. Choose all of the odd answer that cannot complete this sentence: Stress can affect the respiratory system by __________.
    (a) causing stomach problems
    (b) causing asthma
    (c) a loss of carbon dioxide
    (d) causing breathing problems

DIRECTIONS (Qs. 31-37) : *Read the short story and answer the question that follow.*   **(2018)**

MYSTERIOUS STRANGER

My name is Oliver and I live in a small beach town. The town is famous for its huge fishing nets and many tourists come to see the nets every year.

One day I saw a boy. He really did look like a tourist, with a small camera in one hand and a bottle of water in the other. The slim boy sat on the bench by the tree, sipping water and pretending to look at a glossy cruise brochure. His thick glasses masked his eyes, but I knew he wasn't looking at the brochure. He hadn't turned a page for the last ten minutes.

As I walked up to him to say hi, he looked at me briefly and pretended that his

parents were calling him and walked away. I tried not to stare at the tiny scar just above his left eyebrow, I walked back to where I was sitting under the tree shaking my head. He looked familiar, but I couldn't quite place him.

Then it hit me. The bicycle accident. The mysterious stranger who helped me get up and park my bicycle on the side of the road. I rushed back to the bench and saw the water bottle along with a card left on the bench. The card said:

I am deeply indebted to you. The evening of your bicycle accident, I was looking for my parents as I had lost them in the crowd, Helping you made me stay in the same spot for sometime and because of that my parents spotted me. We are going back to our home today. Hope you are better now. Thank you Rajan.

I felt glad that my little accident brought a family together again. I said a silent prayer for him and got back home, smiling.

31. Who is the mysterious stranger?
     (a) The person from the beach town.
     (b) The owners of the fishing net.
     (c) The boy with the thick glasses.
     (d) The parents of the tourist boy.

32. What was the slim boy faking to do?
     (a) Sip water.
     (b) Look at the nets.
     (c) Mask him eye.
     (d) Read a brochure.

33. The boy had a mark on his skin on his __________.
     (a) hand
     (b) forehead
     (c) ear
     (d) eyelid

34. Oliver was shaking his head as he walked back because _______.
     (a) he couldn't recognise who Rajan was
     (b) Rajan couldn't find his parents anywhere
     (c) of the pain from the scar over his eyebrow
     (d) Rajan had taken his seat under the tree

35. What was Oliver hit by?
     (a) By the mysterious stranger
     (b) By the memory who Rajan was
     (c) By the bench on which he sat
     (d) None of these

36. How did Rajan's parents find him?
     (a) Rajan stayed in the same place because of the accident.
     (b) Rajan helped the mysterious stranger.
     (c) Oliver helped Rajan find his parents in the crowd.
     (d) The accident happened in the market.

37. What did Oliver do in the end?
     (a) Spotted his parents
     (b) Bought the family together
     (c) Felt better after the accident
     (d) Said a prayer for Rajan

DIRECTIONS (Qs. 38-42) : *Read the passage and answer the questions that follow.*   **(2020)**

1. What is global food security? Global food security means providing every individual in the world with enough food to eat. This means having enough calories to function and right nutrients to have a healthy life. The modern challenge is doing this with a growing population and sustainably, given that in the future there will likely be less land available for agriculture and climate change will mean we need to use the Earth's resources more efficiently.

2. Food production is dependent on water and there is overwhelming evidence that water will be the major barrier to production of increased amounts of food to meet the expanding world population. The majority of the world is currently experiencing or is at risk of experiencing water shortages. At the moment 925 million people in the world are estimated to experience hunger, with limited or no access to the major macronutrients in the major food groups such as carbohydrates, fats and protein.

3. It is estimated that a further billion could be suffering from "hidden hunger" in which important micronutrients (such as vitamins and minerals) are missing from their diet, with consequent risks of physical and mental impairment.

4. It is projected that world population will reach roughly 9 billion, around 2050. However, despite what most people sometimes assume, population growth isn't the key problem in food security. Consumption patterns are an issue that needs to be addressed much more urgently, as not all food requires the same amounts and types of resources to be produced.

5. People in the developed world consume far more resources per capita than people in the developing world.

6. Threats to global food and water security have been predicted as a "looming storm" of population growth, changeability of food price, political instabilities and climate change. Many

of these issues will affect African states and communities particularly hard, in places where food and water insecurity has historically been exacerbated by civil war, state weakness, and under-development.

7. Water, food and energy are the key to human well-being. They are interlinked in a nexus which is central to sustainable development. The security of all three leads to social and economic benefits, which all increase the standard of living and quality of life.

8. Food is vital for providing energy and its availability depends on climate, soil and level of technology. Malnourishment and undernourishment lead to disease and, ultimately, death. It can mean that children underperform at school and then experience a decreased economic wellbeing in life. They can make adults be less productive and, consequently, impact on their country's economic worth and growth.

38. Choose an appropriate title or heading for the passage.
    (a) Food Security
    (b) Lack of Food and Water
    (c) Global Food Security and its Importance
    (d) Climate Change and its Affect on Food

39. Food availability depends on __________
    (a) climate change
    (b) climate, soil and level of technology
    (c) global warming
    (d) lack of rain

40. Hidden hunger means the lack or deficiency of________   in the food.
    (a) carbohydrates
    (b) protein
    (c) vitamins and minerals
    (d) fats

41. The security of water, food and energy leads to social and __________ benefits.
    (a) geographical
    (b) natural

(c) economic
(d) logical

42. Which of the following words given in the 6th paragraph means 'aggravated'?
    (a) Looming   (b) Changeability
    (c) Insecurity   (d) Exacerbated

DIRECTIONS (Qs. 43-47) : *Read the passage and answer the questions that follow.*   **(2021)**

Some virus experts might not consider viruses to be alive. Yet viruses can reproduce. To do so, they hijack the cells of a host. They borrow the "machinery" in the host's cells to copy the virus' genetic code. Those host cells may spit out hundreds or thousands -even millions - of copies of the original virus. These new viruses then go on to infect more cells. May be the host will also sneeze out the viruses or otherwise release some to infect other potential hosts. And those hosts might be anything from people or plants to bacteria.

But each time a virus is copied, there's some risk the host's cell will make one or more errors in the genetic code of that virus. These are known as mutations. Each new one alters the genetic blueprint of the virus a bit. Mutant viruses are known as variants of the original.

Many mutations won't affect how a virus works. Some might be bad for the virus. Others might improve how well the virus can infect a cell, or help the virus evade its host's immune system. A mutation might even allow the virus to resist the effects of some therapy. Scientists refer to such new-and-improved variants as strains.

And although coronavirus variants made news throughout much of the COVID-19 pandemic, any virus runs the risk of spawning new variants through mutation. Indeed, mutations are one basis of evolution. Mutations that don't benefit an organism (or virus), often die out. But those that make an organism more fit -better adapted to its environment -tend to become more dominant.

Scientists refer to some new versions of the coronavirus as "variants of concern". Compared to the original virus, these variants might infect or spread between people more easily, respond less well to treatments or impair how well vaccines work against the virus. A more serious class of viruses are so-called "variants of high consequence".

Treatments or precautions work far less well against these viruses than they had against earlier forms of the virus. For instance, the new variants might resist current vaccines. They may not show up well in current tests. They might even cause more severe disease.

43. Choose the best title or heading for the passage.
    (a) Virus-Variants and Strains
    (b) Virus Mutations
    (c) Covid-19 Pandemic
    (d) Variants of Concern

44. Mutations that don't benefit an organism often _____
    (a) pass over   (b) carry on
    (c) die out   (d) leave out

45. Mutant viruses are known as _______ of the original.
    (a) copies   (b) distribution
    (c) variants   (d) organism

46. Choose the correct synonym of the given word.
    Variant
    (a) Alternative   (b) Common
    (c) Correct   (d) Similar

47. Variants of viruses can also impact the efficacy of
    (a) infection   (b) spread
    (c) vaccines   (d) illness

DIRECTIONS (Qs. 48-52) : *Read the passage and answer the questions that follow.*   **(2022)**

Having a luxurious car like Jaguar, Aston Martin, Bentley, Ferrari or Lamborghini in itself is a matter of pride for their owners because these vehicles are not just cars but symbol of power, comfort and luxuriousness mounted in one unit. There would be hardly an owner of such cars who will intend to go for any modification in his beloved car, but interestingly in recent years, it is witnessed that the next generation-owners of these cars are not satisfied with the features that are packed by their respective car makers in their vehicles.

These generation next car drivers are always in hunt for such techniques that are helpful in deriving much from their powerful giants. Interestingly, nowadays the trend of car tuning has gained huge popularity across the world, facilitating the car owners to enjoy enhanced performance of their car to its full extent.

What is car tuning: In simple words, car tuning may be defined as the method of modifying certain features of the car depending upon your requirements and preferences. This might surprise most of the car owners, including both expert and novice drivers, that there are various components in a car which can be modified depending upon the choice of the car owner. Some of the common components which can be modified are spoilers, air vents, engine, wheels which can be tuned depending upon the requirements of the car owner.

In other words, it can be said that tuning the car facilitates the car owner to personalize the car by making it compatible to his needs. For instance, if by following the trend of buying an expensive luxurious car, you bought a car with an engine configuration of 4.0 litre, but after some time you realize that you are not able to cater to its fuel requirement by driving it regularly then by tuning the car you can change its engine configuration to 2.0 litre and enjoy not only its regular drive, but also notice the huge savings on fuel investment.

Factors to consider before getting your car tuned : Although the fashion of tuning the car is flourishing at dynamic speed across the world, especially among the youth, it doesn't mean that following the blind race, you should also join the team and find yourself cheated after driving it. Therefore, to avoid any such problem in future it would be better to get yourself acquainted with complete knowledge related to the subject. For this you can consider the following factors:

1. Forums: As referred above today as the trend of car tuning has gained huge popularity among the car enthusiasts, there are various online forums which are assisting the novice drivers in making them aware about the benefits of car

tuning and teaching them about the whole process. Joining these forums will help in getting all your doubts cleared by experts and you will also get feedback from the car owners who have had their cars tuned according to their requirements.

2. Seeking the help of an expert: Consulting an expert will help you in broadening your knowledge about car tuning in a much better way. Contacting an expert will benefit you in having a face to face interaction with him and discussing your doubts in a broader way. Moreover, going through the condition of your car the expert will be able to suggest you necessary modifications that could be implemented on your car.

48. Choose the appropriate title for the given passage.
    (a) The importance of cars
    (b) Car Tuning: Understanding the Concept
    (c) Luxurious Cars
    (d) Types of Cars

49. According to the passage, which of the following car components can be modified?
    (i) Spoilers   (ii) Motor
    (iii) Air vents   (iv) Engine
    (v) Wheels
    (a) (i) and (ii) only
    (b) (ii), (iii), (iv) and (v) only
    (c) (i), (iii), (iv) and (v) only
    (d) (iv) and (v) only

50. What are the luxurious cars symbolic of?
    (i) Power
    (ii) Energy
    (iii) Comfort
    (iv) Luxuriousness
    (v) Kindness
    (a) (i), (ii) and (iii) only
    (b) (iii), (iv) and (v) only
    (c) (iv) and (v) only
    (d) (i), (iii) and (iv) only

51. What is the meaning of the word 'personalize'?
    (a) To problematise the whole field of study
    (b) To critically examine one's method of thinking
    (c) Mark something in a way to show it belongs to someone
    (d) To logically analyse a series of arguments

52. Select the incorrect statement about the factors to be considered before getting a car tuned
    (a) One should blindly follow the fashion of tuning a car because it is popular.
    (b) One should get acquainted with complete knowledge related to car tuning.
    (c) One should join forums which will help clearing doubts and getting feedback from experts.
    (d) One should consult an expert in the field of car tuning.

DIRECTIONS (Qs. 53-57) : *Read the passage and answer the questions that follow.* **(2022)**

A phobia is an irrational and excessive fear of an object or situation, according to the American Psychiatric Association (APA). More often than not, phobia involves a sense of endangerment or a fear of harm. For example, somebody suffering from agoraphobia will dread being trapped in an inescapable place or situation.

Here, we discuss 8 most common phobias that people suffer from:

1. **Agoraphobia:** It is a phobia which is quite common. It is a fear of open or crowded spaces. It creates a vicious cycle and the sufferer gets panic attacks when nearing any event that necessitates facing such circumstances.

2. **Acrophobia:** It is a fear of heights. It is an irrational fear of heights or the fear of falling. In severe cases, a victim may even suffer panic attacks.

3. **Aerophobia:** It is the fear of flying. Almost 6.5 percent of the world's population has this fear. This phobia is closely linked with agoraphobia and claustrophobia (fear of small and restricted spaces). In extreme cases, this may affect a

person's professional and personal life when air travel becomes inevitable.

4. **Mysophobia:** It is a fear of germs. This fear is also akin to obsessive-compulsive disorder (OCD). A person may suffer from both these disorders at the same time. Sufferers often become isolated in mysophobia.

5. **Claustrophobia:** The fear of small spaces, this phobia is common as 5-7 percent ofthe world population suffers from claustrophobia. This phobia is related to fear of suffocation or the fear of restriction. Very few sufferers seek treatment in this phobia and majority of them go untreated.

6. **Cynophobia:** The fear of dogs is called cynophobia. Many people fear dogs and there is no harm in that. But cynophobia is an extreme and uncommon fear about dogs. It is one of the most common animal phobias in the world. It is estimated that about 36 percent of the sufferers seek treatment for cynophobia.

7. **Astraphobia:** The fear of thunder and lightning is called astraphobia. It is true that thunderstorm and lightning can make even the brave run for cover, but for an individual suffering from astraphobia, it is altogether a different case. Starting in childhood, this fear can continue into adulthood.

8. **Arachnophobia:** The fear of spiders afflicts a lot of people in the society. This is an extreme fear of spiders and other arachnids like scorpions. This causes a lot of embarrassment to the victims.

Managing phobias

A little of fear and phobia is normal. However, when it goes beyond control and begins to affect the daily activities of a person, it becomes a concern. Phobias are mental conditions which qualify for intervention. One should see a psychiatrist if faced with an extreme phobia of any kind. In fact, phobias are mostly related to anxiety disorder in a person.

53. Choose the appropriate title for the passage.
    (a) Phobia and Its Origins
    (b) Agoraphobia
    (c) American Psychiatric Association
    (d) Most Common Phobias

54. Match the columns, based on the passage.

Column-1	Column-11
(A) Astraphobia	(i) Fear of heights
(B) Claustrophobia	(ii) Fear of germs
(C) Mysophobia	(iii) Fear of thunder and lightning
(D) Acrophobia	(iv) Fear of small paces

    (a) A - (iii), B - (iv), C - (ii), D - (i)
    (b) A - (i), B - (ii), C - (iii), D - (iv)
    (c) A - (ii), B - (iv), C - (iii), D - (i)
    (d) A - (iv), B - (iii), C - (ii), D - (i)

55. Which fear is akin to obsessive compulsive disorder (OCD)?
    (a) Agoraphobia
    (b) Aerophobia
    (c) Mysophobia
    (d) Cynophobia

56. What is the percentage of sufferers that seek treatment for Cynophobia?
    (a) 50%
    (b) 36%
    (c) 47%
    (d) 5-7%

57. What is the meaning of word 'endangerment ' as used in the passage?
    (a) To be kind
    (b) To be angry
    (c) To behave unreasonably
    (d) To put somebody/something in a situation of harm/danger

HINTS & EXPLANATIONS

LEVEL-1

1. (c) Unity in Diversity
2. (a) They get common feeling of unity
3. (a) sacrifies, truth and prosperity
4. (b) 2nd October
5. (b) Yes, everyone should respect our national flag
6. (d) a set of principles or religious beliefs, people of all races
7. (b) making the beginning of important thing
8. (d) India & Pakistan
9. (a) Poonam Raut
10. (a) Archana Das and N. Niranjan
11. (c) Guangzhou
12. (b) Indian bowlers
13. (c) October 2, 1869
14. (a) barrister
15. (d) S. Africa
16. (d) to treat people on the basis of colour of skin.
17. (a) 1919, 1947
18. (d) 1915
19. (c) Sanskrit
20. (a) Common people were not in a position to understand Sanskrit
21. (d) Under this system treatment of people was based on their community.
22. (a) to strongly criticise
23. (a) They had to bear insult throughout their life
24. (b) Mahavir and Gautam Buddha
25. (d) the sun descends in the west
26. (d) a flower vase
27. (a) a flower
28. (b) give blessing and joy
29. (d) the occupants are asleep without any care
30. (b) Daredevil Russians
31. (c) Get a tattoo of the company's logo
32. (b) 100 free pizzas yearly for 100 years
33. (b) 300+
34. (d) Eventually
35. (a) Fireworks for the Visually Impaired
36. (c) Feeling Fireworks
37. (b) Canada
38. (c) sixty six
39. (a) Shining
40. (b) Importance of School Library
41. (d) "It provides a place to have recreational activities during classes" is incorrect.
42. (c) Synonym of enrich is endow.
43. (c) reading
44. (a) intellectual, artistic and social
45. (b)
46. (d)
47. (a)

LEVEL - 2

1. (a) he gave me gold here means jewels
2. (a) money
3. (c) The poor man gave food to the poet and took care of him day and night
4. (b) The poor man blessed the charity of the poet.
5. (a) charity
6. (a) holds it in its lap
7. (c) thread the dews like pearls
8. (c) pretty tunes
9. (a) It has so little to do.
10. (d) Hay dreams each day away, and so does the poet.
11. (d) spices gone to sleep
12. (a) because both are small and round
13. (d) She had a dream about the grass.
14. (b) "to move"
15. (c) to explain what happens to grass when it dies
16. (c) It has some rhyming lines.
17. (b) 5

18. (b) I was familiar with every bit of the cell
19. (c) The prisoner's conscious efforts to overcome the loneliness
20. (a) It is possible to adjust oneself to uncongenial surroundings.
21. (c) So far nobody climbed that high.
22. (b) There was not enough air to breathe.
23. (a) They took off their gloves because it was not very cold
24. (b) The passage was full of smoke
25. (d) Saved a life
26. (b) anecdotal problems
27. (a) the arms
28. (d) all of the above
29. (d) whimsy
30. (a) causing stomach problems
31. (c) The boy with the thick glasses
32. (d) Read a brochure
33. (b) forehead
34. (a) he couldn't recognise who Rajan was
35. (b) By the memory who Rajan was
36. (a) Rajan stayed in the same place because of the accident
37. (d) Said a prayer for Rajan
38. (c) Global Food Security and its Importance
39. (b) climate, soil and level of technology

40. (c) vitamins and minerals
41. (c) economical
42. (d) Exacerbated
43. (a) Virus-Variants and Strains
44. (c) die out
45. (c) variants
46. (a) Synonym of variant is alternative.
47. (c) vaccines
48. (b) Car Tuning : Understanding the Concept
49. (c) (i), (iii), (iv) and (v) only
50. (d) (i), (iii) and (iv) only
51. (c) Mark something in a way to show it belongs to someone
52. (a) "One should blindly follow the fashion of tuning a car because it is popular" is incorrect.
53. (d) Most Common Phobias
54. (a) a – (iii), b – (iv), c – (ii), d – (i)
55. (c) Mysophobiais akin to obsessive compulsive disorder (OCD).
56. (b) 36%
57. (d) To put somebody/something in a situation of harm/danger.

CHAPTER 12

ADVERTISEMENT/ GRAPHS/IMAGES

ADVERTISEMENT

Advertising brings a product (or service) to the attention of potential and current customers. Advertising is focused on one particular product or service. Thus, an advertising plan for one product might be very different from that for another product. Advertising is typically done with signs, brochures, commercials, direct mailings or e-mail messages, personal contact, etc.

Advertising is the activity of drawing public attention to a product or service in order to encourage people to buy it.

GRAPHS

Graphs, charts, and tables are ways of presenting information. Graphs and charts are pictures which show numbers or figures, and tables are just rows and columns of information.

This is a table. It shows the population of the world's top ten cities in 2011.

1	Tokyo	Japan	32,450,000
2	Seoul	South Korea	20,550,000
3	Mexico City	Mexico	20,450,000
4	New York City	USA	19,750,000
5	Mumbai	India	19,200,000
6	Jakarta	Indonesia	18,900,000
7	São Paulo	Brazil	18,850,000
8	Delhi	India	18,680,000
9	Osaka/Kobe	Japan	17,350,000
10	Shanghai	China	16,650,000

One of the most important things to do is get the main idea of the graph. First, identify the main features of the graph. What is happening? What are the biggest numbers? If it is a time graph, what are the biggest changes? What are the trends?

Ideally you need to find one main idea and, if possible, one or two smaller ideas.

- Don't have too much information.
- Don't analyse or explain everything in the graph.
- Don't go from left to right, explaining everything. Instead pick the main ideas.
- Use the biggest and next biggest - don't mention everything in between.
- Don't mention the small or unimportant stuff.
- Pick an idea and find information that supports it.

WHAT A GRAPH CAN TELL YOU

On a graph you get an overall shape of a variable or the relationships between variables.

A line graph represents a numerical or mathematical relationship and so has more information "buried" in it than other graphs.

Line graphs can sometimes be used to make predictions for values that were not measured, by interpolating or extrapolating the trend, or by looking at the shape.

Limitation

Graphs can tell you a lot about the design of an investigation, but they don't tell you everything. For example, they don't usually tell you which variables were controlled, the sample size, or the method of measurement. So there are lots of questions to ask to find out about validity and reliability, and also about the actual context of the investigation.

TYPES OF GRAPHS

You are likely to meet only two types of graphs in English tests - time and comparison graphs. (Sometimes you can get both in the same test!)

- In time graphs you have to describe changes over time.
- In comparison graphs you have to compare different items - countries, people, products, places, etc.

The vocabulary for each kind of graph is different:

- In time graphs you use time vocabulary to describe change: rose, fell, declined, shot up, increased, remained steady, etc.
- In comparison graphs you compare: twice as much as, more than, less than, the same amount, both X and Y have the same figure, etc.

IMAGES

The word image is in the broader sense means any two-dimensional figure such as a map, a graph, a pie chart, or a painting. In this wider sense, images can also be rendered manually, such as by drawing, the art of painting, carving, rendered automatically by printing or computer graphics technology, or developed by a combination of methods, especially in a pseudo-photograph.

***Example*:**

Description : This advertisement shows a simple gray car in a gray background. The big words say, "The Only One You'll Need." The smaller text says, "Experience the freedom and peace of mind knowing you've made a great investment. Essentially, you are buying a car for life. Twenty years from now it will still get you from point A to B."

Interpretation : It seems that the message is clear that this car will last a long time. The text, "Experience the freedom and peace of mind knowing you've made a great investment," seems to speak to older people who think responsibly about their purchases. It seems to say that this is the smart thing to do. Also, when it says that it gets you from "Point A to B" seems to mean that the most important consideration in buying a car is reliability. Because of this, this ad is definitely meant for older people (age 50+).

LEVEL 1

DIRECTIONS (Qs. 1-4) : *Read the following advertisment and answer the questions that follow.*

Wayfinders

New batch for basic Travel and tourism course commencing shortly.
* Three months duration
* Convenient timings
* Easy payment options
* Online training on computer Reservation System.
* Ensures 100% placement assistance

Our Courses include
* Airhostess
* Flight steward course
* Airline sales and Marketing
* Airport functions
* Fundamentals of Air Transportation

Call or visit us at:
Wayfinders Aviation Pvt. Ltd.
12, Gurgaon (behind The Marriot Hotel)
www.wayfindersaviation.com

---

1. Which of the following about this training programme is false?
   (a) It gives training to pilots
   (b) It provides courses to become air hostess.
   (c) It gives training on airline marketing
   (d) It also trains in air transportation.

2. What do you think is the purpose of this advertisement?
   (a) To inform people about its programme.
   (b) To give publicity to its programme.
   (c) To convince the people.
   (d) To fill a page in the newspaper.

3. This advertisement mentions a landmark to reach its office, what is that?
   (a) A hostel   (b) A hotel
   (c) A school   (d) A temple

4. This advertisement promises its trainees ___________.
   (a) Full payment on time
   (b) Assistance in placement
   (c) 100% placement guarantee.
   (d) In campus placement.

DIRECTIONS (Qs. 5-8) : *Read the following advertisement and answer the questions that follow.*

CLIMATE RECORDS 2014

NEWSICLE

The annual State of the Climate report is out: it shows record heat, record sea levels, more hot days and fewer cool nights, surging cyclones, unprecedented pollution, and rapidly diminishing glaciers. The US National Oceanic and Atmospheric Administration issues the report compiling the latest data gathered by 413 scientists from 58 countries around the world. Here's a look at some of the climate highlights from 2014:

Temperatures set a new record

Four independent data sets show that **last year was the hottest** in 135 years of modern record keeping. More than 20 countries in Europe set new heat records, with Africa, Asia and Australia also experiencing near-record heat. **The annual mean temperature for India was 0.52°C above the 1961-90 average.** The east coast of North America was the only region to experience cooler than average conditions

Sea levels surge to a record

The **global mean sea level continued to rise,** keeping pace with a trend of 3.2mm per year over the last two decades. Eight of the world's 10 largest cities are near a coast

Glaciers retreat for the 31st consecutive year

Data from over 36 mountain glaciers show that 2014 was the 31st straight year of glacier ice loss worldwide. Most alarming: The rate of loss is accelerating over time

More hot days and fewer cool nights

Climate change doesn't just increase the average temperature — it also **increases the extremes**

Record greenhouse gases fill the atmosphere

By burning fossil fuels, humans have cranked up **concentrations of carbon dioxide in the atmosphere by more than 40% since the Industrial Revolution.** Carbon dioxide reached a concentration of 400 parts per million for the first time in May 2013

THE OCEANS ABSORB CRAZY AMOUNTS OF HEAT OCEANS ARE ABSORBING EVEN MORE GLOBAL WARMING THAN THE SURFACE OF THE PLANET, CONTRIBUTING TO RISING SEAS, MELTING GLACIERS, AND DYING CORAL REEFS AND FISH POPULATIONS

In 2015 the world has moved into an El Nino warming pattern in the Pacific Ocean. El Nino phases release some of the ocean's stored heat into the atmosphere, causing weather shifts around the world. El Nino hasn't peaked yet this year, but by some measures it's already the most extreme ever recorded for this time of the year and could mean 2015 may set even more climate records

5. What among the following is not a cause for global warming? **(Tricky)**
   - (a) Illiteracy
   - (b) Burning of fossil fuels.
   - (c) Pollution
   - (d) Deforestation

6. What among the following is not getting affected by climate change?
   - (a) Glaciers
   - (b) Fish populations
   - (c) World weather
   - (d) The production of cars and other vehicles.

7. Which among the following statements is not true about climate change?
   - (a) It is just increasing the average temperature and nothing more than it.
   - (b) It has increased the extremities of weather.
   - (c) It has raised the sea levels.
   - (d) The mountain glaciers are melting.

8. What are greenhouse gases?
   - (a) Gases green in colour
   - (b) Gases that are found in green houses.
   - (c) Any gaseous substance capable of absorbing infrared radiation and trapping it.
   - (d) Carbon dioxide and oxygen.

DIRECTIONS (Qs 9-12) : *Look at the table below and answer the questions that follow. Choose the answers from the options given below.*

(2013)

9. The above table on esteem of a country is based on _______.
   (a) Honesty of the people.
   (b) The corruption levels in a country.
   (c) The performance of government, economy and environment of a country.
   (d) The flora and fauna of a country.

10. This table presents a survey done on how many people?
    (a) 10000 people
    (b) 1000 people
    (c) More than 25,000 people
    (d) More than 30,000 people.

11. Which of the statements is false?
    (a) India is far ahead of Pakistan in terms of esteemed countries.
    (b) Reputation of India took the highest jump.
    (c) Pakistan is lagging behind China
    (d) This is a survey done on all the countries of the world.

12. What is meaning of esteem?
    (a) Honesty
    (b) Venerate
    (c) Scorn
    (d) Happy

DIRECTIONS (Qs. 13-16) : *Read the following advertisment and answer the questions.*

13. What do you mean by a solitaire?
    (a) Diamond   (b) Gold
    (c) Alone   (d) Many.

14. What is the purpose of Laser here?
    (a) For treatment of eyes.
    (b) It Is used as a technology for making diamond
    (c) It Is a technique to manufacture gold.
    (d) A device that is used for metal cutting.

15. How much does this jeweller promise to charge for making a piece of jewellery?
    (a) 8% flat on any piece
    (b) 8% per gram on any item.
    (c) 8% on carving of diamonds
    (d) 8% only on selected items

16. What is meant by assaying here?
    (a) Attempt
    (b) Determine the quality and content of metal.
    (c) Analyse
    (d) Try

DIRECTIONS (Qs. 17-25) : *Read the following passage and answer the questions that follow.*

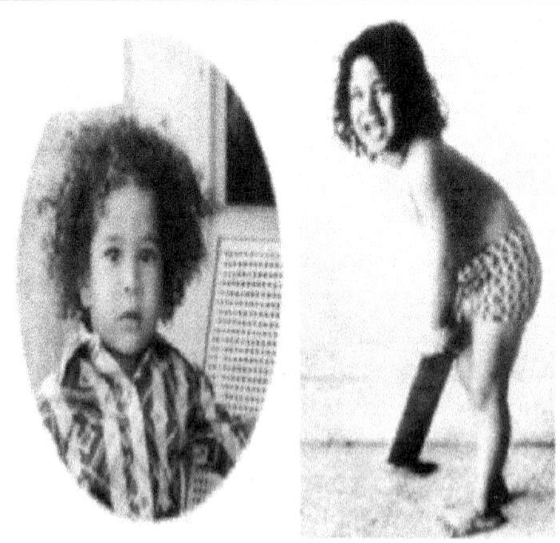

He was born on April 23, 1973 at the Nirmal Nursing Home in Dadar, Mumbai. His father was one of the most famous novelists of Maharashtra, Ramesh Tendulkar, and his mother Rajni was an insurance professional. His father named him after Sachin Dev Burman who happened to be his favorite music director. He was the youngest among 4 siblings - elder brothers Nitin and Ajit and elder sister Savita.

The first few years of his life were spent at the Sahitya Sahawas Cooperative Housing Society in Bandra East. As a young kid he was completely opposite to how he is nowadays - at school he was not averse to picking a fight or two against children who had come there for the first time and this led him to be regarded as a bully of sorts.

In his teens he was a big fan of John McEnroe, one of the prominent tennis stars from the US who was also known for his fits of temper. Ajit decided to do away with the bullying and mischievous nature of his and so he introduced him to cricket during 1984. He took him to Ramakant Achrekar, who was one of the most well known club cricketers of his time as well as a top coach. He used to teach at Shivaji Park, Dadar. Achrekar liked what he saw with the young child and asked him to change his school to Sharadashram Vidyamandir (English) High School, which was located in Dadar itself. The school was a top name in local cricketing circles and had gifted many famous cricketers at that time. Before this, he had been studying at the Indian Education Society's New English School in Bandra East.

He used to practice for hours at end and whenever he became tired Achrekar used to place a one rupee coin at the top of his stumps. The condition was that he could keep them if he did not get out and he collected 13 coins this way, which he still regards as being among his most treasured possessions. It was at this time that he decided to stay with his uncle and aunt who lived close to Shivaji Park in order to deal with a tiring schedule. At school he was regarded as a child prodigy and was a common point of discussion in the cricketing circles of Mumbai. He was a constant feature for his school team in the well known Matunga Gujarati Seva Mandal Shield. He attended the MRF Pace Foundation in Madras at the age of 14 so that he could train and become a fast bowler. However, Dennis Lillee who was heading the proceedings was not impressed at the least by the young kid and asked him to focus on his batting instead. It was during this time that he was not able to win the Best Junior Cricketer

Award of the Mumbai Cricket Association and was distraught but he received a pair of ultra light pads from a certain Mr. Sunil Gavaskar who wrote to him as well and said that he himself had not been able to win it as well at that age. In an effort to gee up the young talent he also stated that he had not done too badly as a cricketer himself. He stated after he had eclipsed Gavaskar's record of 34 test centuries that it had acted as possibly the greatest encouragement for him at that point in time.   **(2012)**

17. His father was:
     (a) poet   (b) novelist
     (c) dramatist   (d) cricketer

18. He was named after the famous musician:
     (a) Sachin Dev Burman
     (b) R.D. Burman
     (c) Laxmikant Pyarelal
     (d) Khayam

19. In his childhood he was:
     (a) calm   (b) shy
     (c) kind   (d) a bully

20. John McEnroe was one of the prominent was a
     (a) base ball player
     (b) footballer
     (c) tennis stars
     (d) golfer

21. His mentor was
     (a) Ajit Tendulkar
     (b) Ramakant Achrekar
     (c) Sunil Gavaskar
     (d) Dillip Vengsarkar

22. MRF Pace Foundation is located in
     (a) Tamil Nadu   (b) Australia
     (c) Madras   (d) Delhi

23. He still regards as being among his most treasured possessions; what is the possession?
     (a) 13 coins
     (b) his hundreds
     (c) winning the world cup
     (d) his sister Savita

24. He was a child prodigy. What does the phrase mean?
     (a) mischievous   (b) born genius
     (c) lazy   (d) friendly

25. MRF Pace Foundation in Madras is headed by
     (a) Javagl Srinath   (b) Allan Border
     (c) Shane Warne   (d) Dennis Lillee

LEVEL 2

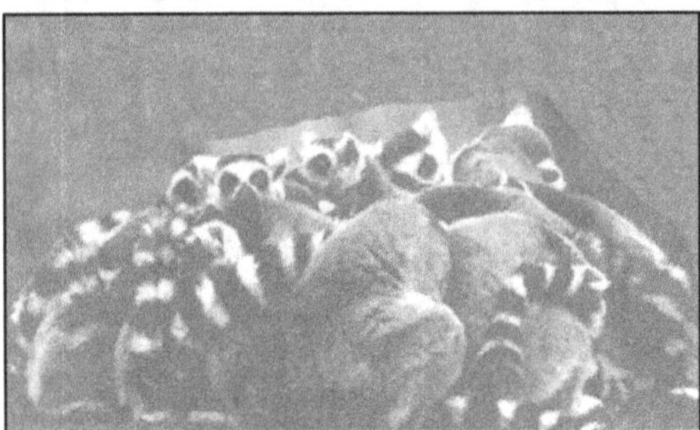

CONFERENCE IN PROGRESS

Lesiure Hotels presents interesting venues for out-of-the ordinary business conferences & corporate training programs. Picturesque destinations, all fully equipped with the latest state-of-the-art conferencing facilities combined with the best in Indian hospitality await you. At each of our resorts, you will find a panel of experts with customised and metilculous planning capability ready to make any event not just sucessful, but also an enjoyable and memorable experience for the participants. So get ready. It's time to change the corporate rules a bit and take a few tips from Mother Nature.

ELEPHANT/JEEP SAFARIS • NATURE WALKS/TREKS/HIKES • BIRDWATCHING • ROCK CLIMBING/ RAPPELLING • RIVER CROSSING • SLITHERING • SPA THERAPIES & MASSAGES • MULTI-CUSINE RESTAURANTS & PATISSERIE • GRILLS & BAR-BE-CUES • LOUNGE BARS • LIVE MUSIC & BAND • FOLK SHOWS • WILDLIFE MOVIES & SLIDE SHOWS • THEME NIGHTS

1. What is meant by " state of the art" conferencing facilities?
   (a) The state that has some art.
   (b) Modern, using the latest ideas.
   (c) Best and perfect ideas.
   (d) Art that has a status.
2. What is rappelling and slithering as mentioned here?
   (a) Rappel is something to do with repulsion and slithering to go up.
   (b) They are names of animal devices
   (c) They are kinds of wildlife safari.
   (d) They are adventure sports.

3. This advertised hotel books venues for________.
   (a) Family.
   (b) Corporate training programmes.
   (c) Wedding parties.
   (d) Birthday parties.
4. A scientist who studies birds is called________.
   (a) Birder   (b) Birdwatcher
   (c) Ornithologist   (d) Ornithist

MAHINDRA RISE

BRING HOME THE LUXURIOUS REXTON TODAY.

The Reston. The flagship SUV form SsangYong-the leading South Korean premium SUV manufacturer that is part of the Mahindra group. A perfec combination of luxury, style and performance, it will wow you like it has everyone across 120 countries.

Benefits upto ₹ 1.65 Lakhs*

High on luxury.

• 184 Bhp (137 kW) • E-tronic Automatic Transmission with Mercedes-Benz™ technology • All Wheel Drive • Sunroff • 4 Airbags • Leather upholstery • ESP • Powered driver seat with memory " Touch screen Infotainment with Navigation • Also available in Manual Transmission

(Tricky, 2014)

5. What do you understand by flagship store?
   (a) A ship with a flag in a store.
   (b) A store to showcase a brand
   (c) A store to sell its products.
   (d) Best store
6. What is the purpose of airbags in a car?
   (a) To provide protection to the passengers from outside pollution.
   (b) To fill air in its bags
   (c) To provide protection to the driver during a collision
   (d) None of these
7. The advertisement mentions a word that is the opposite of 'frugality' What is that word?
   (a) Luxury
   (b) Leading
   (c) Benefits
   (d) performance

8. The full form of ESP is 'Electronic Stability Control', how do you think is it helpful in a car?
   (a) It prevents air pollution
   (b) It makes the car automatic electronically
   (c) It stabilises a car from sliding
   (d) It gives extra power to the engine.

DIRECTIONS (Qs. 9-12) : *Read the following advertisement and answer the questions that follow.*

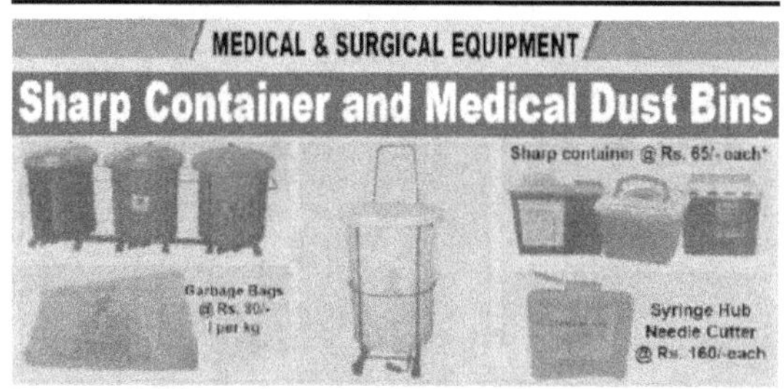

Have a look at the advertisement given below and answer the questions that follow. Choose the answers from the options given below.   **(2012)**

9. The above advertisement mentions needle cutters, why do we need them?
   (a) To cut stitching needle so that they don't hurt anyone.
   (b) To dispose the syringe needle.
   (c) To make a large number of needles for multiple usage.
   (d) None of these.

10. What is the significance of the colour of the Dust Bins?
    (a) They specify the type of waste to be disposed as to house waste or office waste.
    (b) They have no other significance apart from looking good.
    (c) They specify the waste as biodegradable and non-biodegradable.
    (d) None of these.

11. Waste disposal is proving to be a menace to the cities nowadays, what can be done to get rid of this menace?
    (a) We should keep the garbage in plastic bags.
    (b) We must throw the garbage in the corners of the lanes.

(c) We must dig pits in the centre of the residential areas to get rid of it instantly.
(d) Waste must be disposed off in landfills.

12. Which among the following is not the correct way to dispose of waste?
    (a) Sort out the garbage before disposing.
    (b) Turn kitchen and garden waste into compost.
    (c) Waste that be reused should be sorted.
    (d) Put the waste in plastic bags and throw it in a far off place not close to your own house.

DIRECTIONS (Qs. 13-16) : *Read the following paragraph and answer the questions that follow.*

Divya Public School, Navjeevan Vihar A ceremony was held for the newly elected council members for the session 2015-16. The chief guest for the day was RN Mattoo, Director (Spl Exams and CTET Unit), CBSE, Delhi. The members brimmed with confidence as they shouldered their assigned duties. Raghav Chawla and Aruna were elected as the head boy and head girl respectively. All the leaders pledged to deliver their duties with sincerity and efficiently.

13. What do we understand by shoulder their duties?
    (a) They put their badges on their shoulders.
    (b) They took up their responsibilities
    (c) They found a shoulder to cry on
    (d) They promised to fight together.

14. Find out a word in the report that is the opposite of deficient.
    (a) Brimmed   (b) Pledged
    (c) Assigned   (d) Full

15. Who were the leaders who took the pledge?
    (a) The PM and the Ministers.
    (b) The head boy and the head girl
    (c) The Political leaders.
    (d) The Head of the school.

16. As you can see the head boy and the head girl take a pledge, what does that pledge signify?
    (a) It assures their loyalty towards their country.
    (b) It assures their promise to fulfil their duties.
    (c) It insures secrecy of office.
    (d) It insures against discrimination.

DIRECTIONS (Qs. 17-20) : *Read the following advertisement carefully and answer the questions that follow.*

CODE-DECODE

SAARC SATELLITE

Indian Space Research Organisation (ISROI) chief AS Kiran Kumar has confirmed that the space agency will launch the first SAARC by next year..

THE SATELLITE : A brainchild of PM Narendra Modi who proposed the idea of a satellite serving the needs of SAARC member nations during his visit to Nepal in August 2014, the SAARC satellite is communication-cum-meterorology satellite to aid neighbouring countries with their need for satellite transponders for communication and weather forecasting.

INDIA TO LEAD : The satellite will launched by ISRO next year. India is bearing all costs of the communication satellite that will weight approximately 2,000 kg, and is presently close to completion. It will help provide tele-education, tele-medicine, and communication during disasters.

The South Asian Association for Regional Cooperation (SAARC) was established in 1985. This organisation has a key focus on economic and developmental issues. SAARC has eight members: Afghanistan, Bangladesh, Bhutan, India, Maldives, Nepal, Pakistan and Sri Lanka. Additionally, there are some nations with observer status, including the United States, Australia, Japan, and China.

Did you **Know** *?*

WHY IS INDIA KEEN FOR IT ? It is believed that India is keen to counter the growing demand for Chinese space services in India's neighbourhood by coming up with a SAARC satellite. Pakistan and Sri Lanka has launched communication satellites with China's help. Another SAARC member, Afghanistan, has leased a part of the French telecommunication satellite, Eutelsat 48D. Bangladesh has hired a Us-based space consultancy firm to lunch its own satellite, Bangabandhu 1, by 2017. India has been ignored by its neighbours even as countries from Europe and the Americas have south ISRO's services.

17. How many members are there in SAARC?   **(Critical Thinking)**
    (a) Eight
    (b) Nine
    (c) Twelve
    (d) Fifteen
18. What will be the name of the satellite that Bangladesh is going to launch in 2017?
    (a) ISRO
    (b) Bangladeshi
    (c) Bangabandhu
    (d) Bengabandhu
19. Which of the following purposes is not served by a satellite?
    (a) Weather forecasting
    (b) Communication
    (c) Tele -education
    (d) Peace
20. Which word in the above article means the opposite of repudiate?
    (a) Confirm
    (b) Forecasting
    (c) Completion
    (d) Issues

DIRECTIONS (Qs. 21-24) : *Read the following advertisement carefully and answer the questions that follow:-*

DOES YOUR CAR HAVE A
LIFETIME ENGINE WARRANTY?

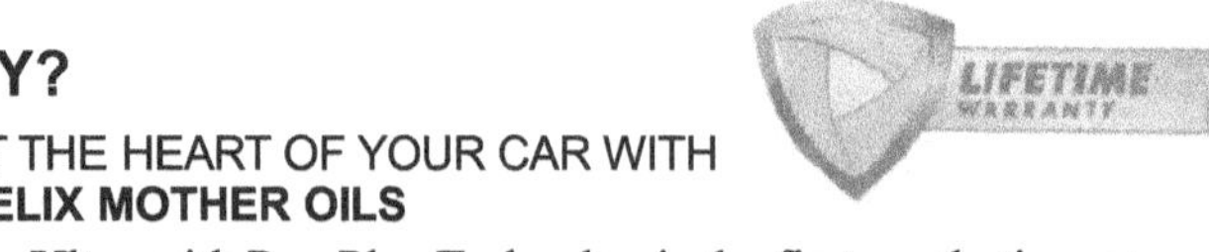

PROTECT THE HEART OF YOUR CAR WITH
SHELL HELIX MOTHER OILS

Shell Helix Ultra with PurePlus Technoloy is the first synthetic motor oil designed from Natural Gas, that gives on exceptional protection to your engine. We are so confident of this unique PurePlus Technolgy present in Sheel Helix Ultra that we are offering you a Lifetime Engine Warranty. So, go ahead and give your car's engine the exceptional protection it deserves!

To know more about this :
TOLL FREE NO. 1800 103 9481
SMS 'WARRANTY' TO 56363
www.shell.com/warranty

21. Which of the following statements is not true about the advertisement?
    (a) It gives lifetime Engine guarantee.   (b)   It gives lifetime Engine warrantee.
    (c) It is designed from natural gas.   (d)   It protects your engine.
22. How is natural gas extracted?
    (a) Through the process of hydraulic fracturing
    (b) Through filtration process
    (c) Through sedimentation
    (d) Through decantation
23. Find out the word from the above advertisement that is the opposite of conventional.
    (a) Protection   (b) Exceptional   (c) Ahead   (d) Deserves
24. Why do we need to use engine oil in a car?
    (a) To prevent overheating of the of parts of an engine caused by their rubbing together
    (b) To prevent pollution caused by overheating of the engine.
    (c) To prevent the fuel leakage
    (d) To maintain speed of the engine.

DIRECTIONS (Qs. 25-28) : *Read the following table and answer the questions that follow.*

TABLE ON GROWTH OF POPULATION

Country	July 1, 2015 Projection	Estimated Doubling Time (In Years)	Official Figure	Date of Last Figure	Source
China	1,370,793,000	141	1,371,160,000	July 26, 2015	Official population clock
India	1,299,499,000	43	1,210,854,977	March 1, 2011	Final 2011 census result
Indonesia	255,462,000	50	255,461,700	2015	Official estimate
Pakistan	191,785,000	35	191,164,000	July 26, 2015	HYPERLINK "http://www.pwd.punjab.gov.pk/" Official Population Clock
Bangladesh	158,762,000	51	158,935,000	July 26, 2015	Official population clock
Japan	126,950,000	-	126,950,000	July 1, 2015	Monthly official estimate
Philippines	102,965,000	33	102,965,300	2015	Official estimate
Vietnam	91,812,000	60	90,493,352	April 1, 2014	Official estimate
Iran	78,778,000	54	78,525,000	July 26, 2015	Official population clock
Turkey	78,214,000	52	77,695,904	December 31, 2014	Official estimate
Thailand	68,387,000	91	65,926,261	September 1, 2010	2010 census results
Burma	52,280,000	57	51,486,253	March 29, 2014	2014 census results
South Korea	50,617,000	181	50,617,045	2015	Official estimate
Iraq	36,575,000	24	36,575,000	2015	Official estimate

(Critical Thinking, 2013)

25. What is the difference between official estimate of population and official population clock?
    (a) Both are basically same.
    (b) One is a calculation on a rough basis and the other is exact.
    (c) Official clock keeps adding to the birth every second whereas official estimate is based on a survey done.
    (d) Official population clock is an estimated birth every minute and estimated population is the counting done on the basis of registered births.
26. According to this table India stands second in terms of population ; what can be the hazards of overpopulation?
    (a) Lack of opportunities.
    (b) Stress on environmental resources
    (c) Economic growth is retarded.
    (d) All of these.
27. Which of the following statements is not true?
    (a) China is the world leader in population.
    (b) In 2058 India's population will have doubled itself.
    (c) South Korea will show fastest growth in population.
    (d) Iraq will be far ahead of India in growth of population in the coming decades.
28. What is meant by census?
    (a) Official counting of people and compilation of economic social and other data.
    (b) Survey of people and their backgrounds.
    (c) Report of population by census officers.
    (d) Counting of the mainstream population.

DIRECTIONS (Qs. 29-36) : *Observe the image given below and read the passage. Answer the questions that follow.*

MISSION SWACHH BHARAT

Narendra Modi

On the occasion of Mahatma Gandhi's 145th birth anniversary, Prime Minister Narendra Modi launched the first-ever nation-wide 'Clean India' campaign (Swachh Bharat Campaign). Modi weilded a broom to kick off the campaign that he had announced during his Independence Day speech. The aim of this campaign is to make India 'clean' by 2019, which will mark Gandhi's 150th birth anniversary. Under the campaign, every city, town and village will be facilitated with pucca toilets, safe drinking water, waste disposal systems and clean roads.

The campaign is also meant to create awareness about the importance of sanitation and cleanliness, and civil society and social organisations are expected to participate in the campaign. Several companies have also donated funds for the campaign.

More than 30 lakh central government and state government employees will pledge to carry the campaign forward. Hundreds of school and college students will also join the campaign.

One of Modi's main thrust areas in the campaign is providing toilets to all, given that 53 percent of households are still without toilets as per the 2011 census.   **(2014)**

29. What is the name of the mission referred here?
    (a) Swachh Bharat Campaign
    (b) Mission Swachh Bharat
    (c) Modi mission
    (d) Clean mission
30. What does the Prime Minister appeal?
    (a) Every citizen of India to dedicate 100 hours a year towards cleanliness
    (b) To pay money for the success of the mission
    (c) To be different to filth and dirt.
    (d) To avoid speeches and debates on the topic.
31. Mahatma Gandhi's 150 th birth anniversary falls in
    (a) 2025   (b) 2017
    (c) 2020   (d) 2019\
32. The campaign will spread the message of
    (a) sanitation   (b) education
    (c) economics   (d) democracy
33. One of Modi's main thrust areas in the campaign is
    (a) providing money to all
    (b) providing medicine to all
    (c) providing toilets to all
    (d) providing house to all
34. Swaccha Bharat Mission is started by
    (a) Narendra Modi   (b) Mahatma Gandhi
    (c) Arun Jaitly   (d) None of the above
35. The Prime Minister makes special appeal to
    (a) military   (b) scavengers
    (c) students   (d) lawyers
36. The goal of the mission is
    (a) to make India clean
    (b) to make India rich
    (c) to make India free from poverty
    (d) to make India strong

HINTS & EXPLANATIONS

LEVEL - 1

1. (a) It gives training to pilots
2. (b) The purpose of any advertisement is always to give publicity and thereby to promote its sales.
3. (b) Marriot Hotel
4. (b) It only promises assistance in placement and not guarantee placement.
5. (a) Illiteracy is not a direct cause of global warming, though it might be unawareness about creating causes for it.
6. (d) The production of cars is not at all getting affected by it. In fact it might be adding to it.
7. (a) It is not only increasing average world temperature but also leading to other devastating phenomena.
8. (c) Greenhouse gases are any gaseous substance present in the atmosphere that absorbs infrared radiation and traps it.
9. (c) The above survey was done on the performance of the government , economy and environment of countries.
10. (c) This report is based on a survey done on 27,000 people.
11. (d) This survey was done in 55 countries of the world.
12. (b) esteem means venerate or respect.
13. (c) Solitaire literally means lonely or alone when used in context of diamonds it means a single piece of a diamond.
14. (d) Laser means Light Amplification by Stimulated Emission OF Radiation. It is used for diverse purposes like CD writing/reading, communications, land mapping and here it is used to cut metals.
15. (a) 8% flat on any piece.
16. (b) The advertisement claims to mention the self-determined quality and content of the metal on the pieces made by the jeweller.
17. (b) 18. (a) 19. (d) 20. (c)
21. (b) 22. (c) 23. (a) 24. (b) 25. (d)

LEVEL - 2

1. (b) State of the art means the usage of modern and latest ideas and methods.
2. (d) Rappelling is to slide down a rope, and slithering is to slip or slide for example on a bridge. Both are adventure sports.
3. (b) The hotel has specifically mentioned in its advertisement that it offers its venue for conferences and corporate training programmes.
4. (c) A scientist who studies about birds is known as an ornithologist.
5. (b) A flagship store is a store to showcase a brand and does not focus on earning profit.
6. (c) Airbags protect the driver during a collision.
7. (a) 'Frugal' means poor whereas the word 'luxury' is just the opposite.
8. (c) ESP on a car is more like ABS and stabilises a car from sliding.
9. (b) Needle cutters are used to dispose of syringe needles as each time a new syringe has to be used to avoid the spread of diseases.
10. (c) They are used to categorise waste as the one that is biodegradable and the non-biodegradable.
11. (d) Landfills should be made far away from the residential areas . The waste collected in the landfill generates, methane a flammable and explosive gas.
12. (d) Waste should not be disposed in this manner.
13. (b) Shouldered their duties here means took up their responsibilities.
14. (a) brim means full and is an opposite of deficient meaning lacking.
15. (b) Here it is clearly mentioned that the head boy and the head girl took up the pledge.
16. (b) Here the pledge signifies that the head boy and the head girl will fulfil their assigned duties .

17. (a) There are eight countries that are a participant of SAARC .

18. (c) Bangladesh has hired a US based agency to launch its own satellite Bangabandhu

19. (d) Peace is not served by a satellite.

20. (a) Repudiate means to deny and is the opposite of confirm.

21. (a) It gives only warrantee that if anything goes wrong they will be responsible and not guarantee that the car engine cannot fail.

22. (a) Natural Gas is extracted through a process of hydraulic fracturing or fracking.

23. (b) The opposite of conventional is exceptional.

24. (a) To prevent overheating of parts.

25. (d) Official population clock is an estimate of population based on births per minute , deaths per minute and migrations. Whereas official estimate refers to the data collected of births as registered.

26. (d) Overpopulation is proving a hazard to the ecology of the world around, putting a lot of stress on the environmental resources.

27. (c) South Korea's population will double in 181 years so it will show the least growth of population.

28. (a) Census means data collection of a population.

29. (b)   30. (a)   31. (d)   32. (a)   33. (c)

34. (a)   35. (c)   36. (a)

CHAPTER 13

DRAWING CONCLUSIONS AND INFERENCES

DEFINITION

When we read a text, the author does not always tell us everything. The author may leave out details on purpose. He may also depend on the reader's general knowledge to fill in the blanks.

Inference: an idea that is suggested by the facts or details in a passage

Conclusion: a decision about what may happen or about the result an event may have

Making an inference and drawing a conclusion are very similar skills. Each requires the reader to fill in blanks left out by the author. An author may not include information for several reasons: they may think you already know it, it may not seem important to them, or they may want you to find the result.

How to make an inference or draw a conclusion

*   Observe all the facts, arguments, and information given by the author

*   Consider what you already know from your own experiences

*   When faced with multiple choice answers, determine whether each is true or false based on the information in the passage

Example

The woman waited nervously in line. When the counter was empty, she carefully unloaded her items from her cart. Lines creased her forehead as if to show the calculations ringing up in her head. Finally, the cashier began ringing up the items as the woman clutched her purse.

Inference/conclusion: The woman may not have enough money to cover the cost of her groceries.

*   Think about the facts of the passage and what may result from them

*   Think about causes and effects

The writer may only provide a list of effects, so you have to figure out the cause.

The child stood on the sidewalk clenching her ice cream cone. Beads of sweat collected on her little nose as she furiously licked at the ice cream dripping down her hand.

Inference/conclusion: It must be a hot day because her ice cream is melting, and she is sweating.

- Try saying "If ...then"

If the girl is sweating, then it may be warm outside.

Remember

- Most writing suggests more than it says

- By making inferences, you get more from the story

- Conclusions may be missing from the things you read, so you have to draw your own

PRACTICE ACTIVITIES

Sujata almost wished that she hadn't listened to the radio. She went to the closet and grabbed her umbrella. She would feel silly carrying it to the bus stop on such a sunny morning.

1.   What probably happened?

    (a)   Sujata realised that she had an unnatural fear of falling radio parts.

    (b)   Sujata had promised herself to do something silly that morning.

    (c)   Sujata had heard a weather forecast that predicted rain.

    (d)   Sujata planned to trade her umbrella for a bus ride.

"Larry, as your boss, I must say that it's been very interesting working with you," Miss Sharma said. "However, it seems that our company's needs and your performance style are not well matched. Therefore, it makes me very sad to have to ask you to resign your position effective today."

2.   What was Miss Sharma telling Larry?

    (a)   She would feel really bad if he decided to quit.

    (b)   He was being fired.

    (c)   He was getting a raise in pay.

    (d)   She really enjoyed having him in the office.

Bill and Jessica were almost done taking turns choosing players for their teams. It was Jessica's turn to choose, and only Kurt was left. Jessica said, "Kurt."

3.   We can infer that

    (a)   Kurt is not a very good player.

    (b)   Jessica was pleased to have Kurt on her team.

    (c)   Kurt was the best player on either team.

    (d)   Jessica was inconsiderate of Kurt's feelings.

MENDING

A giant hand inside my chest

Stretches out and takes

My heart within its mighty grasp

And squeezes till it breaks.

A gentle hand inside my chest,

With mending tape and glue,

Patches up my heart until

It's almost good as new.

I ought to know by now that

Broken hearts will heal again.

But while I wait for glue and tape,

The pain!

The pain!

The pain!

4. The poem is probably about

   (a) a woman.

   (b) a man.

   (c) a broken heart.

   (d) heart surgery.

5. It can be inferred that the subject of the poem is

   (a) a lot of physical pain.

   (b) enjoying arts and crafts.

   (c) a good friend.

   (d) broken heart

LEVEL 1

1. In a one day cricket match, the total runs made by a team were 200. Out of these 160 runs were made by spinners.   **(2015)**

   Conclusions:

   I.   80% of the team consists of spinners.

   II.   The opening batsmen were spinners.

   (a)   Only conclusion I follows

   (b)   Only conclusion II follows

   (c)   Either I or II follows

   (d)   Neither I nor II follows

2. The old order changed yielding place to new.

   Conclusions:

   I.   Change is the law of nature.

   II.   Discard old ideas because they are old.

   (a)   Only conclusion I follows

   (b)   Only conclusion II follows

   (c)   Either I or II follows

   (d)   Neither I nor II follows

3. Population increase coupled with depleting resources is going to be the scenario of many developing countries in days to come.   **(2013)**

   Conclusions:

   I.   The population of developing countries will not continue to increase in future.

   II.   It will be very difficult for the governments of developing countries to provide its people decent quality of life

   (a)   Only conclusion I follows

   (b)   Only conclusion II follows

   (c)   Either I or II follows

   (d)   Neither I nor II follows

4. Prime age school-going children in urban India have now become avid as well as more regular viewers of television, even in households without a TV. As a result there has been an alarming decline in the extent of readership of newspapers.

   Conclusions:

   I.   Method of increasing the readership of newspapers should be devised.

   II.   A team of experts should be sent to other countries to study the impact of TV. on the readership of newspapers.

   (a)   Only conclusion I follows

   (b)   Only conclusion II follows

   (c)   Either I or II follows

   (d)   Neither I nor II follows

   (e)   Both I and II follow

5. The T.V. programmes, telecast specially for women are packed with a variety of recipes and household hints. A major portion of magazines for women also contains the items mentioned above.

   Conclusions:

   I.   Women are not interested in other things.

   II.   An average woman's primary interest lies in home and specially in the kitchen.

   (a)   Only conclusion I follows

   (b)   Only conclusion II follows

   (c)   Either I or II follows

   (d)   Neither I nor II follows

6. The distance of 900 km by road between Bombay and Jafra will be reduced to 280 km by sea. This will lead to a saving of ` 7.92 crores per annum on fuel.   **(2016)**

   Conclusions:

   I.   Transportation by sea is cheaper than that by road.

   II.   Fuel must be saved to the greatest extent

   (a)   Only conclusion I follows

   (b)   Only conclusion II follows

   (c)   Either I or II follows

   (d)   Neither I nor II follows

7. The manager humiliated Sachin in the presence of his colleagues. **(2014)**

   Conclusions:
   I. The manager did not like Sachin.
   II. Sachin was not popular with his colleagues.
   (a) Only conclusion I follows
   (b) Only conclusion II follows
   (c) Either I or II follows
   (d) Neither I nor II follows

8. National Aluminium Company has moved India from a position of shortage to self-sufficiency in the metal. **(2015)**

   Conclusions:
   I. Previously, India had to import aluminium.
   II. With this speed, it can soon become a foreign exchange earner.
   (a) Only conclusion I follows
   (b) Only conclusion II follows
   (c) Either I or II follows
   (d) Both I and II follow

9. Jade plant has thick leaves and it requires little water.

   Conclusions:
   I. All plants with thick leaves require little water.
   II. Jade plants may be grown in places where water is not in abundance.
   (a) Only conclusion I follows
   (b) Only conclusion II follows
   (c) Either I or II follows
   (d) Neither I nor II follows

10. Use "Kraft" colours. They add colour to our life. - An advertisement. **(2014)**

    Conclusions:
    I. Catchy slogans do not attract people.
    II. People like dark colours.
    (a) Only conclusion I follows
    (b) Only conclusion II follows
    (c) Either I or II follows
    (d) Neither I nor II follows

11. Modern man influences his destiny by the choice he makes unlike in the past.

    Conclusions:
    I. Earlier there were fewer options available to man.
    II. There was no desire in the past to influence the destiny.
    (a) Only conclusion I follows
    (b) Only conclusion II follows
    (c) Either I or II follows
    (d) Neither I nor II follows

12. Water supply in wards A and B of the city will be affected by about 50% on Friday because repairing work of the main lines is to be carried out. **(2015)**

    Conclusions:
    I. The residents in these wards should economise on water on Friday.
    II. The residents in these wards should store some water on the previous day.
    (a) Only conclusion I follows
    (b) Only conclusion II follows
    (c) Either I or II follows
    (d) Both I and II follow

13. People who speak too much against dowry are those who had taken it themselves. **(2013)**

    Conclusions:
    I. It is easier said than done.
    II. People have double standards.
    (a) Only conclusion I follows
    (b) Only conclusion II follows
    (c) Either I or II follows
    (d) Both I and II follow

14. The national norm is 100 beds per thousand population but in this state, 150 beds per thousand are available in the hospitals. **(2012)**

    Conclusions:
    I. Our national norm is appropriate.
    II. The state's health system is taking adequate care in this regard.
    (a) Only conclusion I follows
    (b) Only conclusion II follows
    (c) Either I or II follows
    (d) Neither I nor II follows

15. Money plays a vital role in politics.

   Conclusions:

   I.   The poor can never become politicians.

   II. All the rich men take part in politics.

   (a) Only conclusion I follows

   (b) Only conclusion II follows

   (c) Either I or II follows

   (d) Neither I nor II follows

16. Vegetable prices are soaring in the market.

   Conclusions: **(2016)**

   I.   Vegetables are becoming a rare commodity.

   II. People cannot eat vegetables.

   (a) Only conclusion I follows

   (b) Only conclusion II follows

   (c) Either I or II follows

   (d) Neither I nor II follows

17. The serious accident in which a person was run down by a car yesterday had again focused attention on the most unsatisfactory state of roads.

   Conclusions:

   I.   The accident that occurred was fatal.

   II. Several accidents have so far taken place because of unsatisfactory state of roads.

   (a) Only conclusion I follows

   (b) Only conclusion II follows

   (c) Either I or II follows

   (d) Both I and II follow

DIRECTIONS (Qs. 18 - 25) : *Read the clues and choose the correct answer from the options given.*

18. With pointed fangs I sit and wait; with piercing force I crunch out fate; grabbing victims, proclaiming might; physically joining with a single bite. What am I?   **(Tricky)**

   (a) snake   (b) cat

   (c) stapler   (d) none of the above

19. What has 13 hearts, but no other organs?

   (a) crocodile   (b) parakeet

   (c) a deck of cards   (d) none of the above

20. A green man lives in the green house. A blue man lives in the blue house. A red man lives in the red house. Who lives in the white house?

                                        (2012)

   (a) The white man   (b) Mr. President

   (c) nobody   (d) none of the above

21. In a one-storey pink house, there was a pink person, a pink cat, a pink fish, a pink computer, a pink chair, a pink table, a pink telephone, a pink shower– everything was pink! What color were the stairs?

   (a) Pink   (b) green

   (c) white   (d) no stairs

22. What has hands but cannot clap?

   (a) two left hands   (b) a clock

   (c) monkeys   (d) none of the above

23. Train A leaves from Delhi, heading towards Pune at 120 km/h. Three hours later, train B leaves Pune heading towards Delhi at 180 km/h. Assume there's exactly 6000 kilometers between Pune and Delhi. When they meet, which train is closer to Delhi? **(Tricky, 2013)**

   (a) A   (b) B

   (c) Both   (d) None of the bove

24. If there are 3 apples and you take away 2, how many do you have?

   (a) 3   (b) 2

   (c) 5   (d) 7

25. Who is silent in the parliament?

   (a) The speaker

   (b) Mr. Prime minister

   (c) Letter A

   (d) None of the above

26. My new book is in a completely different __________ to what I usually read.   **(2019)**

   (a) practice   (b) code

   (c) genre   (d) mode

LEVEL 2

DIRECTIONS (Qs. 1-18) : *In each of the following questions, one or two statements are given, followed by two conclusions I and II. You have to consider the two statements to be true, even if they seem to be at variance from commonly known facts. You have to decide which of the given conclusions, if any, follow from the given statements.*

1. **Statements:** The best evidence of India's glorious past is the growing popularity of Ayurvedic medicines in the West.
   Conclusions:
   I. Ayurvedic medicines are not popular in India.
   II. Allopathic medicines are not popular in India.
   (a) Only I follows
   (b) Only II follows
   (c) Both I and II follow
   (d) Neither I nor II follows

2. **Statements:** Some dogs bark. All dogs bite.
   Conclusions:
   I. Those dogs who do not bark, also bite
   II. Those dogs who do not bark, not necessarily bite.
   (a) Only I follows
   (b) Only II follows
   (c) Either I or II follows
   (d) Neither I nor II follows

3. **Statements:** A room with flowers looks beautiful. **(2012)**
   Conclusions:
   I. Flowers are grown for decoration of rooms.
   II. Rooms without flowers look ugly.
   (a) Only conclusion I follows
   (b) Only conclusion II follows
   (c) Both conclusions I and II follow.
   (d) Neither conclusion I nor conclusion II follows

4. All students are boys. No boy is dull.
   Conclusions:
   I. There are no girls in the class.
   II. No student is dull.
   (a) Only conclusion I follows
   (b) Only conclusion II follows
   (c) Both conclusions I and II follow
   (d) Neither conclusion I nor conclusion II follows

5. **Statements:**
   1. All children are students.
   2. All students are players.
   Conclusions:
   I. All cricketers are students.
   II. All children are players.
   (a) Only conclusion I follows
   (b) Only conclusion II follows
   (c) Both conclusions I and II follow.
   (d) Neither conclusion I nor II follows.

6. **Statements:** **(2013)**
   1. No teacher comes to the school on a bicycle.
   2. Anand comes to the school on a bicycle.
   Conclusions:
   I. Anand is not a teacher.
   II. Anand is a student.
   (a) Conclusion I alone can be drawn.
   (b) Conclusion II alone can be drawn.
   (c) Both conclusions can be drawn.
   (d) Both conclusions can not be drawn.

7. **Statements:** Teaching is an art. Drawing is also an art. **(2014)**
   Conclusions:
   I. All artists are teachers.
   II. All artists know how to draw pictures.
   (a) Only conclusion I follows.
   (b) Only conclusion II follows.
   (c) Neither conclusion I nor II follows.
   (d) Both conclusions I and II follow.

8. **Statement:** Tension is detrimental to physical and mental health. **(2016)**
   Conclusions:
   I. To be healthy one should be free from tension.
   II. Mental health depends upon the tension one experiences.
   (a) Only I follows
   (b) Only II follows
   (c) Neither I nor II follows
   (d) Both I and II follow

9. **Statement:** Religious-minded and God-fearing people will not cheat.   **(2013)**
   Conclusions:
   I.   Those who cheat are atheists.
   II.   Religion nurtures virtues.
   (a)   Only I follows
   (b)   Only II follows
   (c)   Both I and II follow
   (d)   Neither I nor II follows

10. **Statement:** India is a multilingual country. Hindi is the national language of India.
    Conclusions:
    I.   All Indians should learn many languages.
    II.   To be an Indian one needs to learn Hindi.
    (a)   Only I follows
    (b)   Only II follows
    (c)   Neither I nor II follows
    (d)   Both I and II follow

11. **Statements:**
    1.   Some human creatures are angels.
    2.   All doctors are angels.
    Conclusions:
    I.   Some human creatures are doctors.
    II.   Some doctors are humane creatures.
    (a)   Only I follows
    (b)   Only II follows
    (c)   Either I or II follows
    (d)   Neither I nor II follows

12. **Statement:** Many people feel nervous when they talk before a group.   **(2015)**
    Conclusions:
    I.   Many people can talk confidently before a group.
    II.   Very few people can talk confidently before a group.
    (a)   Only I follows
    (b)   Only II follows
    (c)   Neither I nor II follows
    (d)   Both I and II follow

13. **Statement:** No children are voters.
    Conclusions: **(2012)**
    I.   All adults are voters.
    II.   No voters are children.
    (a)   Only conclusion II follows
    (b)   Only conclusion I follows
    (c)   Both conclusions I and II follow
    (d)   Neither conclusion I nor II follows

14. **Statements:**
    1.   Some children like candies.
    2.   All ice-creams are liked by children.
    Conclusions:
    I.   Some children like ice-creams
    II.   Some candies are liked by children.
    (a)   Only conclusion I follows
    (b)   Only   conclusion II follows
    (c)   Neither conclusion I nor II follows
    (d)   Both conclusions I and II follow

15. **Statements:**
    1.   Science teachers do not use plastic bags.
    2.   Plastic bags are not used by some Engineers
    Conclusions: **(2012)**
    I.   All Science teachers are Engineers.
    II.   All Engineers do not use plastic bags.
    (a)   Only conclusion I follows
    (b)   Only conclusion II follows
    (c)   Both conclusions I and II follow
    (d)   Neither conclusion I nor II follows

16. **Statements:**
    1.   All poets are intelligent.
    2.   All singers are intelligent.   **(2013)**
    Conclusions:
    I.   All singers are poets.
    II.   Some intelligent persons are not singers.
    (a)   Only conclusion I follows
    (b)   Only conclusion II follows
    (c)   Either conclusion I or II follows
    (d)   Neither conclusion I nor II follows

17. **Statement:** All philosophers are men. Socrates was a philosopher.   **(2014)**
    Conclusions:
    I.   Socrates was a man.
    II.   Women cannot become philosophers.
    (a)   Only I is valid
    (b)   Only II is valid
    (c)   Both are not valid
    (d)   Both are valid

18. **Statements:**
    1.   All virtuous persons are happy.
    2.   No unhappy person is virtuous.   **(2016)**
    Conclusions:
    I.   Happiness is related to virtue.
    II.   Unhappy person is not virtuous.
    (a)   Only I follows
    (b)   Only II follows
    (c)   Neither I nor II follows
    (d)   Both I and II follow

DIRECTIONS (Qs. 19-25) : *Read the questions and choose the correct option to answer.*

19. A donkey behind another donkey
    I'm behind that second donkey
    But there is a whole nation behind me
    It is a murder you can describe in a word.
    (a) Assassination   (b) murder   **(2014)**
    (c) homicide   (d) pantomime

20. A man is sitting in a pub feeling rather poor. He sees the man next to him pull a wad of ₹500 notes out of his wallet.

    He turns to the rich man and says to him,

    'I have an amazing talent; I know almost every song that has ever existed.'

    The rich man laughs.

    The poor man says, 'I am willing to bet you all the money you have in your wallet that I can sing a genuine song with a lady's name of your choice in it.'

    The rich man laughs again and says, 'OK, how about my daughter's name, Janani Shanti Priya?'

    The rich man goes home poor. The poor man goes home rich.

What song did he sing?   **(Tricky)**
(a) hasta la vista   (b) Happy Birthday
(c) National Anthem   (d) None of the above

21. I have keys but no locks. I have a space but no room. You can enter, but can't go outside. What am I?
    (a) Keychain   (b) key stand
    (c) Keyboard   (d) none of the above

22. My first is often at the front door.
    My second is found in the cereal family.
    My third is what most people want.
    My whole is one of the United States.
    What am I?
    (a) Corn bread   (b) Matrimony
    (c) amazon   (d) None of the above

23. Marten is a butcher. He is 5'10" tall. What does he weigh?   **(Tricky, 2014)**
    (a) 89 kgs
    (b) meat
    (c) not enough information
    (d) none of the above

24. A plane crashes on the border of India and Nepal. Where do they bury the survivors?
    (a) India   (b) Nepal
    (c) Graves   (d) none is buried

HINTS & EXPLANATIONS

LEVEL - 1

1. **(d)** According to the statement, 80% of the total runs were made by spinners. So, I does not follow. Nothing about the opening batsmen is mentioned in the statement. So, II also does not follow.

2. **(a)** Clearly, I directly follows from the given statement. Also, it is mentioned that old ideas are replaced by new ones, as thinking changes with the progressing time. So, II does not follow.

3. **(b)** The fact given in I is quite contrary to the given statement. So, I does not follow. II mentions the direct implications of the state discussed in the statement. Thus, II follows.

4. **(d)** The statement concentrates on the increasing viewership of TV. and does not stress either on increasing the readership of newspapers or making studies regarding the same. So, neither I nor II follows.

5. **(b)** Clearly, nothing about 'other things' is mentioned in the statement. So, I does not follow, Also, since it is mentioned that programmes and magazines for women are stuffed with kitchen recipes and other household hints, it means that women have special interest in these areas. So, II follows.

6. **(b)** According to the statement, sea transport is cheaper than road transport in the case of route from Bombay to Jafra, not in all the cases. So, conclusion I does not follow. The statement stresses on the saving of fuel. So, conclusion II follows.

7. **(d)** The manager might have humiliated Sachin not because of his dislike but on account of certain negligence or mistake on his part. So, I does not follow. Also, nothing about Sachin's rapport with his colleagues can be deduced from the statement. So, II also does not follow.

8. **(d)** According to the statement, National Aluminium Company has moved India from a position of shortage in the past to self-sufficiency in the present. This means that previously, India had to import aluminium. So, I follows. Also, it can be deduced that if production increases at the same rate, India can export it in future. So, II also follows.

9. **(b)** The statement talks of jade plants only and not 'all plants with thick leaves'. So, I does not follow. Also, since jade plants require little water, so they can be grown in places where water is not in abundance. So, II follows.

10. **(d)** The slogan given in the statement is definitely a catchy one which indicates that catchy slogans do attract people. So, I does not follow. Nothing about people's preference for colours can be deduced from the statement. Thus, II also does not follow.

11. **(a)** Clearly, I directly follows from the statement while II cannot be deduced from it.

12. **(d)** Clearly, the information has been given beforehand so that the residents can collect water on the previous day and use less water on Friday. So, both I and II follow.

13. **(d)** The statement clearly implies that it is easier to say than done and what people say is different from what they do. So, both I and II follow.

14. **(b)** Whether the national norm is appropriate or not cannot be said. So, I does not follow. However, more number of beds per thousand population are available in the state. So, II follows.

15. (d) Neither the poor nor the rich, but only the role of money in politics is being talked about in the statement. So, neither I nor II follows.

16. (d) The availability of vegetables is not mentioned in the given statement. So, I does not follow Also, II is not directly related to the statement and so it also does not follow.

17. (d) Since the accident has caused concern, it must be fatal. So, I follows. The use of the word 'again' in the statement justifies the fact mentioned in II. So, II also follows.

18. (c) A stapler

19. (c) A deck of cards has 13 hearts

20. (b) The President of the United States lives in the White House.

21. (d) There weren't any stairs; it was a one storey house

22. (b) A clock.

23. (c) Both trains would be at the same spot when they meet therefore they are both equally close to Delhi.

24. (b) If you take 2 apples, than you have of course 2.

25. (c) letter 'a'

26. (c) genre

LEVEL - 2

1. (d) 2. (a) 3. (d) 4. (c) 5. (b)
6. (a) 7. (b) 8. (d) 9. (b)
10. (c)
11. (d) 12. (d) 13. (b)
14. (c)
15. (d)
16. (b)
17. (d)
18. (d)
19. (a) Assassination
20. (b) Happy birthday!
21. (c) Keyboard
22. (b) Matrimony (mat rye money). This is certainly a united state!
23. (b) meat
24. (d) none is buried - the survivors are alive, we don't burry the people who are alive.

CHAPTER 14

WRITING SKILLS

Grammar, vocabulary and correct spelling are essential tools in written communication. In this chapter, we shall learn the following forms of written communication.

* Paragraph writing

* Story writing

* Notice writing

* Letter writing

* Message writing

* Report writing

* Diary entry

The reader will comprehend according to the content presented and errors are likely to lead them to misinterpretation. Therefore, it is essential to pen the thoughts coherently.

PARAGRAPH WRITING

Paragraph writing is a base for any other form of writing, you may indulge in (story, essay, letter, etc.) It contains all the ideas intended to be presented. The length of the paragraph depends on the purpose of writing. For instance, when writing an essay - a paragraph should not exceed 3-5 sentences. Similarly, when writing a report, it could be up to 3 or 4 sentences. A paragraph is used to break the ideas and control the flow of writing.

A good paragraph contains the following:

1. One Main Idea

2. Topic Sentence

3. 5-7 Sentences

4. Closing Sentence

5. No errors related to grammar, spelling and punctuation

A Good Paragraph

Example   topic sentence

There are several serious health hazards directly linked to smoking. The link between smoking and cancer is well known. As well smoking is linked to other lung diseases like emphysema and bronchitis. Smokers also have a greater risk of heart disease later in life. This is evidenced in recent court cases in the USA where smokers have been awarded damages from tobacco companies. Further, there is substantial research that even passive smoking can have long term effects on health. Clearly smoking is a dangerous habit and should be avoided.

supporting sentences   concluding sentence

EXAMPLE PARAGRAPH

The festival of Christmas undoubtedly holds a great significance across the world, especially for those who follow Christianity. Everyone, particularly children, eagerly wait for the, festival as they receive loads of gifts, sweets and surprises on this day. Christmas, an annual festival is celebrated on 25th of December, in the honour of Jesus Christ who taught the path of peace and harmony to people. This is an occasion for people to meet their loved ones, leave behind all their worries and come together for merry-making. It is declared a gazetted holiday in India and the celebration of this festival is highly noticeable at places where Christians are in majority. People exchange sweets with each other; the entire city gets illuminated with star like lights. People decorate their houses, including their surroundings and some follow the native rituals by displaying clay figures and decorating huge Christmas trees, which are usually an evergreen conifer such as fir, pine or spruce. Christmas tree and Santa Clause are an indispensable part of this festival.

STORY WRITING

Story writing is a creative form of expression. It is purely based on imagination. A story that is meant to be read in a single sitting needs to be brief. To write a good story, you need to have a clear plot in your mind.

The main elements of the story include:

* Setting - Where is the story taking place?

* Plot - The sequence of events

* Conflict - The opposition of forces connecting the events

* Climax – The turning point of the story

* Theme - The central idea of the story

To help you start given below is a worksheet. Once you fill the worksheet, use the details and weave your story together.

Elements of a Story

Name: _______________________

PLOT
What happens in the story?

____

____

____

____

CHARACTERS	THE STORY	SETTING
Name and Describe	Title	Where and When?
	Author	

PROBLEM
Describe the problem in the story.

____

____

____

____

____

SOLUTION
Describe how the problem is solved.

____

____

____

____

____

THE FROGS' RACE
By Dulce Rodrigues
One day, a group of frogs decided to make a race and get to the top of a high tower.

A lot of people came to see them and give them their support, but the race had just begun and everybody was already saying that the frogs would not get there: "It doesn't make any sense going on! You'll never reach the top of the tower! "

Little by little, the frogs felt disappointed and discouraged, except for one of them that continued to run. And everybody cried out: "Give up! Give up! You'll never get to the top!" Listening repeatedly to these negative words led the frogs to abandon the race after all, except for the one frog that, despite what people were saying, and though alone and with great pain, continued to run and finally reached the top.

Deeply astonished, the other frogs wanted to know how she had managed to do it. They came to her and asked her what her secret was.

And it was then that they found out that… she was deaf!

Take a healthy life attitude: Never listen to people who are negative in their intentions. Be deaf to discouraging words and always follow your dreams to the end.

NOTICE WRITING

Let's assume that you lost your watch on the school playground. What can you do to find your watch?

In this situation, you can display a notice on the school notice board to request other students to return it to you. Notices are generally pasted, published or clipped at a place where many interested people can view it easily and get the required information. You might have seen notices in your school about the exam dates, essay competition, change in syllabus or educational tour.

Notices are generally pasted, published or clipped at a place where many interested people can view it easily and get the required information. This place can be a reception desk of an office, bank, court, school, websites of govt. department or companies, a column of a newspaper or any place where people come frequently.

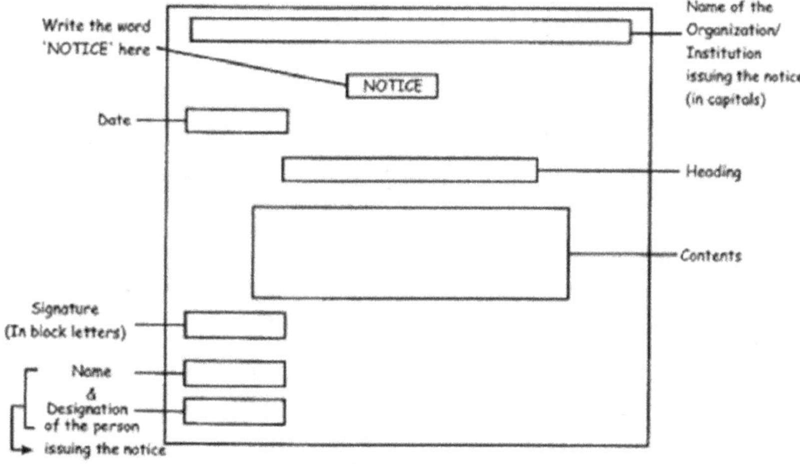

Sample notice is given below.

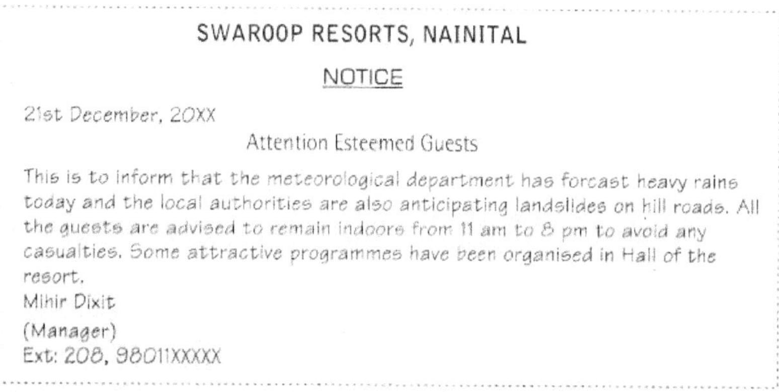

LETTER WRITING

In the age of digital world, though we write more e-mails and send text messages, we still need to write letters some times. Letters of complaint, job applications, thank you letters, letters requesting changes or making suggestions.

There are two types of letters.

* Formal letters
* Informal letters

Formal Letter:

Formal letters are written to banks, government officials, editor of a newspaper or magazine, principal, etc,. There are certain rules to be followed while writing a formal letter.

The tone of a formal letter is serious and most of the sentences add specific meaning to the writing. The format of a formal letter is standard and applicable to all.

A formal letter comprises of the following elements.

* Address (Sender's/Receiver's)
* Date
* Salutation
* Subject
* Body Text
* Closing

1) *Address*

Senders' Address: It should be written on the left-hand corner and should include your street address, city, state, pin code.

EXAMPLE

B-45, Anupam Apartments

Civil Lines, Pitampura

New Delhi, 110015

October 20, 2018

Receiver's Address – Mention the recipient's address just below the date.

2) *Date and Salutation*

Date: The date should be placed just below the sender's address with a line gap.

Salutation: "Dear Sir/Madam" suffices, if you know the name of the person, address him/her directly. Make sure that you address them formally using "Rev.", "Dr.", "Mr.", "Mrs.", or "Ms.", and include their full name.

EXAMPLE

Dear Mr. Amir Ali

3) *Subject and Body*

Subject – Write the subject of the letter, keep it brief and if possible, in one line only.

Body Text – Organise the writing into paragraphs. The writing should include sophisticated vocabulary, standard spellings and punctuation.

The first paragraph should be short and to the point conveying the purpose of the letter.

The second paragraph needs to give the details, explaining the reason for writing the letter.

The final paragraph should talk about the action that the recipient is expected to take.

4) *Closing*

Sign off with appropriate closing statement followed by your signature and full name. The most preferred salutations include:

Yours Faithfully

Yours Sincerely

EXAMPLE

Write a letter to your civic body, asking permission to send garbage trucks frequently in your residential area.

6C, Kaveri Apartments

West Maredpally, Secunderabad

Telangana, 500025

November 22, 2017

The Municipal Corporation

Secunderabad, 500025

Telangana

Dear Sir

Subject: Request letter to send garbage trucks.

I live in West Maredpally. For the past 1 year, I have been complaining about the filthy roads of this area, but every time my efforts goes down the drain as the concerned department fails to take any action. The garbage trucks have become an out of the ordinary thing in this area as they seldom arrive.

The situation is getting worse day by day as now not only the beauty of the landscape but the health of the residents is getting affected. The mound of garbage serves as a breeder of mosquitoes. The foul smell filled in the air around, is solely responsible for the headache and nausea reported by the residents. People living on the ground floor are majorly affected as the heaps of garbage lie just outside their kitchens or living areas because of which children and aged people find it hard to breathe.

The best one can do in this regard is making the garbage trucks more frequent in this area, from thrice a month to daily. It will take time for this area to go back to what it was.

Therefore, I would request the authorities to take an intense and long-lasting step for the upliftment of this area.

I request you, sir, to kindly do the needful.

Yours Faithfully

Ms Anuradha Singh

Informal letter:

Informal letters are personal letters, written to friends and relatives.

An informal letter comprises of the following elements.

* Address (Personal/Recipient's)
* Date
* Salutation/Greeting
* Beginning
* Main Content
* Conclusion
* Closing

1.) *Address*

Write your address on the top right corner and don't miss out on the pin code.

EXAMPLE

B,38 Agnipath Apartments

Allahabad, Uttar Pradesh, 211001

India

November 22, 2017

Dear Radhika

2.) Date

It is very important that you mention the date in correct format while writing a letter on the right hand side, just below your address. The correct format is mentioned below.

September 19, 2017

3.) Salutation

'Dear' is the most commonly used salutation. Write the first name of the recipient, followed by a comma after the name; don't write 'Dear friend' but always write a name. Since it's an informal letter, you may use nicknames that are used to address the person by you personally.

EXAMPLE

- Dear Shivani
- Dearest Dad

4.) *Beginning*

Unlike formal letters, the beginning of an informal letter is friendly. It always contains questions relating to the receiver's well-being as well as that of those around. The most commonly used ones include:

- How are you?
- How have you been?
- How is life treating you?
- I hope you are doing well

5.) *Body*

It is the soul of the letter. You may write all the details regarding the purpose of your writing.

6.) *Closing*

Once you have conveyed your message, summarise the matter and end your letter using a nice and warm closing statement like the following:

- I am looking forward to seeing you.
- I am looking forward to hearing from you.
- I can't wait to see you soon.

Sign off from writing using a nice phrase and then just below that write your name.

EXAMPLE

Lots of love

Anuradha Singh

EXAMPLE

Write a letter to your younger brother advising him on saving money and being financially aware.

B38 Agnipath Apartments

Allahabad, Uttar Pradesh, 211001.

India

November 22, 2017

Dear Rakesh

How are you? I hope you are doing fine; mother and father are also doing well. It's been a while since we got in touch so I finally decided to write you a letter. You seem to be having such a great time in your new school and city that you chose to stay back in school even during vacations.

Yesterday father was upset after you called. He didn't say a word but I could sense how disappointed he was! Not like an elder sister but as a friend I would advise you to check on your expenses. I understand the enthusiasm of being all by oneself in a new city, yet we have to be thoughtful.

Parents are willingly paying for all the expenses as they don't want you to lose any opportunity and experience but it is you who should be taking care of how wisely the money is used. Chalk out a list of your daily expenses and strike out all the unnecessary ones. Try to stick by the list for a week or so, gradually you will be able to cut down the extras.

As they say "a penny saved is a penny earned", therefore, handle the money given to you with maturity and yet continue to live life king size as the best things in life are free. At the end, I would like to wish you all the luck with your studies and other endeavours. We all miss you badly so try to come as we all can't wait to see you.

Yours Loving
Sunita

MESSAGE WRITING

It is a method of conveying information in a short, simple and clear manner. It is usually written in the absence of the person concerned.

A message should always contain the following details:

* Who called
* Why did the person call
* Follow up action required

A sample format is given below.

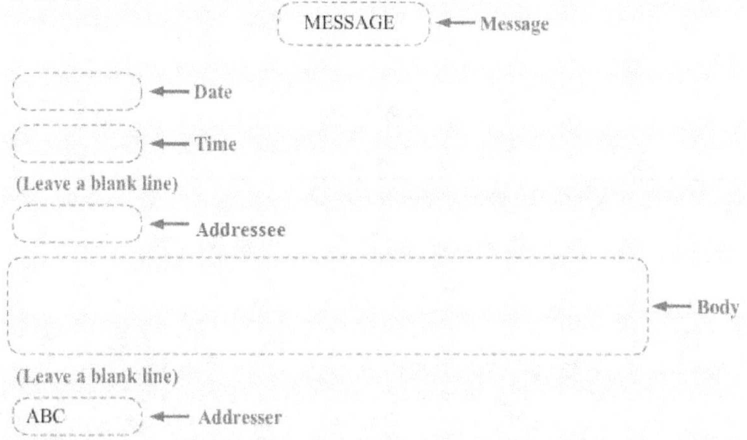

Look at the example given.

Anita had been cleaning up the back yard as instructed by her mother who had gone to the gym. While she was busy cleaning up, she got a call from one of her mother's friend, Mrs. Sherawat. She called to inform her mother about the slight change in their plan of having a meeting in the evening; instead they would now have the meeting in the next day morning at 7.30. After finishing her work, Anita has to go for her dance class. So, she decided to leave a message for her mom. Write the message in not more than 50 words.

MESSAGE
24th May 2018
12 : 30 PM
Mother,
While cleaning the backyard, I received a phone call from your friend, Mrs. Sherawat. She informed me that your meeting with her, scheduled for today evening, is now postponed for tomorrow morning 7 : 30. I will go to my dance classes after I have finished cleaning the backyard.
Anita

REPORT WRITING

A report is a short account of an event which has taken place in the past or recent past. It helps in keeping a record of the important events that happen in the world around us.

A report gives us first-hand experience of an event. It states what happened, along with opinions and ideas of the writer.

Different kinds of reports are: **news reports, medical reports, literary reports** etc.

> **Please note:** A report is a formal piece of writing.

Points to Remember While Writing a Report

* Mention the place, date, time and other important facts about the event.
* Include information given by people present at the site of the event.
* Write the name of the reporter.
* Give your report a suitable heading.
* Write in past tense.
* Use indirect speech and passive voice.
* Write in a less formal tone and more descriptive manner while writing a report for a school magazine.

Format of Report Writing

<table>
<tr><td colspan="3" align="center">Title:</td></tr>
<tr><td>Date:</td><td></td><td align="right">By______________</td></tr>
<tr><td colspan="3" align="center">**Content**</td></tr>
</table>

Sample report: Report a car crash that happened on your street.

Horrible Car Crash Leaves Three Injured

By – Ritu Sharma

10.10. 2012

At 9 p.m. yesterday, when many people were out on the streets for their walk after dinner, the driver of a black sedan lost control of the car, injuring three people and a dog. This incident happened in the Rajiv Nagar area of North Delhi. Witnesses said that they saw the car coming towards them at really fast speed. Many saved themselves by moving away from the road. But a few were not able to do so. Two men and one woman, along with her dog, were injured badly. Mr. Sharma, one of the victims, broke his arm, while Mr. Nautiyal and Miss. Kapoor faced injuries on their legs and back respectively. Miss Kapoor's dog broke its leg too. This incident has shaken the residents of Rajiv Nagar. A few of them said that they don't feel safe anymore. The driver, who was the main accused of this accident, was found to be under the influence of alcohol. This incident again reminds us how dangerous it is to drink and drive. Hopefully, this will be a reminder to many who do not follow the traffic laws.

DIARY ENTRY

Diary writing is a hobby where people write about their everyday life in a diary. It records a person's day to day events, observations, feelings or a list of their personal activities. It is an informal kind of writing.

Old diaries have proven to be very helpful in telling us about the past. By reading old diaries, we can learn about the lifestyle of people who lived in those times. One of the most famous diaries is **Anne Frank's- Diary of a Young Girl**. This diary told the sad tale of a young girl, Anne Frank, who lived during the world war.

It is a good habit to write a page or two in your diary every day. Here is how you can do it.

Steps of Diary Writing

1. Begin the entry with a general statement describing the day or momentary feelings.

2. In the body, you may discuss an event, your feelings towards it, how it is likely to affect your future plans etc.

3. Conclude with final remark and future course of action.

Format and Sample Diary Writing

<table>
<tr><td>

12 September, 2016 _______________ | Date |

Monday ____________ | Day |

9:00 a.m. ____________ | Time |

Dear Diary, ____________ | Opening |

</td></tr>
<tr><td>

I feel so tired today. Yesterday was a busy day for all of us. We were packing our clothes and other things from morning till night. I don't want to leave this house. It feels that I am leaving a part of myself here. I don't know if the new city will be as good as this one. And I am too scared to think about my new school. I will miss my friends a lot, especially Tina. I hope to see her again soon.Now, I will go and help mummy. She is packing all my toys and I don't want to leave even a single one here.

</td></tr>
<tr><td>

Charu ←— | Writers Name |

</td></tr>
</table>

LEVEL 1

1. **The body of a letter to the Editor is given with four blanks I, II, III and IV which should be filled by statements P, Q, R and S. Choose your answer in the correct order from the following options.**
   Through the column of your esteemed newspaper _______I _______________of terrorism. Present world has been facing many problems, ________II _______________. Almost everyday there is a blast or attack taking place all over the world. People are afraid of coming out of their houses. Once they come out, they don't know whether they will be return back safely or not. It is a big challenge in front of us. _______________III ___________.
   I hope that the governments and the civilized people of the world will work collectively ___________IV _____________ so that this beautiful world can be made much safer place to live in.
   Yours faithfully
   Smith
   P: We need to address its root cause to eradicate it
   Q: to solved this problem
   R: I would like to express my views on the issue
   S: terrorism is one of them
   I II III IV
   (a) S R Q P   (b) R S P Q
   (c) P S R Q   (d) Q R P S   **(2014)**

2. **A notice is given with four blanks I, II, III and IV which should be filled by the statements given as P, Q, R and S. This notice is for the school notice board to inform the students about the blood donation camp that will be organised at the school. Choose your answer from the given options.**
   ABC School   16th May, 2018

   NOTICE
   <u>Blood Donation Camp</u>

   It is _______________ I ___________ that our school is going to organise a blood donation camp _________II ___________ as per the following schedule.
   Date : 30th May, 2018
   Time : 8 AM to 2 PM
   Venue: __________ III __________
   Age group: 18 years and above
   Students are requested ___________ IV ___________ to come forward and donate the blood for noble cause.
   Rakesh
Science Secretary

   P: to mobilise their parents and the people in their neighbourhoods
   Q: hereby informed
   R: With the help of Red Cross Society of India
   S: School Auditorium
   I   II   III   IV
   (a) S R Q P   (b) R P Q S
   (c) P S R Q   (d) Q R S P

DIRECTIONS (Qs. 3-9) : Read the following telephonic conversation and complete the message with the help of the options given below.

Arya : Hello ! Is it 2345687?

Namrata : Yes, Who is calling please?

Arya : I am Arya. Could I speak to Malini?

Namrata : I am sorry; She has just gone out. I am Namrata, her sister. Anything important?

Arya : Yes, she has my Maths Project File and I have to submit it to the teacher tomorrow. Please ask her to bring it to school positively.

Namrata : I am going out of station just now, but I will make sure that she gets your message.

Arya : Thank you very much.

Namrata : You are welcome.   **(2015)**

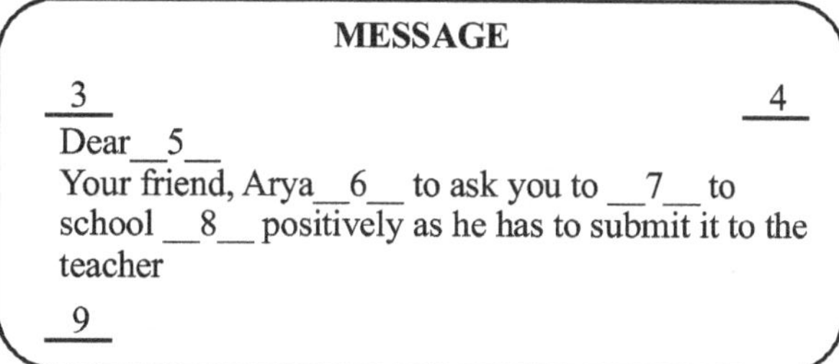

3. (a) 27th April, 20XX
    (b) 5 : 30 P.M.
    (c) 27. 01.
    (d) 01 - 05 - 20XX

4. (a) Thursday
    (b) 5 : 30 P.M.
    (c) 27th April, 20XX
    (d) None of these

5. (a) Namrata   (b) Arya
    (c) Teacher   (d) Malini

6. (a) is calling   (b) called up
    (c) was calling   (d) has been called

7. (a) take his Maths Project File
    (b) for taking his Maths Project File
    (c) to come to school positively
    (d) to submit the Project File

8. (a) yesterday   (b) the following
    (c) tomorrow   (d) the previous day

9. (a) Arya   (b) Malini
    (c) Namrata   (d) Yours affectionately

10. A diary entry may not include

     (a) date

     (b) salutation

     (c) Complementary closing

     (d) signature

11. As a member of the NSS group of your school, write a report for your school magazine on a recently organised blood donation camp. You are Kritika.

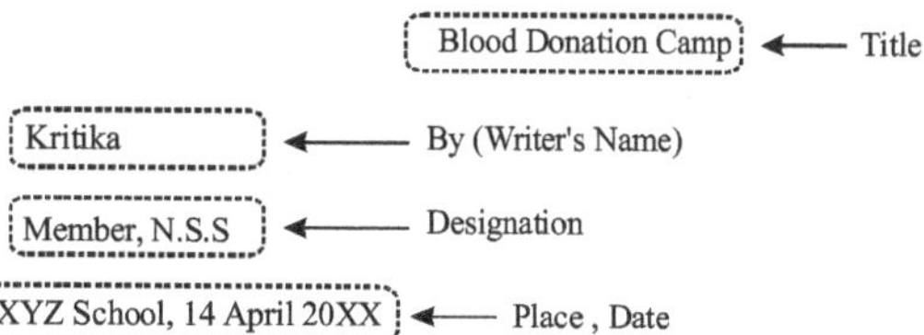

> A blood donation camp was organised on Oct 13, 20XX. The activites of the camp were carried out by the N.S.S wing of the school and the 'Blood of India' blood bank. The chief guest for this occasion was the noted senior doctor of Apollo Hopital, Mr. Bhatt. He inaugurated the event by donating blood himself. For a week before the camp, special efforts were put in to create awareness. This encouraged people to donate blood without any apprehension. Consequently, the number of blood donors surpassed the estimated number. 'Blood of India' appointed ten doctors for the event. They worked throughout the day to collect blood. The donors were given juice and fruits after the donation. Later, the chief guest presented the appreciation certificates to the N.S.S volunteers. He congratulated this noble event.

← Body

Given here is an example of

(a) letter
(b) message
(c) report
(d) diary entry

DIRECTIONS (Qs. 12-15) : *Read the following diary entry and answer the questions that follow. Choose the answers from the options given below.*

April 29, 2018

Dear Diary,

Me and my family were really very saddened by the news. Later today an earthquake hit the city and there were screams of people dying. We knew we weren't alone....As we were running for our lives, we saw our friends getting crushed under bookshelves. We have been trained to save ourselves in an incident of an earthquake. By the time it got over it had killed more than 10,000 people. Luckily, we received aids from many countries to help with the shock. I hope that there are no further shocks!

12. What is an earthquake?   **(2013)**

    (a) It is the vibration caused by rocks breaking under pressure

    (b) It is something related to changing weather phenomena.

    (c) It is the movement of earth away from the rest of the planets.

    (d) It is earth quacking for survival.

13. What among the following is not a protective measures during an earthquake?

    (a) Cover you head and neck under a table.

    (b) Come out of the building and go in an open area like a park, away from the buildings.

    (c) Hold on to your shelter till the tremor stops.

    (d) Lock yourself in a room.

14. In the last few years, the incidents of earthquakes have risen, what do you think can be a reason for it?

    (a) Changing weather conditions

    (b) Excessive drilling of earth for oil and gas extraction.

    (c) Rising level of pollution.

    (d) Deforestation.

15. Find out the word from the above diary entry that means 'convulsion'.

    (a) Earthquake   (b) Saddened

    (c) Crushed   (d) Incident

16. Anil "Since they've won the lottery they've stopped talking to us."   **(2018)**
    (a) They need to get their heats around it

    (b) All the money has gone to their head

    (c) yeah they have a price on their heads

    (d) They were never right in the head.

17. Son : Mum, where are the scissors?   **(2019)**
    Mom : I couldn't say. I scarched _______ for them yesterday.
    (a) in and over   (b) near and far

    (c) high and fow   (d) left and east

LEVEL 2

1. **The body of a letter to the Editor is given with four blanks I, II, III, and IV which should be filled by statements P, Q, R and S. Choose your answer from the given options.**

    ___________ I ______________ I would like to express my views on the issue of law and order problem in our area. The crime graph in our area has been increasing day by day. __________ II __________ have been rapidly increasing. We are feeling insecure in our own houses. We are confused and terrified over the prevailing situation. _________III _________ but no action has been taken yet. Therefore, on the behalf of all the residents I am requesting you to pay attention_____________IV__________.

    Yours faithfully
Sushma

    P: Incidents like chain snatching, eve teasing, robbery, theft, etc.
    Q: through the column of your esteemed newspaper
    R: We have already complained to the concerned authorities
    S: towards our problem so that law and order can be maintained properly.
    I II III IV
    (a) S R Q P   (b) R P Q S   (c) Q P R S   (d) Q R P S

2. **A notice is given with four blanks I, II, III and IV which should be filled by the statements given as P, Q, R and S. This notice is for the school notice board to inform the students about Annual Day celebration. Choose your answer from the given options.**   **(2015)**

    ABC School   16th Oct, 2013

    Notice
Annual Day Celebration

    It is __________________ I ______________ that our school is going to celebrate its annual day __________ II ______________.

    Date: 25th April, 2018
    Time : 4 PM to 6 PM
    Venue : School Auditorium
    Chief Guest : Governor
    You all _________ III __________.
    Please_________ IV __________.

    Monica
Cultural Secretary

    P : collect your pass from the undersigned
    Q : hereby informed
    R : are cordially invited
    S : as per schedule
    I II III IV
    (a) S R Q P   (b) R P Q S   (c)   P S R Q   (d)   Q S R P

DIRECTIONS (Qs. 3-10) : *Choose the most appropriate option.*

3. An informal letter should _________ contain the subject line.
   - (a) sometimes
   - (b) always
   - (c) compulsorily
   - (d) never

4. For a formal letter, arrange the following in the correct sequence:
   - (A) Recipient's address
   - (B) Sender's address
   - (C) Date
   - (D) Salutation
   - (a) A-B-C-D
   - (b) A-D-C-B
   - (c) B-C-A-D
   - (d) A-C-B-D

5. In a formal letter, the salutation is: "Dear Sir" What would be the closing in such a letter?
   - (a) Yours sincerely
   - (b) Yours truly
   - (c) Yours faithfully
   - (d) Yours only

6. Where is a greeting positioned in a formal letter? **(Tricky)**
   - (a) Top centre
   - (b) Bottom centre
   - (c) Bottom left corner
   - (d) None of the above

7. In the body of a formal letter, what should be the content of the first few lines? **(2014)**
   - (a) Summary of the letter
   - (b) Introduction and reason for writing
   - (c) Detailed explanation
   - (d) None of the above

8. A short note taken on a person's behalf
   - (a) letter
   - (b) notice
   - (c) report
   - (d) message

9. A writing which is personal and kept for personal record or reference –
   - (a) letter
   - (b) diary entry
   - (c) message
   - (d) notice

10. A formal communication –
    - (a) letter
    - (b) message
    - (c) report
    - (d) diary entry

DIRECTIONS (Qs. 11-14) : *Read the following letter and answer the questions that follow.*

(2016)

The Principal

St. Peters School

M.G Road,

Delhi

15 May 2015

Dear Sir,

Sub : Coaching Classes for hockey and cricket.

My name is Arun Kumar. I study in Class IX A and I am the Sports Captain of the school. As you know, our hockey and cricket teams have been selected to play the inter-state tournaments in the month of July. I feel that both our teams stand a very good chance of winning the tournaments. However, the players feel that if we discontinue practice during the holidays, our performance may be affected adversely.

Therefore, I request you on behalf of the players, to arrange for special coaching during the summer vacation for both hockey and cricket. I am happy to inform you that we have already obtained permission from Mr. More, the Head of Sports, to hold practice sessions and he has promised to supervise the classes personally. I sincerely hope you will consider my request.

Yours faithfully,

Arun Kumar

Sports Captain

Encl. Letter of permission.

11. State which of these statements is false?

    (a) This letter is addressed to the school principal.

    (b) The two teams have been selected to inter-state tournaments.

    (c) The Dean of Sports has given permission to hold practice sessions.

    (d) The Sports Captain wants the teams to practice during the vacations also.

12. Find out the word that has the same meaning as 'earnest'.

    (a) Adverse   (b) Sincerely

    (c) Permission   (d) Request

13. Sports or games are an essential aspect of growth. How?

    (a) They help in physical and mental development of a person

    (b) They teach you sportsmanship.

    (c) They help you learn team spirit or joint responsibility.

    (d) All of these.

14. Can you name one of the greatest hockey players that India has produced?

    (a) Milkha Singh

    (b) Dhyan Chand

    (c) Ben Johnson

    (d) Giani Singh

15. Salesgirl : " _________ This is our brand new range.   **(2018)**

    (a) Can I tell you to try this? It's new

    (b) Do you have one minute. Try this

    (c) Might I suggest you try this new model, sir?

    (d) You can try this if you want, your choice.

16. Pallavi : "Is it a difficult game?"   **(2018)**

    (a) There's nothing to it

    (b) So fat, so good

    (c) Yes, very much so

    (d) Mmm, that figures

17. Given below is a notice with four blanks. Fill those blanks with the options provided in P, Q, R and S to make it a sensible one.

    5th January, 2022   **(2022)**

    Notice

    Debate Competition

    All the students are hereby informed that I has organized an interschool debate competition on 15th January, 2022, at 9 am, II . Topic for the III '. Interested candidates can IV to the undersigne.

    P: the debating society of our school

    Q: give their names

    R: debate is 'The importance of Indian army'

    S: at our school auditorium

    (a) PSRQ   (b) QSRP

    (c) RSPQ   (d) SPQR

HINTS & EXPLANATIONS

Level - 1

1.	(b)	2.	(d)
3.	(a)	4.	(b)
5.	(d)	6.	(b)
7.	(a)	8.	(c)
9.	(c)	10.	(c)
11.	(c)		

12. **(a)** An earthquake is a violent shaking of earth's ground as a result of movement within earth's crust.

13. **(d)** During an earthquake there are a few safety measures to be adopted, 1. We must come out of the building to an open area. 2. Sit under a table or get inside a closet.

14. **(b)** It has been proved that excessive drilling of earth to extract minerals is proving to be a major reason for the eruption of earthquakes.

15. **(a)** Earthquake is another word for convulsion that means violent disturbance.

16. **(b)** All the money has gone to their heads

17. **(c)** 'high and low' which means 'everywhere'.

Level - 2

1.	(c)	2.	(d)
3.	(d)	4.	(c)
5.	(c)	6.	(c)
7.	(b)	8.	(d)
9.	(b)	10.	(a)

11. **(c)** It is not the Dean of Sports but the Head of the Sports who has given permission.

12. **(b)** Sincerely means to be earnest or honest.

13. **(d)** Sports helps in the overall development of a person.

14. **(b)** The greatest hockey player that India has produced is Dhyan Chand.

15. **(c)** Might I suggest you try this new model, sir?

16. **(a)** Their's is nothing to it.

17. **(a)**

CHAPTER 15

PARAGRAPH COMPLETION/ ERROR FINDING/ QUESTION TAGS

PARAGRAPH COMPLETION

Paragraph completion has been an important component of the verbal section. For those who have not had any encounter with paragraph completion in the past, it refers to the question type where a paragraph is given and a sentence from the given paragraph is removed (In most of the cases, the last sentence is removed).

All you have to do is to complete the paragraph i.e., you have to choose the option which completes the given paragraph in the best manner from the given options.

Solving Passage Completion questions is all about how much one can comprehend from the given paragraph. The more you understand the paragraph, the easier it becomes for you to solve the question. It becomes easier for you to solve these types of questions if you are a good reader.

Go through the paragraph and try to catch the essence of the paragraph. Figure out what the paragraph is all about. Try to understand the keywords used in the passage.

Some Important Pointers to keep in mind while solving a PC question

There are no pre-defined formulaes to solve Passage Completion type questions. But there are some important points we need to remember while solving them.

(1) Find the essence of the passage

Once you are able to find it, Passage Completion would become an easy affair.

(2) Notice the tone of the passage

Think about it. If an author is being sarcastic in his writing, wouldn't it be logical to choose the option which has sarcasm in it? Remember however that there might be multiple options that comply with the author's tone.

Hence, always keep in mind that Tone is Important but not the only criteria.

(3) Do not pick an option that brings an external idea

Never pick an option which talks about things that are not mentioned in the paragraph. The correct option will be the one which relates itself to the core information mentioned in the paragraph.

(4) Reject the options that are contradictory

Whenever you see an option which contradicts the idea of passage, eliminate it.

(5) Maintain the flow of the paragraph

Always make sure you are maintaining the flow of ideas in the passage. Never pick an option which breaks or suddenly changes the flow to some other direction.

(6) Pay Special Attention to the line before the blank

The line before the blank pays an important role in PC. Sometimes, the correct option is the one which is in agreement with that line. So it would be wise if one also pays close attention to what that line is talking about.

ERROR FINDING (EDITING)

Editing simply means correcting the mistakes you have found. While editing one should look for mistakes and make the text error free. Error correction means looking for grammar, punctuation and spelling mistakes in your writing. These could be mistakes related to subject-verb agreement, sentence fragments, incorrect singular or plurals, etc.

Tips for Editing

* Identify the error/omission keeping in mind the PPACTS rule.

   P – Preposition

   P – Pronoun

   A – Article/determiner

   C – Conjunction

   T – Tense/Verb Forms (singular/plural)

   S – Spelling

* After reading the passage, identify the tense and see whether it is appropriate to the context.
* Check the subject-verb agreement.
* Check the areas where word is missing, in case of omission and check the errors as mentioned above for error correction.

EXAMPLE

1. Edit the following passage, underlining the mistake present in every line, by writing the correct word in the blank space.

My day begins on five O'clock in the morning a) ______

It has been so since the last forty years b) ______

except for the two years of which I was c) ______

very ill. I wake up at the sound of an d) ______

alarm clock bought at 1952. e) ______

From then until today, it has never f) ______

let me down. My routine, however turns topsy-turvy

in holidays when I cannot sleep for ten O'clock. I have g) ______

maintained a fairly regular routine over my working years. h) ______

When I retire on two years' time, I hope I will be i) ______

able to continue this practice.

2. The following passage is incomplete. One word has been omitted in every line against which there is a blank. Indicate the place where the word has to be inserted with a / and write the word in the space provided.

Suresh and his friends planning a trip a) ______

during the summer vacations. While all of them b) ______

keen to get away from the heat, none them were able to suggest which place to visit. c) ______

It only draw of lots which could finally decide the matter. d) ______

They decided on Shimla as it neither too far away nor too crowded e) ______

The date of departure and the duration of their stay still to be decided. f) ______

The announcement of their final exam date sheet still two weeks away. g) ______

Until then, each of them resolved h) ______

collect information about hill station. i) ______

Key to the passages:

1.   (a)   on - at   (b) has - had

      (c)   for - of   (d) at - by

      (e)   at- in   (f) from - since

      (g)   for - till   (h) over - during

      (i)   on - after

2. word before   missing word   word after

word before	missing word	word after
(a) friends	are	planning
(b) them	are	keen
(c) none	of	them
(d) only	was	draw
(e) it	was	neither
(f) stay	is	still
(g) sheet	is	still
(h) them	are	resolved
(i) _	to	collect

QUESTION TAGS

Question tags are the short questions that we put on the end of sentences. We use them to either confirm something we already know or get permission. These are in general used in spoken English.

Positive/negative

If the main part of the sentence is positive, the question tag is negative.

    She is a teacher, isn't she?

    You are hungry, aren't you?

If the main part of the sentence is negative, the question tag is positive.

    You haven't met him, have you?

    She isn't coming, is she?

While using auxiliary verbs the question tag uses the same verb as the main part of the sentence. If this is an auxiliary verb ('*have*', '*be*') then the question tag is made with the auxiliary verb.

    They've gone away for a few days, haven't they?

    They weren't here, were they?

    He had met him before, hadn't he?

    This isn't working, is it?

If the main part of the sentence **doesn't have an auxiliary verb**, the question tag uses an appropriate form of '*do*'.

    You don't want me to come, do you?

    She sings well, doesn't she?

With modal verbs, if there is a modal verb in the main part of the sentence the question tag uses the same modal verb.

    They couldn't hear me, could they?

    You won't tell anyone, will you?

Question tags for sentences that start with '***I am***' is '*aren't I?*'

    I'm the fastest, aren't I?

    I'm not going to the party, am I?

LEVEL 1

DIRECTIONS (Qs. 1-30) : *In each of the following passages, there are blanks, each of which has been numbered, these numbers are again printed below the passages and against each five words are suggested, one of which fits the blank appropriately in the context of the whole passage. Find out the appropriate word.*

I. It was never talked about, but in the weeks that _________(1) the party, my relationship with Brittany, _________ (2) and I returned to doing normal things with kids of my own _________ (3). I thought it was almost a _________(4) to not have to worry about another party or situation where I would_________(5) out of my league. I was at the beach with friends several months later when 1 _________(6) talking to a girl. As we _________(7), I _________(8) I was strangely happy just _________(9) to her and _________ (10) her.

1. (a) followed   (b) ended
   (c) continued   (d) began
   (e) flopped
2. (a) began   (b) started
   (c) ended   (d) closed
   (e) shut
3. (a) year   (b) age
   (c) form   (d) old
   (e) young
4. (a) strain   (b) worry
   (c) pressure   (d) relief
   (e) problem
5. (a) forget   (b) abstain
   (c) remember   (d) leave
   (e) feel
6. (a) started   (b) stopped
   (c) began   (d) left
   (e) took
7. (a) crooned   (b) talked
   (c) blabbed   (d) blurted
   (e) leaked
8. (a) know   (b) follow
   (c) realized   (d) missed
   (e) understood

9. (a) hearing   (b) whispering
   (c) attending   (d) listening
   (e) missing
10. (a) watching   (b) seeing
    (c) looking   (d) gazing
    (e) locating

II. When I was five years old, I_________ (11) an extreme _________(12) to my sister's toys. It made little _________(13) that I had a trunk _________ (14) with dolls and toys of my own. Her _________ (15) girl treasures were much _________ (16) to break, and much more _________(17). Likewise when I was ten and she was twelve the earrings and make-up that she was _________(18) being permitted to ______ (19) with held my _________(20).   **(2013)**

11. (a) took   (b) snatched
    (c) stole   (d) gave
    (e) got
12. (a) loving   (b) liking
    (c) disliking   (d) dislike
    (e) fondness
13. (a) similarity   (b) change
    (c) difference   (d) lack
    (e) importance
14. (a) overflying   (b) leaking over
    (c) dwindling   (d) overflowing
    (e) empty
15. (a) bigger   (b) great
    (c) large   (d) giant
    (e) big
16. (a) easier   (b) easy
    (c) easiest   (d) simple
    (e) simpler
17. (a) attractive   (b) appealing
    (c) gladdening   (d) unappealing
    (e) pleasureable
18. (a) slow   (b) fast
    (c) slowly   (d) quickly
    (e) little

19. (a) do   (b) fool
    (c) experience   (d) experiment
    (e) test

20. (a) attention   (b) pleasure
    (c) attraction   (d) distraction
    (e) obsession

III. After brushing my teeth, I stooped to _________ (21) the cool water streaming from the faucet, _________ (22) back to that _________ (23) summer. It was the summer when life _________ (24), the summer I turned sixteen. I had my own car, _________ (25) with a brand-new _________ (26). It was not the _________ (27) of a new (28) that _________ (29) to me, but that of him _________ (30) over me with a laughing grin. **(2015)**

21. (a) drink   (b) gulp
    (c) lap   (d) swallow
    (e) sip

22. (a) floating   (b) drifting
    (c) flying   (d) flowing
    (e) running

23. (a) unforgivable   (b) forgetful
    (c) unforgettable   (d) noticeable
    (e) forgettable

24. (a) emerged   (b) ended
    (c) began   (d) ensued
    (e) arrived

25. (a) away   (b) while
    (c) almost   (d) along
    (e) nearly

26. (a) fairy   (b) ghost
    (c) elf   (d) spirit
    (e) soul

27. (a) memory   (b) rememberance
    (c) remembering   (d) recollection
    (e) vision

28. (a) right   (b) privilege
    (c) duty   (d) responsibility
    (e) favour

29. (a) moved   (b) dashed
    (c) rushed   (d) pounced
    (e) sprang

30. (a) looming   (b) hovering
    (c) appearing   (d) stirring
    (e) flowing

DIRECTIONS (Qs. 31 - 47): *Underline each error and write the correction in the space provided.*

Passage I

One morning, the Nawab call 31) _________

his minister and said him 32) _________

that I wanted the length and 33) _________

breadth from the earth 34) _________

measured. He also feel the 35) _________

need to have the stars on the 36) _________

sky counted. The minister says 37) _________

that the task he have been 38) _________

set being impossible. 39) _________   **(2014)**

Passage II

I entered the manager's office and sat down.

I have just lost five hundred rupees and I felt very upset. 40) _______

"I leave the money in my desk," I said, 41) ______

"and it is not there now". The manager was very sympathetic

but he can do nothing. "Everyone loses money these days", 42) ______

he said, He start to complain about this wicked world, 43) ______

but is interrupted by a knock at the door. 44) ___   ___

A girl came in and puts an envelope on his desk.
45) _______

It contains five hundred rupees. "I found this
46) _______

outside this gentleman's room," she said.

"Well! I say to the manager, "there is still some 47) ____
honesty in this world !"

DIRECTIONS (Qs 48 - 55): *Read the sentences and supply the correct question tags by choosing the correct options.*

48. Mr. Ashok is from Kolkata, _________? **(2015)**
   (a) isn't he
   (b) is he
   (c) are he
   (d) did he

49. The car isn't in the garage, _________?
   (a) isn't it   (b) is it
   (c) are they   (d) is there

50. You are Sanjay, _________?   **(2012)**
   (a) are you   (b) is you
   (c) aren't you   (d) none

51. She went to the library yesterday, _________?
   (a) isn't she   (b) didn't she
   (c) are she   (d) did she

52. He didn't recognize me, _________? **(2016)**
   (a) isn't he   (b) is he
   (c) are he   (d) did he

53. Cars pollute the environment, _________?
          (2014)
   (a) isn't they   (b) don't they
   (c) are they   (d) did they

54. The trip is very expensive, _________?
   (a) isn't it   (b) is it
   (c) are it   (d) did it

55. He won't tell her, _________?
   (a) isn't he   (b) is he
   (c) will he   (d) did he

56. We've never been to Spain _______ we?
          (2018)

   (a) has   (b) have
   (c) haven't   (d) had

57. "You surely don't need all this paper, do you"
       _______ Frank.   **(2018)**
   (a) yelled   (b) said
   (c) told   (d) asked

58. Mohan will complete his work, _______?
          (2018)
   (a) Will you   (b) Won't you
   (c) Shall he   (d) Won't he

59. Find the part which has an error in the given sentence   **(2018)**
   God helps those who help themself.

   (a) God helps

   (b) Those who

   (c) Help

   (d) Themself

60. I can't stand the thought of being up all night, _______ you?   **(2019)**
   (a) thought   (b) can
   (c) are   (d) have

61. Ritu: Hello.   **(2020)**
   Suharsh: Could I speak to Mr. Solanki?
   Ritu:_______. Can I take your message?
   (a) If you don't mind
   (b) I'm afraid he is not at home
   (c) In case it is not urgent
   (d) But why do you want that

62. We _______ waiting for you at the bus stop, weren't we?   **(2021)**
   (a) are
   (b) was
   (c) have
   (d) were

63. Choose the correct question tag for the given sentence.   **(2022)**
   He did not help me, _______?
   (a) does he
   (b) do he
   (c) did he
   (d) didn't he

LEVEL 2

DIRECTIONS (Qs. 1-39) : *In each of the following passages, there are blanks, each of which has been numbered, these numbers are again printed below the passages and against each five words are suggested, one of which fits the blank appropriately in the context of the whole passage. Find out the appropriate word.*

I. My class was two weeks _______(1) from the _______(2) night of our play _______(3) Sherry walked into my classroom and in a _______(4) voice announced that she would have to _______(5). Hundreds of reasons for _______(6) a declaration rushed _______(7) my mind, _______(8) illness, death in the family, a terrible family crisis. The _______(9) on my face prompted a _______(10) explanation.

1.   (a) away   (b) far
    (c) near   (d) along
    (e) later

2.   (a) starting   (b) opening
    (c) beginning   (d) closing
    (e) shutting

3.   (a) while   (b) where
    (c) when   (d) until
    (e) whenever

4.   (a) unwilling   (b) hesitatingly
    (c) slow   (d) hesitant
    (e) unsure

5.   (a) break   (b) close
    (c) stop   (d) exit
    (e) quit

6.   (a) such   (b) thus
    (c) just   (d) any
    (e) such like

7.   (a) across   (b) through
    (c) between   (d) throughway
    (e) throughout

8.   (a) tragically   (b) sad
    (c) tragic   (d) sorrowful
    (e) tragedy

9.   (a) look   (b) show
    (c) ideas   (d) expression
    (e) expressing

10.   (a) further   (b) more
    (c) further more   (d) farther
    (e) additional

II. When I was fifteen, I stood in _______(11) of my English class and _______(12) an essay I had written. I talked about how_______ (13) all my friends were to be _______(14) drivers education and getting drivers licenses I was _______(15). I know I'd _______ (16) be walking _______ (17) on others to _______(18) me. I am _______(19) blind.

11.   (a) front   (b) before   **(2013)**
    (c) early   (d) behind
    (e) facing

12.   (a) reading   (b) read
    (c) interpreted   (d) understanding
    (e) understood

13.   (a) excitable   (b) interested
    (c) excited   (d) exciting
    (e) stimulated

14.   (a) taken   (b) take
    (c) took   (d) taking
    (e) receiving

15.   (a) grudging   (b) envy
    (c) jealously   (d) jealousy
    (e) jealous

16.   (a) always   (b) at all times
    (c) evermore   (d) ever
    (e) everywhere

17.   (a) everyday   (b) everywhere
    (c) ever more   (d) all places
    (e) for all places

18.   (a) addicted   (b) survive
    (c) dependent   (d) independent
    (e) free

19. (a) legally   (b) legalistic
    (c) illegally   (d) lawfully
    (e) legal

III. When the late Father Aurelins Maschio __________ (20) the 60,000 square metres __________ (21) ground on the __________ (22) of Mumbai in Matunga, his __________ (23) were rather __________ (24) of him. During a meeting in Chennai this Italian priest heard of the explosion that had ________ (25) the Bombay Docks. Rushing back to Mumbai , Father Maschio.

__________ (26) with the British commander to __________ (27) the rubble on his marshy ground. Begging for donations he sat __________ (28) letter after letter to his friends and acquaintances. He went about organizing __________ (29) to collect funds. His knees knelt hours before the Madonna praying for help.

(Tricky)

20. (a) purchased   (b) received
    (c) bargained   (d) got
    (e) hired
21. (a) marshes   (b) marshy
    (c) wet and soft   (d) sandy
    (e) marsh
22. (a) fortier   (b) border
    (c) outskirts   (d) farflung
    (e) boundary
23. (a) friendships   (b) friendly
    (c) confederates   (d) confreres/friends
    (e) accomplices
24. (a) critiques   (b) crucial
    (c) criticising   (d) critics
    (e) critical
25. (a) struck   (b) striking
    (c) stricken   (b) strove
    (e) strike
26. (a) plead   (b) pleaded
    (c) beg   (d) begged
    (e) pledged
27. (a) dumping   (b) put
    (c) dump   (d) drops
    (e) down
28. (a) typed up   (b) type
    (c) scribbling   (d) typing
    (e) penning

29. (a) raffles   (b) sales
    (c) fetes   (d) lotteries
    (e) rafting

IV. This IPS Officer __________ (30) his own food. Travelling in the second __________ (31) by train and bus, he __________ (32) an hour to reach his __________ (33) village. Nazrul Islam has not __________ (34) his humble beginnings. He had to earn __________ (35) wages of ` 4 to support his __________ (36) family. Though his brothers __________ (37) out, Nazrul __________ (38) in school besides __________ (39), in other's fields.   **(2015)**

30. (a) cooks   (b) bakes
    (c) fries   (d) steam
    (e) boil
31. (a) degree   (b) class
    (c) division   (d) bogey
    (e) standard
32. (a) hops   (b) trudges
    (c) strolls   (d) walks
    (e) jumps
33. (a) local   (b) indigenous
    (c) native   (d) innate
    (e) natural
34. (a) left   (b) thrown
    (c) deleted   (d) remembered
    (e) forgotten
35. (a) daily   (b) everyday
    (c) yearly   (d) weekly
    (e) monthly
36. (a) paucity   (b) poor
    (c) rich   (d) poverty
    (e) penniless
37. (a) slipped   (b) went
    (c) dropped   (d) got thrown
    (e) fell
38. (a) determined   (b) tried
    (c) achieved   (d) persevered
    (e) persisted
39. (a) labouring
    (b) relaxing
    (c) sleeping
    (d) struggle
    (e) basking

DIRECTIONS (Qs 40 - 49): *The following passage contains 10 mistakes, such as grammatical errors, wrong prepositions and conjunctions. Correct the mistakes and rewrite the correct version of this passage.*   **(Critical Thinking)**

Varanasi (40) are locate on the north eastern part of India. Hindu pilgrims go (41) to there to purify their souls. To the Hindus Varanasi is (42) one of the holiest pilgrimage centers (43) all. Thousands of pilgrims visit this (44) wholly city every year.

As early as four o'clock in the morning the pilgrims are seen (45) make their way to the famous bathing steps known as Ghats. From there they board row boats to the holy river Ganges. By this time, pilgrims (46) have already bathing in the holy river. (47) In doing this the pilgrims believe their sins (48) shall be (49) wash away.

DIRECTIONS: (Qs. 50 - 54): *Read the sentences and supply the question tags by choosing the correct option.*

50.   David is still a bachelor, ___________?
    (2014)
    (a) isn't he   (b) isn't she
    (c) isn't they   (d) none

51.   It is dangerous for Mary to come at this time, ___________?   **(2015)**
    (a) isn't she   (b) isn't it
    (c) aren't they   (d) none

52.   I like to list
en to radio, ___________?
    (a) am I   (b) aren't I
    (c) don't I
    (d) none

53.   His health seems good, ___________?
    (2016)
    (a) doesn't it   (b) isn't she
    (c) isn't they   (d) none

54.   The staff meeting will be held at 2 p.m, ___________?
    (a) aren't it
    (b) isn't she
    (c) won't it
    (d) none

55.   These orders from the manager may put the lives of many workers in a danger.   **(2019)**

(a)   These orders from
(b)   the manager may put
(c)   the lives of many
(d)   workers in a danger.

DIRECTIONS (Qs. 56-58) : *Choose the correct option to complete each conversation.*   **(2020)**

56.   Bobby: What if Nirupa hadn't turned up with the umbrella the other night?

    Prateek: ___________

    (a)   Oh God, when I think of her my heart sinks.

    (b)   No way, seriously Nirupa will do that to you?

    (c)   She could have turned around and gone home.

    (d)   We both would have got drenched completely.

57.   Library attendant: Dear member, we are closing down the library. We sincerely apologise for the inconvenience.

    Your membership will be returned.

    You: ___________

    (a)   I would be grateful if my money was refunded.

    (b)   Give my money back immediately, or else ...

    (c)   That is nonsense. The library was open yesterday.

    (d)   Why are you talking about library closing?

58.   Choose the correct option to complete the conversation.

    George: I'm going to an art gallery tonight.

    Katherine: That's cool.

    George: My cousin, Jessica, is ________.

    She's displaying her work there.

    Katherine : ___________ . I paint in my spare time.

    (a)   a doctor / I love skating

    (b)   a teacher / I love teaching

    (c)   an artist / I love art

    (d)   a playwright / I love plays

59. Choose the most suitable option to complete the conversation.   **(2021)**

    Sarita : With today's announcement, she _____ as the leader.

    (a) appoints

    (b) will appoint

    (c) has been appointed

    (d) have appointed

    For questions 21 and 22, choose the appropriate meaning for the idioms/ proverbs.

60. The signpost at the gate of the garden read : 'Trespassers will be persecuted'.   **(2022)**

    (a) The signpost at.

    (b) the gate of the garden.

    (c) read : 'Trespassers will.

    (d) be persecuted.

61. This small table will collapse if you will stand on it.   **(2022)**

    (a) This small table

    (b) will collapse

    (c) if you will

    (d) stand on it.

62. Choose the most suitable option to complete the conversation.

    James : Many people have an ________ to tattoos.   **(2022)**

    Thomas : It's true.

    (a) adaptation

    (b) averswn

    (c) assurance

    (d) afflicted

63. Find the part of the sentence given below which contains a grammatical error.   **(2022)**

    We should abide (1)/ to the promise that (2)/ we make. (3)/ No error (4)

    (a) 1   (b) 2
    (c) 3   (d) 4

HINTS & EXPLANATIONS

LEVEL - 1

1. (a)   2. (c)   3. (b)   4. (d)   5. (e)
6. (a)   7. (b)   8. (c)   9. (d)   10. (c)
11. (a)   12. (b)   13. (c)   14. (d)   15. (e)
16. (a)   17. (b)   18. (c)   19. (d)   20. (a)
21. (a)   22. (b)   23. (c)   24. (c)   25. (d)
26. (e)   27. (a)   28. (b)   29. (c)   30. (a)
31. call - called
32. said him- said to him
33. I - he
34. from - of
35. feel - felt
36. on - in
37. says - said
38. have - has
39. being - is
40. have - had
41. leave - left
42. can - could
43. start - started
44. is - was
45. puts - put
46. contains - contained
47. say – said
48. a) isn't he
49. (b)   is it
50. (c)   aren't you
51. (b)   didn't she
52. (d)   did he
53. (b)   don't they
54. (a)   isn't it
55. (c)   will he
56. (b)
57. (d)
58. (d)   Won't he
59. (d)   'themselves' should be used at the place of 'themself'.
60. (b)   can
61. (a)   If you don't mind
62. (d)   were
63. (c)

LEVEL - 2

1. (a)   2. (b)   3. (c)   4. (d)   5. (e)
6. (a)   7. (b)   8. (c)   9. (d)   10. (a)
11. (a)   12. (b)   13. (c)   14. (d)   15. (e)
16. (a)   17. (b)   18. (c)   19. (a)
20. (a)   21. (b)   22. (c)   23. (d)   24. (e)
25. (a)   26. (b)   27. (c)   28. (d)   29. (a)
30. (a)   31. (b)   32. (d)   33. (c)   34. (e)
35. (a)   36. (b)   37. (c)   38. (d)
39. (a)
40. is located
41. (No preposition)
42. The
43. Of
44. holy
45. making
46. were
47. By
48. would
49. washed

Varanasi is located on the north eastern part of India. Hindu pilgrims go there to purify their souls. To the Hindus, Varanasi is one of the holiest pilgrimage centers of all. Thousands of pilgrims visit this holy city every year. As early as four o'clock in the morning the pilgrims are seen making their way to the famous bathing steps known as Ghats. From there they board row boats to the holy river Ganges. By this time, pilgrims were already bathing in the holy river. By doing this the pilgrims believe their sins would be washed away.

50. (a) isn't he

51. (b) isn't it

52. (c) don't I

53. (a) doesn't it

54. (c) won't it

55. (d) 'workers in danger' is right usage.

56. (d) We both would have got drenched completely.

57. (a) I would be grateful if my money was refunded.

58. (c) an artist / I love art

59. (c) has been appointed.

60. (d) be persecuted'. The correct sentence is: The signpost at the gate of the garden read : 'Trespassers will be prosecuted'.

61. (c) if you will. The correct sentence is: This small table will collapse if you stand on it.

62. (b) aversion

63. (b)

CHAPTER 16

ANALOGY & CLASSIFICATION

An analogy is a comparison in which an idea or a thing is compared to another thing that is quite different from it. It aims at explaining that idea or thing by comparing it to something that is familiar. Metaphors and similes are tools used to draw an analogy. Therefore, analogy is more extensive and elaborate than either a simile or a metaphor.

Consider the following example:

"Structure of an atom is like a solar system. Nucleus is the sun and electrons are the planets revolving around the sun."

Here an atomic structure is compared to a solar system by using "like". Therefore, it is a simile. Metaphor is used to relate the nucleus to the sun and the electrons to the planets without using words "like" or "as'. Hence, similes and metaphors are employed to develop an analogy.

Examples of analogy from everyday life

We use analogy in our everyday conversation. Some common analogy examples are given below:

- Life is like a race. The one who keeps running wins the race and the one who stops to catch a breath loses.
- Just as a sword is the weapon of a warrior, a pen is the weapon of a writer.
- How a doctor diagnoses diseases is like how a detective investigates crimes.
- Just as a caterpillar comes out of its cocoon, so we must come out of our comfort zone.
- You are as annoying as nails on a chalkboard.

Writers use analogies to link an unfamiliar or a new idea with common and familiar objects. It is easier for you to comprehend a new idea, which may have been difficult to understand otherwise. Your comprehension of a new idea picks up the pace when you observe its similarity to something that is familiar to you. In addition, by employing this literary tool, writers catch the attention of their readers. Analogies help increase readers' interest as analogies help them relate what they read in their life.

ANALOGY KINDS

Opposites Analogies

Opposites are exactly as the word suggests things that are opposite to each other. These are exactly as the word suggests things that are opposite to each other

Examples : crying - laughing, question - answer, day - night etc.

Object and Related Object Analogies

The related object in this "object and related object" analogy is an obvious relation however the object are not inseparably intertwined to one another like for example a knife and a fork. The objects in this analogy type have a relation to one another however; the correct relation should be determined by looking at the concerning question and answers.

Examples : cat & kitten, plant & seed, dog & puppy.

Object and Group Analogies

These are objects which form a specifically named group when several are put together. Several wolves together form a pack, several trees together form a forest etc.

Examples : wolf & pack, tree & forest, seagull & flock

Degrees of a Characteristic Analogies

The "degrees of a characteristic" relation in analogies can best be explained by looking at an example. Let's use the warm and hot from below. One degree higher than warm can be hot, another degree higher could be burning. We can also go the other way around like from cold to freezing. This analogy type mostly consists of adjectives but this does not always have to be the case like the flat to skyscraper example depicts.

Examples : flat & skyscraper, tired & exhausted, warm & hot, cold & freezing

Cause and Effect Analogies

The similarity in these types of analogies derives from the cause on one side and its indisputably connected effect on the other side. If you spin you'll get dizzy whether you like it or not, this is a side effect of spinning since you will not likely spin just to become dizzy.

Examples: spin & dizzy, fire & burn, read & learn, etc.

Effort and Result Analogies

The difference between this analogy type and "cause and effect" type, which is explained above, is the fact that for the effort and result connection an actual effort has to be made. If you put your hand in fire it will burn without effort. A painting on the contrary has to be painted and painting is an effort somebody has to perform and it has to be performed in a certain way.

Examples : paint & painting, build & house, write & letter.

Problem and Solution Analogies

Some problems have very obvious solutions like for example if you have an itch (problem) you can scratch (solution) to solve that problem. These problems and solutions are used in word analogy problems.

Examples : itch & scratch, unemployment & job application, tired & sleep.

Verb Tenses Analogies

This is exactly as the word says a type of analogy in which two tenses of a verb are analogous to two of the same tenses of another verb. These are pretty simple and easily recognizable types.

Examples: walk & walked, eat & ate, send & sent.

Performer and Action Analogies

This is again a very straightforward analogy type which is based on taking two sets of performers and their corresponding actions. The relation between a painter and to paint is the same as the relation between a soldier and to fight.

Examples : painter & to paint, soldier & to fight, scientist & to research.

Object and Part of the Whole Analogies

Be careful not to confuse this type of analogy with the object and group analogy which is described above. The difference derives from the fact that in the object and part of a whole relation the "object" is not automatically the "whole" when lots of the objects are brought together. For example glass and window match the description of object and part of a whole, but glass could just as easy match light bulb so the glass will only be a light bulb if you process it in certain ways. Examples: brick & wall, glass & window, glass & light bulb, page & book.

Object and Function Analogies

Some objects have designated functions which are inseparably connected to the concerning object for example you use a keyboard for typing and a telephone for calling. These relations are often used in analogy test problems.

Examples: keyboard & to type, telephone & to call, paintbrush & to paint.

Object and Location Analogies

In this relation objects are designated to their most logical location. This is not always strictly defined e.g., a tree can be in the forest but it can just as easily be in the park. You will have to find the correct answer again by carefully analysing the analogy problem and its possible solutions.

Examples: plane & hangar, dog & doghouse, tree & forest.

Things that Go Together Analogies

Some objects for example salt and pepper are indisputably connected to each other. These "sets" of objects are used in modern verbal analogies.

Examples: salt & pepper, statue & socket, fork & knife.

Rhyme Analogies

Rhyme comes in lots of different shapes and is used sometimes in word analogies. Keep in mind that not only the standard perfect rhymes can be used but also other types like syllabic rhyme or half rhyme can be encountered.

Examples: deer & steer, red & rod, glasses & mosses.

LEVEL 1

DIRECTIONS (Qs. 1-10) : *Pick the right word which means differently from the following group of words.*

1. Prohibit, Prevent, Block, Forbid, Allow, Deny **(2014)**
   - (a) Prevent
   - (b) Allow
   - (c) Block
   - (d) Deny
2. Profit, Gain, Failure, Improvement, Utility, Value
   - (a) Failure
   - (b) Utility
   - (c) Gain
   - (d) Profit
3. Sustain, Maintain, Keep, Block, Uphold, Bear
   - (a) Uphold
   - (b) Maintain
   - (c) Sustain
   - (d) Block
4. Decline, Increase, Advancement, Growth, Development, Progression
   - (a) Growth
   - (b) Progression
   - (c) Decline
   - (d) Increase
5. Associate, Companion, Familiar, Partner, Pal, Opponent
   - (a) Companion
   - (b) Pal
   - (c) Opponent
   - (d) Familiar
6. Honour, Renown, Disgrace, Splendour, Fame, Brilliance **(2013)**
   - (a) Fame
   - (b) Renown
   - (c) Splendour
   - (d) Disgrace
7. Gladness, Joy, Rapture, Cheer, Delight, Distress
   - (a) Cheer
   - (b) Distress
   - (c) Rapture
   - (d) Delight
8. Right, Appropriate, Proper, Unfit, Fair, Decent
   - (a) Proper
   - (b) Unfit **(2016)**
   - (c) Appropriate
   - (d) Fair
9. Raise, Uplift, Erect, Grow, Arouse, Decrease
   - (a) Decrease
   - (b) Uplift
   - (c) Erect
   - (d) Arouse
10. Settle, Displace, Transfer, Separate, Shift, Displant **(2015)**
    - (a) Transfer
    - (b) Displant
    - (c) Displace
    - (d) Settle

DIRECTIONS (Qs. 11 -16) : *In each of the following questions four words have been given out of which three are alike in some manner, while the fourth one is different. Choose the word which is different from the rest.*

11. (a) Chicken   (b) Snake **(2013)**
    (c) Frog   (d) Crocodile
12. (a) Cap   (b) Turban **(2015)**
    (c) Helmet   (d) Veil
13. (a) Kiwi   (b) Eagle
    (c) Emu   (d) Ostrich
14. (a) Rigveda   (b) Yajurveda **(2012)**
    (c) Atharvaveda   (d) Ayurveda
15. (a) Curd   (b) Butter
    (c) Oil   (d) Cheese
16. (a) Potassium   (b) Silicon **(2014)**
    (c) Zirconium   (d) Gallium

DIRECTIONS (Qs. 17-25) : *There is some sort of functional relationship between the two words asked in the question. Choose the same sort of relationship between the words given in the four alternatives and complete the set.*

17. Antlers : Stag : : _______ : _______. **(2016)**
    - (a) Hoofs : Horse
    - (b) Mane : Lion
    - (c) Wings : Eagle
    - (d) Horns : Bull
18. Waiter : Tip : : _______ : _______.
    - (a) Discipline : Student
    - (b) Scholar : Book
    - (c) Student : Marks
    - (d) Teacher : Class
19. Yawn : Boredom **(2013)**
    - (a) Anger : Madness
    - (b) Dream : Sleep
    - (c) Smile : Amusement
    - (d) Impatience : Rebellion
20. Chain ; Punish : : _______ : _______. **(2012)**
    - (a) Switch : Chastise
    - (b) Birth : Reward
    - (c) Whip : Flay
    - (d) Pigeon : Peace
21. Clarify : Baffle : : ______ : ______. **(2014)**
    - (a) Crop : Field
    - (b) Garbage : House
    - (c) Coward : Dastard
    - (d) Diffidence : Confidence
22. Branch : Tree **(2016)**
    - (a) Crest : Wave
    - (b) Bulb : Filament
    - (c) Clothes : Cupboard
    - (d) Water : Tap

23. Apiary : Bees : : __________ : ________ .
    (a) Asylum : Mentally ill
    (b) Aerie : Insects
    (c) Byre : Burial for dead
    (d) Dock : Duck

24. Trumpet : Elephant : : __________ : __________ .
    (a) Twitter : Squirrels
    (b) Coo : Crows
    (c) Neigh : Horses
    (d) Howl : Monkeys

25. Troop : Horsemen : : __________ : __________ .
    (a) Bunch : Flowers   **(2013)**
    (b) Shoal : Fish
    (c) Band : Soldiers
    (d) Team : Followers

DIRECTIONS (Qs. 26 -35) : *Below are given four choices (A), (B), (C) and (D). Out of these four choices, 3 are similar in nature but one of them is different. Choose the different one and write the answer.*

26. (a) Screw   (a) Hammer
    (c) Needle   (b) Pin
27. (a) Up   (b) Down   **(2014)**
    (b) Small   (d) Below
28. (a) Tiger   (b) Dolphin
    (c) Wolf   (d) Crocodile
29. (a) Man   (b) Wife
    (c) Husband   (d) Sister

30. (a) ABE   (b) LMP   **(2012)**
    (c) STW   (d) HIM

31. Chalk is to black board as Pen is to...................
    (a) Paper   (b) Book
    (c) Table   (d) Student

32. Players are to team as Flowers are to..................
    (a) Rose   (b) Bouquet   **(2016)**
    (c) Tree   (d) Bush

33. Sheep is to lamb as Dog is to......................
    (a) Domestic   (b) House
    (c) Bitch   (d) Puppy

34. Gravity is to Pull as Magnetism is to..................
    (a) Repulsion   (b) Separation **(2015)**
    (c) Attraction   (d) Push

35. ....is to Land as Navy is to.......................
    (a) Ship-Infantry   (b) Army-Sea
    (b) Ground-Sea   (d) Arrive-Depart

36. Choose the correct answer based on the given hint.
    Child: Childhood : : Boy : ________? **(2018)**
    (a) Boys   (b) Boyish
    (c) Boyhood   (d) Girlish

37. Select the correct match.   **(2022)**
    CLOSE : DNRWJ : : OPEN : _______?
    (a) PJRO   (b) RPJB
    (c) PRRH   (d) PRHR

LEVEL 2

DIRECTIONS (Qs. 1-20) : *In each of the following questions find out the alternative which will replace the blank.*

1. Anthology : Collection of Writings : : Anecdote : _________.

    (a) A pithy saying

    (b) A short narrative of a private life

    (c) A quotation selected from book

    (d) The concluding section of book

2. Infanticide : Killing of a child : : Fratricide : _________. **(Tricky)**

    (a) Killing of a racial group

    (b) Killing of one's own father

    (c) Killing of other's father

    (d) Killing of one's own brother

3. Earth : Axis : : Wheel : _________. **(2014)**

    (a) Hub   (b) Car

    (c) Road   (d) Tyre

4. Courage : Fearful : : Clever : _________.

    (a) Smart   (b) Dunce

    (c) Illiterate   (d) Ignorant

5. Gynocracy : Government by women : : Hierocracy : _________. **(2016)**

    (a) Government by priests or other religious ministers

    (b) Government by ranked people

    (c) Government by one person

    (d) Government by a tyrant

6. Borrow : Plagiarise : : Steal : _________.

    (a) Obtain   (b) Extort

    (c) Pilfer   (d) Snatch

7. Formula : Constituent : : Equation : _________.

    (a) Variables   (b) Constant **(2012)**

    (c) Term   (d) Method

8. Fanatic : Enthusiastic : : Fastidious : _________.

    (a) Fateful   (b) Particular

    (c) Talkative   (d) Boastful

9. Zenith : Bottom : : Zest : _________.

    (a) Reluctance   (b) Relish **(2014)**

    (c) Avidity   (d) Eagerness

10. Uncouth : Refined : : Usurp : _________.

    (a) Expropriate   (b) Seize

    (c) Appropriate   (d) Surrender

11. Adjective : Adverb : : _________ : _________. **(Tricky, 2017)**

    (a) Onomatopoeia : Personification

    (b) Conjunction : Simile

    (c) Noun : Metaphors

    (d) Alliteration : Interjection

12. Inattentive : Circumspect : : Ponderous : _________. **(Tricky)**

    (a) Weighty   (b) Trivial

    (c) Dull   (d) Laborious

13. Ant : Industrious : : _________ : _________.

    (a) Cat : playful   (b) Fox : Cunning

    (c) Vixen : Cute   (d) Horse : runner

14. Medieval : Primeval : : _________ : _________.

    (a) Revelation : Evolution

    (b) Ice : Snow

    (c) Rose : Thorn

    (d) Dragon : Dinosaur

15. Spasm : Convulsion :: _________ : _________ .

    (a) Emotion : Dispassionate   **(2012)**

    (b) Whisper : Cry

    (c) Happiness : Amusement

    (d) Ire : Fury

16. Symphony : Music   **(2015)**

    (a) Mural : Painting

    (b) Ode : Prose

    (c) Preface : Book

    (d) Editorial Journal

17. Skin : Dermatologist :: _________ : _________ .

    (a) Heart : Cardiologist

    (b) Genes : Genealogist

    (c) Antiques : Archaeologist

    (d) Time : Astrologist

18. Noticeable : Outstanding :: _________ : _________ .   **(2013)**

    (a) Usual : Distinguished

    (b) Conspicuous : Striking

    (c) Disclosed : Hidden

    (d) Glaring : Indistinct

19. Atheist : Religious :: _________ : _________ .

    (a) Dunce : Clever   **(2014)**

    (b) Secular : Parochial

    (c) Free : Stray

    (d) Brilliant : Worthy

20. Wither : Dehydrate :: _________ : _________ .

    (a) Yoke : Freedom   **(Tricky)**

    (b) Scanty : Ample

    (c) Scintillating : Tarnished

    (d) Solidarity : Unanimity

DIRECTIONS (Qs. 21-30) : *Choose the odd one among the given options.*

21. (a) Lion   (b) Cheetah

    (b) Goat   (d) Wolf

22. (a) New Delhi   (b) London

    (c) Chennai   (d) Baghdad

23. (a) History   (b) Geography

    (c) Mathematics   (d) Phone

24. (a) Pencil   (b) Book

    (c) Pen   (d) Teacher

25. (a) Patna   (b) Bengaluru

    (c) Nainital   (d) Bhopal

26. (a) Heart   (b) Hand

    (c) Lungs   (d) Kidney

27. (a) Colonel   (b) Major

    (c) General   (d) Rifle

28. (a) WXYZ   (b) PQST   **(2013)**

    (c) GHIJ   (d) ABCD

29. (a) Tendulkar   (b) Sangkara

    (c) Jadeja   (d) Sania

30. (a) River   (b) Drain   **(2012)**

    (c) Canal   (d) Pond

DIRECTIONS (Qs. 31-38) : *There is some sort of functional relationship as mentioned in the question. Choose the same sort of relationship between the words given in the four alternatives and complete the set.*

31. If Grunt is related to camel then ___________ is related to horse.

    (a) Bray   (b) Crow

    (c) Bleat   (d) Neigh

32. Umpire is related to pitch as field is related to ___________ .

    (a) Crop   (b) Ground

    (c) Farmer   (d) Wheat

33. 'Eye' is to 'See' as 'Ear' is to –

    (a) Sound   (b) Taste

    (c) Ring   (d) Smell

34. 'Carpenter' is related to 'Furniture' in the same way 'Goldsmith' is related to –   **(Tricky)**

    (a) Shoes   (b) Gold

    (c) Jewellery   (d) Metal

35. 'Page' is related to 'Book' as 'Leaf' is related to –

    (a) Root   (b) Tree

    (c) Green   (d) Forest

36. 'Examination' is related to 'Success' as 'Match' is related to –   **(2015)**

    (a) Play   (b) Win

    (c) Refree   (d) Goalkeeper

37. 'Bull' is related to 'Cow' in the same way 'Horse' is related to –   **(2017)**

    (a) Elephant   (b) Mare

    (c) Colt   (d) Lion

38. Paddy is to Field as Steel is to ....?

    (a) Ore   (b) Iron

    (c) Factory   (d) Mines

39. Select the pair from the choices given below that shows the same relationship as in the given pair-   **(2014)**

wick: candle

    (a) Lead : Pencil   (b) Light : Darkness

    (c) Thread : Wool   (d) Rapid : Run

40. Select the pair from choices given below that shows the same relationship as in the given pair –   **(Critical Thinking)**

Tree: Branches

    (a) River : Tributaries   (b) Continent : Island

    (c) Stream : Delta   (d) Ocean : Sea

41. Choose the correct answer based on the given hint.   **(2019)**

Vague: Hazy : : Precarious: _______?

    (a) Smooth   (b) Hard

    (c) Confront   (d) Dangerous

42. Arrange the words given below in the sequence as per the dictionary.   **(2022)**

    i.   Rainbow

    ii. Rancour

    iii. Rattle

    iv. Rainy

    (a) i, iii, ii, iv   (b) i, iv, iii, ii

    (c) i, iv, ii, iii   (d) ii, i, iv, iii

HINTS & EXPLANATIONS

LEVEL - 1

1. (b) All the other words are negative which mean to bar something or prohibitions but allow means let (someone) have or do something which is a positive implication.

2. (a) Failure gives a negative meaning while all other words are positive implications of any business or entrepreneurship

3. (d) All other words mean support physically or mentally while block gives a negative sense and does not match with the group

4. (c) All the options are related with virtues of development while decline is the negative trend which means gradual loss of strength or value

5. (c) Each of a pair of things intended to complement or match each other and opponent is the only exception

6. (d) All the words are good qualities which suggest things morally right but disgrace means loss of reputation or respect as the result of a dishonourable action.

7. (b) Distress means a state of extreme necessity or misfortune or sorrow but all other combinations suggest delightfulness

8. (b) Unfit is not fitting with the sequence as all other words give a sense of modesty

9. (a) Decrease means a diminishing state whereas all other words are related to growth.

10. (d) All the other words means to remove from a position, office, or dignity while settle means to make permanent residence

11. (a) All except Chicken can live in water.

12. (d) All except Veil cover the head, while veil covers the face.

13. (b) All except Eagle are flightless birds.

14. (d) All except Ayurveda are names of holy scriptures, the four Vedas. Ayurveda is a branch of medicine.

15. (c) All except Oil are products obtained from milk.

16. (b) All except silicon are metals.

17. (d) 18. (c)

19. (c) Yawn indicates boredom.
Similarly, smile indicates amusement.

20. (c) 21. (d)

22. (a) First is a part of the second.

23. (a) 24. (c) 25. (c)

26. (b) All except Hammer have a pointed end.

27. (c) Small tells about size and all others tell about sides.

28. (b) Except Dolphin all are wild creatures.

29. (a) Except man all others are family relatives.

30. (d) 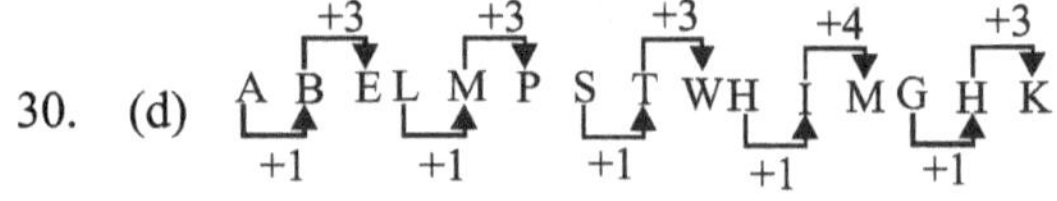

31. (a) 32. (b) 33 (d) 34. (c) 35. (b)

36. (c) Boyhood

37. (d)

LEVEL - 2

1. (b) As anthology means collection of writing likewise anecdote means a short narrative of a private life.

2. (d) As infanticide means killing of a child fratricide means killing of one's brother.

3. (a) As the Earth moves around its axis the wheel moves around its hub.

4. (b) As fearful is the opposite of courage, dunce means a stupid is the opposite of clever.

5. (b) As gynocracy means government by women so also hierocracy means government by ranked people.

6. (c) As borrow means plagiarise (take the work or an idea of someone else and pass it off as one's own) so also pilfer relates to steal which means steal things of little value.

7. (c) In mathematical sense term means each of the quantities in a ratio, series, or mathematical expression. As formula is related with constituent term is related with equation.

8. (b) Fastidious means very attentive to and concerned about accuracy and detail that is to be particular. Fanatic person is enthusiastic.

9. (a) As bottom is contrary to zenith so also reluctance is contrary to zest.

10. (d) As uncouth means lacking refined behaviour so also the opposite of usurp is surrender.

11. (a) As adjective and adverb are parts of speech in grammar so also onomatopoeia and personification are literary devices.

12. (b) As inattentive is related to circumspect so also ponderous is related to trivial.

13. (b) As the quality of ant is industrious so also fox is cunning.

14. (d) Both relations refer to a certain period.

15. (d) As both spasm and convulsion relates to body motion ire and fury relates to emotion.

16. (a) First is a type of the second.

17. (a) The skin specialist is known as dermatologist so also Cardiologist is the specialist of heart.

18. (b) Something out standing means it is noticeable so also something conspicuous means that is striking.

19. (b) Atheist is a person who disbelieves or lacks belief in the existence of God or gods; it is opposite to religious. Parochial means relating to a Church parish and secular is the opposite.

20. (d) As wither means dehydrate so also solidarity means unanimity.

21. (c) Goat is a prey of the other four wild beasts.

22. (c) Chennai is the capital of a Indian state while other four are the capitals of the countries.

23 (d) Phone is an electronic hearing device while other four are subjects.

24. (d) 25. (c) 26. (b) 27. (d) 28. (b)

29. (d) All the rest are male gender and are related to cricket.

30. (d) In all the rest water flows.

31. (d) Camels grunt and horses neigh

32. (c) The farmer works in a field.

33. (a) 34. (c) 35. (b) 36. (b)

37. (b)

38. (c) 39. (a) 40. (a)

41. (d) Dangerous

42. (c)

CHAPTER 17

SITUATION REACTION TEST/ FACT AND OPINION

SITUATION REACTION TEST

Situation Reaction Tests (SRTs) are a type of psychological test which present the test-taker with realistic, hypothetical scenarios and ask the individual to identify the most appropriate response or to rank the responses in the order they feel is most effective. SRTs can be presented to test-takers through a variety of modalities, such as booklets, films, or audio recordings. SRTs represent a distinct psychometric approach from the common knowledge-based multiple choice item.

SRTs tend to determine behavioural tendencies, assessing how an individual will behave in a certain situation, which evaluates the effectiveness of possible responses. These tests could also reinforce the status quo with an organization.

Unlike most psychological tests SRTs are not acquired 'off-the-shelf', but are in fact designed as a bespoke tool, tailor-made to suit the individual role requirements. This is because SRTs are not a type of test with respect to their content, but are a method of designing tests.

The validity of the test corresponds to the types of questions being asked. Knowledge instruction questions correlate more highly with general mental ability while behavioral tendency questions correlate more highly with personality.

Students' knowledge of interpersonal behaviour showed progressive validity over cognitive factors for predicting academic and post academic success. There are many problems within scoring SRTs. "Attempts to address this issue include expert-novice differences, where an item is scored in the direction favouring the experts after the average ratings of experts and novices on each item are compared; expert judgment, where a team of experts decides the best answer to each question; target scoring, where the test author determines the correct answer; and consensual scoring, where a score is allocated to each option according to the percentage of people choosing that option."

No special training, knowledge, or experience is required in order to take this type of test. A candidate's answers should draw on general knowledge and life experience only.

During the test it is important that you read each scenario and each possible response, before answering the question or assigning rankings. The first option available may seem very sensible, but it is important to avoid assigning any rankings until you have considered each option carefully. For example, the last option available may be an even more sensible option and the most effective response.

Bear in mind that you are not being asked to judge if an option is right or wrong, just to evaluate which is the best (and worst) option available to you from those provided. For questions that ask you to rank responses in number order, it is important to note that the ranking is relative. All the available options may be effective, or they may all be ineffective. It is your job to decide on the relative rank, rather than to decide if each option is right or wrong.

Use only the information provided in the question. Do not make assumptions during the SRTs.

FACT AND OPINIONS

Ability to differentiate between a fact and an opinion is an essential reading skill. The writer may be stating a fact or trying to pursue with his/her opinion. How do you tell the difference? It's quite simple. Let's read through and learn.

Fact is something that can be verified. Details supporting the fact are present and confirm the information or statement.

EXAMPLE

- Diamonds are the hardest thing on the earth.

- The greenhouse gases are slowly depleting the Ozone.

How Do You Differentiate Between a Fact and an Opinion?

Statements which can be cross checked are called facts.

Opinion keeps changing from person to person and place to place. *Opinion is purely based on an individual's perspective and may change from time to time.* It may or may not be correct. There are no evidences to prove an opinion. It cannot be verified.

EXAMPLE

- Vegetarians' are healthier than people who eat meat.

- People should not be allowed to use cell phones in a public place.

LEVEL 1

DIRECTIONS (Qs. 1-15) : *Read the following statement and choose the correct option from the given alternatives.*

1. While travelling in a train, you observe some college students pulling the alarm chain simply to get down at their desired point. You would :
   - (a) with the help of some passengers, check them from doing so.
   - (b) let them pull the chain but check them from detraining.
   - (c) inform the guard of the train as soon as it stops.
   - (d) keep quiet and do nothing.

2. You are passing by a river and you know swimming. Suddenly, you hear the cry of a drowning child. You would:
   - (a) dive into the river to save him
   - (b) wait to see if some other person is there to help.
   - (c) look for professional divers.
   - (d) console the child's parents.

3. Your friend has not invited you to his marriage party. You will :
   - (a) hold it against him
   - (b) attend the ceremony
   - (c) send him your best wishes
   - (d) ignore the whole affair

4. While you board a train at the station, you find a suitcase beneath your seat. you would : **(2012)**
   - (a) report the matter to the police.
   - (b) open up the suitcase to look through its contents.
   - (c) try to find out the address of the owner from the papers etc, in the suitcase.
   - (d) finding no one to claim it, take it into your own possession.

5. While attending your friend's party, you see your friend's muffler catching fire from the candle on the table behind him. you would :
   - (a) ask you friend to see behind him.
   - (b) rush to call friend's mother.
   - (c) rush and take out the muffler from his neck, and pour water on it.
   - (d) take out the muffler and throw it away.

6. You find that the person whom you call your friend has been cheating you. What would you do? **(2014)**
   - (a) Break relations with him
   - (b) Give him tit for tat
   - (c) Make him realise his mistake
   - (d) Tell other friends about him

7. While travelling in a train, you notice a man from the coach behind yours fall off the train. You would :
   - (a) pull the alarm chain so that the train may stop and the man may be helped.
   - (b) shout at the falling man asking him to get up quickly and entrain
   - (c) jump off the train to assist the falling man
   - (d) wait till the train stops at the next station and inform the railway authorities there.

8. You are interviewed for a new job. Which of the following is most important to you ?
   - (a) Opportunities for promotion   **(Tricky)**
   - (b) Renumeration you will be paid
   - (c) Scope to develop your ideas and use them to improve the working of the organisation.
   - (d) All the above are equally important.

9. You are living in a college hostel. The dal served to you in the mess has a lot of stones. What would you do?
   - (a) Leave eating the dal altogether.
   - (b) Bring the matter to the notice of mess in-charge.
   - (c) Speak to the cook about changing the dal.
   - (d) Buy your own dal and cook it in your room.

10. You are in a bus. The bus reaches your stop but still you have not purchased the ticket because of heavy rush. What will you do?

(a) Jump out quickly to avoid embarrassment

(b) Call the conductor, give him the money and get the ticket

(c) Hand the money to someone sitting nearby to give it to the conductor.

(d) Give the money to the driver.

11. You are playing in your friend's house, when he gets stuck with a naked electric wire. you would: **(2014)**

(a) hold him by the arms and try to set him free.

(b) hold the wire and pull it away.

(c) pull off the wire with a wooden stick.

(d) send for the doctor.

12. While firing crackers, a child gets severe burns on the hand. What would you do?   **(2015)**

(a) Dip the child's hands in cold water till there is no more burning sensation.

(b) Wash the hands with Dettol.

(c) Send someone to call the doctor.

(d) Apply some ointment on the affected area.

13. You are driving your car on the road when you hit against a fruit vendor's cart. You would :

(a) escape from the site by driving away.

(b) abuse the fruit vendor for putting his cart on the way.

(c) pay the fruit vendor for the damage done to him.

(d) insist that it was not your fault.

14. If in the examination hall, you find that the question paper is too tough to be answered satisfactorily by you, the best thing to do for you is to :   **(Critical Thinking)**

(a) tell the examiner that the questions are out of course.

(b) provoke the candidates to walk out of the examination hall.

(c) try to know something from your neighbour.

(d) try to solve the questions as much as you know with a cool head.

15. You are alone in the house and there is quite a danger of thieves around. Just then, you hear a knock at the door. You would :

(a) Open the door to see who is there.

(b) first peep out from the window to confirm whether you know the person.

(c) not open the door.

(d) ask the servant to see who is there.

DIRECTIONS (Qs. 16 - 20) : *Read the following sentences and state whether its a fact or opinion.*

---

16. The blobfish is made of a jelly like substance and has almost no muscles.

(a) Fact   (b) Opinion

(c) Can't determine   (d) none

17. If you see an owl, that's a sign that something bad will happen to you.   **(2016)**

(a) Fact   (b) Opinion

(c) Can't determine   (d) none

18. Harry Patter is a movie about wizards and their adventures

(a) Opinion

(b) Fact

(c) Can't determine

(d) none

19. Fruits are rich in vitamins and minerals   **(2014)**

(a) Opinion

(b) can't say

(c) Fact

(d) none

20. Happy feet is the best movie ever made.

(a) Fact

(b) Opinion

(c) Can't say

(d) none

DIRECTIONS (Qs. 21 - 25) : *Read the following questions and choose the correct option.*

---

21. Which of the following statement is a fact?

(a) Cats are cuter than any other pet.

(b) Running is the best form of exercise.

(c) Your room is the messiest I have ever seen.

(d) Nigara falls is one of the seven natural wonders of the world.

22. Which of the following is not a FACT?

(a) The LEED Platinum is world's tallest green building.

(b) It houses one of the world's fastest elevators.

(c) The building is modeled after bamboo.

(d) One surely will enjoy its view at night.

23. Which of the following statements are opinions?
    (2015)
    (a) Rabbits are the smartest animals on earth
    (b) Rabbits eat carrots and green vegetables
    (c) Rabbits are extremely messy
    (d) Both choices, 'a' and 'c' are opinions.

24. Which of the following is not a fact?   **(2013)**
    (a) World's tallest growing tree is the coast redwood, growing along the Pacific Coast of US.
    (b) Bamboo is the fastest growing woody plant.
    (c) Flowers make a good gift
    (d) A Sunflower looks like one large flower, but each head is composed of hundreds of tiny flowers.

25. Which of the following is a fact?   **(2012)**
    (a) The rainbow is looking bright and nice
    (b) The first potatoes were cultivated in Peru about 7,000 years ago.
    (c) Sheela's dress was shabby
    (d) Her beauty was more than he could have ever imagined.

26. You want to ask directions for the University. How would you ask?   **(2020)**
    (a) Where is Vidthwata University located?
    (b) Which way can lead Vidthwata University?
    (c) Could you tell me the way to Vidthwata University?
    (d) Can you accompany me to Vidthwata University?

LEVEL 2

DIRECTIONS (Qs. 1-15) : *Read the following statement and choose the correct option from the given alternatives.*

1. Your friends like smoking and influence you to do the same. You will

   (a) smoke only because your friends are smoking

   (b) refuse to smoke

   (c) smoke but only in their presence

   (d) refuse and lie to them that you have asthma

2. The previous day of your interview, your friend comes and tells you that the expert for the interview is a very tough person. You

   (a) stop preparation

   (b) are consoled that you have applied for other posts also

   (c) pray that only simple questions are asked

   (d) are not bothered, as you have prepared well

3. You go to a showroom and like a watch there but it is beyond your budget and is the last of its kind. What do you do?   **(Critical Thinking)**

   (a) You look for a similar but a cheaper watch.

   (b) You borrow money from friends.

   (c) You decide that you cannot afford it and let it be.

   (d) You come back, and after some time try your luck if it is still there.

4. You are a team leader and two of your colleagues are having a strained relationship with each other. As a result, they are not contributing well in group activities. How will you handle such a situation?   **(Tricky)**

   (a) How am I bothered with such petty issues? At least the task is being done by others; so it is fine!

   (b) You will make an explict effort to help them shake hands.

   (c) You will give them complementary tasks in which both have to work together.

   (d) You will punish them for not contributing by keeping them out of the team.

5. Do you think that one should change his job often and face new situation ?   **(2014)**

   (a) No, unless compelled one should not leave his old job

   (b) Yes, every new job is challenging and one should accept the challenge

   (c) No, as it takes time to get adjusted

   (d) No, as the new situation may not suit you

6. What will you do if you find an aged person who has lost his road orientation?   **(2012)**

   (a) Avoid the matter totally

   (b) Help him with some money

   (c) Collect the necessary information related to his destination and guide him accurately

   (d) Just show sympathy and give suggestion to contact the nearest police station

7. You are suffering from diabetes. When you see a whole lot of chocolates, you are tempted to eat them. But you also realise that they are not good for you in the long run. What do you do?

   (a) You would not eat them because you know the harmful effects.

   (b) You decide not to eat them but keep thinking about them.

   (c) You would eat them but feel guilty about what you have done.

   (d) You would give in to the temptation and eat the chocolates without being bothered about the consequences.

8. Your colleague is not performing his duties up to the mark. You will   **(2013)**

    (a) just do your part of the duties and enjoy your work

    (b) take advantage of it to promote yourself

    (c) report to the seniors

    (d) try and handle his customers to maintain the company's status

9. You are a social worker. On visiting an orphanage, there is one child who is not ready to let you go away.

    (a) You ignore the child because you have other kids to attend.

    (b) You leave with no concern.

    (c) You decide to visit him every Sunday.

    (d) You talk to the authorities and arrange for parents who can adopt him.

10. After your graduation, you are offered a well-paid government job. However, your friend says that you have to bribe to get the appointment order. You   **(Tricky)**

    (a) go to some influential politician who can help

    (b) accept the job by paying the bribe, consoling yourself that this is the present social set-up

    (c) accept the job by paying the bribe, but firmly resolve that this is the last time you will pay bribe

    (d) flatly refuse the offer

11. You

    (a) get upset when others do not behave properly

    (b) are least interested about what others are thinking about you

    (c) can keep your face smiling even when you are terribly disgusted

    (d) feel that you should not conceal your attitude from others

12. When someone demands something undersirable, you   **(Critical Thinking)**

    (a) always try to avoid the man

    (b) neglect the person and leave the place

    (c) always try to explain your inability to meet the demand

    (d) try to teach him a lesson so that he does not repeat the same behaviour

13. Suppose your friend visits your home on his way to office. You   **(2012)**

    (a) would not do anything so that he is late

    (b) will compel him to listen to your personal problems

    (c) will request him to have some refreshment

    (d) would ask him to spend at least 15 minutes with you

14. You are in the parking area of a shopping complex. And, suddenly the electricity fails and there is total darkness. You will

    (a) try and take help from someone around

    (b) crawl towards your vehicle

    (c) shout for help

    (d) wait till the lights come

15. In public dealing jobs, one must be   **(2014)**

    (a) a good listener

    (b) quick at taking decisions

    (c) polite and humble

    (d) punctual

DIRECTIONS (Qs. 16 - 21) : *Read the questions and answer by choosing the correct option.*

---

16. Learning to skate is very difficult.   **(2013)**
    (a) Fact   (b) Opinion
    (c) Can't Say   (d) None of the above

17. All cars have four tyres.
    (a) Fact   (b) Opinion
    (c) Can't Say   (d) None of the above

18. Strawberry ice-cream does not taste as good as Vanilla and Chocolate.

    (a) Fact   (b) Opinion

    (c) Can't Say   (d) None of the above.

19. There are 29 states in India.

    (a) Fact

    (b) Opinion

    (c) Can't Say

    (d) None of the above

20. Reena's house is very close to the school.

    (a) Fact

    (b) Opinion   **(2015)**

    (c) Can't Say

    (d) None of the above

21. People of Gujarat are very friendly.   **(2016)**

    (a) Fact

    (b) Opinion

    (c) Can't Say

    (d) None of the above.

DIRECTIONS (Qs. 22 - 26) : *Read the questions and answer by choosing the correct option.*

---

22. For adequate water intake, adults need to drink 6 to 8 glasses of water a day.   **(2016)**

    (a) Fact   (b) Opinion

    (c) Can't say   (d) None of the above

23. Cycling is a truly enjoyable form of exercise.

    (a) Fact   (b) Opinion

    (c) Can't say   (d) None of the above

24. Smoke detectors can help save lives.   **(2014)**

    (a) Fact   (b) Opinion

    (c) Don't know   (d) None of the above

25. The number of people who have high credit card debt is astonishing.   **(2013)**

    (a) Fact   (b) Opinion

    (c) Don't know   (d) None of the above

26. India will win the cricket world cup next year.

    (a) Fact   (b) Opinion   **(2017)**

    (c) Don't know   (d) None of the above

HINTS & EXPLANATIONS

LEVEL - 1

1. (a) 2. (a) 3. (c) 4. (a) 5. (c) 6. (c) 7. (a) 8. (d) 9. (b) 10. (b)

11. (c) 12. (a) 13. (c) 14. (d) 15. (b) 16. (a) 17. (b) 18. (b) 19. (c) 20. (b)

21. (d) 22. (d) 23. (d) 24. (c) 25. (b)

26. (c) Could you tell me the way to Vidthwata University?

LEVEL - 2

1. (b) 2. (d) 3. (d) 4. (b) 5. (b) 6. (c) 7. (a) 8. (d) 9. (d) 10. (d)

11. (c) 12. (c) 13. (d) 14. (b) 15. (a) 16. (b) 17. (a) 18. (b) 19. (a) 20. (b)

21. (b) 22. (b) 23. (b) 24. (b) 25. (b) 26. (b)

SPELL-BEE

CHAPTER 18

It is necessary and also interesting to learn spellings as they form the base of any language. To be a high achiever in this section, students need to increase their vocabulary with correctly spelt words.

The best way to improve your spellings is to practise reading and writing with their correct spellings. If a student reads incorrect spellings, he gets exposure to these misspelt words and his mind learns the incorrect spellings. In this way whenever he writes in future, he makes mistakes in spelling. The learning process of an individual requires the involvement of several senses to learn quickly and in a better way. The individual should be familiar with his weak areas of spellings so as to work on those. The individual should be well aware about the affixes so that he can organize the words and is able to form relevant associations. The next way to improve one's spellings and vocabulary is to bring the words in daily use so that one becomes familiar with the particular words. In case an individual is facing difficulty in learning some words, he can make a list of such words, learn these spellings and frequently use them while speaking and writing.

Group learning is better than solo learning. Individuals in a group ask one another various questions concerning different things, persons and other ideas and practise using new words in such interaction. Thus, they acquire many words without putting much effort in learning them. Group discussion is the most appropriate way to learn one word substitution quickly.

This chapter will help you to:

- Find the correctly spelt word out of incorrectly spelled words.

- Use one word replacing a sentence.

- Fill the letters which are left out to complete the word.

Based on spelling, there are three sets of question in the Olympiad question paper. The first set contains 4 different words having one of them spelled correctly, and the rest of them are incorrectly spelled.

EXAMPLE

1. (a) dependant   (b) profesion   (c) command   (d) admision

2. (a) favourite   (b) plesant   (c) coutious   (d) humur

If one is aware of the correct spelling of all these words, one can easily make out that '(c) command' and '(a) favourite' are the only words which have been spelled correctly in this set. Hence '(c) command' and "(a) favourite' should be marked as the answer.

The second set contains the same word spelled in 4 various ways; one out of them is the correct spelling of the said word.

EXAMPLE

(a) building	(b) belding	(c) bilding	(d) beilding
(a) magagine	(b) megezine	(c) magazine	(d) mageizine

For the student who is familiar with the correct spelling of these words, there would be no hitch in choosing '(a) building ' and '(c) magazine' as the right answer.

And the third set contains only one word in which some blank spaces are provided to insert the right letter(s) taken from the options given.

EXAMPLE

1.   ne – essa – y

(a) a,r	(b) r,i	(c) i,r	(d) c,r

2.   m -- n -- ion

(a) e,r	(b) t,e	(c) e,t	(d) e,e

One who is acquainted with the given words would not hesitate to state that (d) 'c,r' and (c) 'e,t' are the right options because missing places in the first word given require 'c,r' at the blank spaces to make the word 'necessary' while in the second 'e,t' is required to make the word 'mention.'

LEVEL 1

DIRECTIONS (Qs. 1 - 20) : *Choose the correctly spelt word.*

1. (a) construction (b) combenation
   (c) consequense (d) degian

2. (a) neibour (b) industry
   (c) audiense (d) joorie

3. (a) qualeety (b) brigge
   (c) government (d) catagory

4. (a) intenson (b) comunity
   (c) contenuous (d) straight

5. (a) accurate (b) conferrence
   (c) fluantly (d) unanimus

6. (a) camara (b) agreement
   (c) instoll (d) yung

7. (a) mashin (b) energgy
   (c) aeroplane (d) destraction

8. (a) dengerous (b) idantify
   (c) mateerial (d) embassy

9. (a) particular (b) fameeliar
   (c) singuler (d) jewlry

10. (a) palatoon (b) individual
    (c) priveously (d) assosiate

11. (a) funcson (b) resserve
    (c) contrast (d) mineang

12. (a) strenth (b) presscribe
    (c) empolyment (d) introduce

13. (a) challenge (b) lolipop
    (c) floting (d) saveral

14. (a) compelete (b) sentence
    (c) tomoro (d) pracious

15. (a) fynance (b) exsellent
    (c) emphasis (d) enthuseasm

16. (a) hedache (b) ejucation
    (c) suroundings (d) approval

17. (a) special (b) polination
    (c) investiget (d) realige

18. (a) forword (b) document
    (c) madical (d) volantry

19. (a) jurniy (b) bufalo
    (c) rhythm (d) moskuito

20. (a) ansestor (b) neglekt
    (c) vacine (d) beginning

DIRECTIONS (Qs. 21 - 40) : *Select the word which is not misspelt.*

21. (a) violence (b) vilence
    (c) vialence (d) vialance

22. (a) predudice (b) prejudice
    (c) prejudise (d) prajudice

23. (a) exsesive (b) eksesive
    (c) excessive (d) excassive

24. (a) conseder (b) conseeder
    (c) consder (d) consider

25. (a) exhaust (b) exhoust
    (c) ekshaust (d) exhost

26. (a) langage (b) language
    (c) longuage (d) langooage

27. (a) subsiquent (b) subsequant
    (c) subsequent (d) subsikuent

28. (a) concious (b) conseous
    (c) contious (d) conscious

29. (a) tortuous   (b) torchuous
    (c) tertuous   (d) tartuous
30. (a) sergery   (b) surgery
    (c) sergury   (d) serjery
31. (a) tarrible   (b) terribal
    (c) terrible   (d) terible
32. (a) meoseum   (b) musiam
    (c) musiem   (d) museum
33. (a) incapable   (b) inkapable
    (c) incapeble   (d) inkapabal
34. (a) remenent   (b) remnant
    (c) reminent   (d) remaint
35. (a) respactive   (b) raspective
    (c) respective   (d) respectib

36. (a) bihaviour   (b) beheviour
    (c) behabiour   (d) behaviour
37. (a) persuade   (b) pursuade
    (c) pasuade   (d) persuate
38. (a) litral   (b) literal
    (c) letteral   (d) literral
39. (a) ulternate   (b) elternate
    (c) alternate   (d) altrnate
40. (a) dectionary   (b) dictionery
    (c) dicsonary   (d) dictionary
41. Find the word with the incorrect spelling.

(2022)

    (a) Mercenary   (b) Machinery
    (c) Missionery   (d) Visionary

LEVEL 2

DIRECTIONS (Qs. 1 - 10) : *Select the word which can be replaced for the given sentence.*

1. One who introduces performers on stage to the audience ----------
   (a) curator
   (b) compere
   (c) host
   (d) choreographer

2. A place where water is collected and stored -----
   (a) aquarium   (b) reservoir
   (c) water body   (d) scullery

3. An imaginary land with perfect social order --------------
   (a) utopia   (b) zodiac
   (c) sinecure   (d) elysium

4. One who eats too much ----------------
   (a) uneconomical   (b) voracious
   (c) voluminous   (d) glutton

5. Owner of the land or house----------------
   (a) master   (b) landlord
   (c) slave   (d) possessor

6. A heavenly body that changes its shape everyday ---------------------
   (a) star   (b) moon
   (c) earth   (d) sky

7. One who safeguards the border of a country --------------
   (a) leader   (b) police
   (c) soldier   (d) minister

8.   One who is indifferent to pains and pleasures

   (a)   stoic   (b)   recluse

   (c)   hedonist   (d)   hermit

9.   A matter which is kept secret ----------------

   (a)   unknown   (b)   confidential

   (c)   untold   (d)   concealment

10. A person who loves mankind --------------

   (a)   philanthrope   (b)   misanthrope

   (c)   kind   (d)   generous

DIRECTIONS (Qs. 11 - 20) : *Fill in the blanks with the suitable alphabet provided as the option to make a meaningful word.*

---

11. Con __ ersa __ ion

   (a)   t,b   (b)   t,v

   (c)   v,e   (d)   v,t

12. p __ rti __ lly

   (a)   e,a   (b)   e,e

   (c)   a,a   (d)   v,e

13. vo __ unta __ y

   (a)   r,a   (b)   l,r

   (c)   r,a   (d)   l,o

14. ex __ erie __ ce

   (a)   p,n   (b)   o,n

   (c)   n,p   (d)   i,n

15. illegi __ ima __ e

   (a)   d,t   (b)   t,t

   (c)   m,t   (d)   m,m

16. empl __ ye __ s

   (a)   e,e   (b)   o,o

   (c)   o,e   (d)   m,e

17. re __ rima __ d

   (a)   p,n   (b)   o,p
   (c)   n,p   (d)   n,n

18. p __ nc __ uality

   (a)   u,e   (b)   t,u

   (c)   a,u   (d)   u,t

19. or __ ani __ ation

   (a)   s,s   (b)   g,e

   (c)   g,s   (d)   a,s

20. c __ ns __ mer

   (a)   o,u   (b)   a,u

   (c)   e,u   (d)   e,o

DIRECTIONS (Qs. 21-22) : *Choose the option with correct spelling.*   **(2020)**

21. What is the spelling of the word which means 'to show intense enjoyment'?

   (a)   Enthusistic   (b)   Enthoosiastic

   (c)   Anthusiastik   (d)   Enthusiastic

22. What is the spelling of the word which means 'brotherhood'?

   (a)   Kameraderi   (b)   Cameradeeri

   (c)   Camaraderie   (d)   Camaredari

DIRECTIONS (Qs. 23-24) : *Choose the option with correct spelling.*   **(2021)**

23. How do you spell the word which means 'senseless'?

   (a)   Aisine   (b)   Asinine

   (c)   Aseine   (d)   Asinne

24. How do you spell the word which means 'heavily '?

   (a)   Pandurously   (b)   Pondreuosly

   (c)   Ponderously   (d)   Pundarously

DIRECTIONS (Qs. 25-26) : *Choose the word with the correct spelling.*   **(2022)**

25. (a)   Lackadaisicle

     (b)   Lackdaisical

     (c)   Lackadaisical

     (d)   Lackadisical

26. (a)   Equanimity

     (b)   Equanimmity

     (c)   Equannimity

     (d)   Equinimity

HINTS & EXPLANATIONS

LEVEL - 1

1. (a) 2. (b) 3. (c) 4. (d) 5. (a)
6. (b) 7. (c) 8. (d) 9. (a) 10. (b)
11. (c) 12. (d) 13. (a) 14. (b) 15. (c)
16. (d) 17. (a) 18. (b) 19. (c) 20. (d)
21. (a) 22. (b) 23. (c) 24. (d) 25. (a)
26. (b) 27. (c) 28. (d) 29. (a) 30. (b)
31. (c) 32. (d) 33. (a) 34. (b) 35. (c)
36. (d) 37. (a) 38. (b) 39. (c) 40. (d)
41. (c)

LEVEL - 2

1. (b) compere
2. (b) reservoir
3. (a) utopia
4. (d) glutton
5. (b) landlord
6. (b) moon
7. (c) soldier
8. (a) stoic
9. (b) confidential
10. (a) philanthrope
11. (d) v,t
12. (c) a,a
13. (b) l,r
14. (a) p,n
15. (b) t,t
16. (c) o,e
17. (a) p,n
18. (d) u,t
19. (c) g,s
20. (a) o,u
21. (d) 'Enthusiastic' means 'to show intense enjoyment'.
22. (c) 'Camaraderie' means 'brotherhood'.
23. (b) Asinine
24. (c) Ponderously
25. (c) "Lackadaisical" which means "lacking enthusiasm and determination".
26. (a) "Equanimity" which means "a calm mental state".